BUILDING THE NATION

BUILDING THE **NATION**

MISSED OPPORTUNITIES IN IRAQ AND AFGHANISTAN

HEATHER SELMA GREGG

Potomac Books
An imprint of the University of Nebraska Press

Library of Congress Cataloging-in-Publication Data
Names: Gregg, Heather S., author.
Title: Building the nation: missed opportunities in
Iraq and Afghanistan / Heather Selma Gregg.
Description: Lincoln: Potomac Books, an imprint
of the University of Nebraska Press, 2018. | Includes
bibliographical references and index.
Identifiers: LCCN 2018006593
ISBN 9781640120877 (cloth: alk. paper)
ISBN 9781640121386 (epub)
ISBN 9781640121393 (mobi)
ISBN 9781640121409 (pdf)
Subjects: LCSH: Nation-building—Iraq. | Postwar
reconstruction—Iraq. | Iraq—Politics and
government—2003– | Nation-building—Afghanistan. |
Postwar reconstruction—Afghanistan. | Afghanistan—
Politics and government—2001– | Iraq—Foreign
relations—United States. | United States—
Foreign relations—Iraq. | Afghanistan—Foreign
relations—United States. | United States—Foreign
relations—Afghanistan.
Classification: LCC DS79.769 .G74 2018 |
DDC 956.7044/31—dc23 LC record available
at https://lccn.loc.gov/2018006593

Set in Scala OT by E. Cuddy.

For my students at the Naval Postgraduate School.
Thank you for all that you have taught me.

And in memory of U.S. Army Lieutenant Colonel Todd Clark,
and U.S. Army Major Benny Romero.

CONTENTS

TABLES

BUILDING THE NATION

1

BRINGING THE NATION BACK INTO NATION-BUILDING

On June 5, 2014, the Islamic State in Iraq and Levant (ISIL) launched a major offensive into Iraq from neighboring Syria and captured Samarra, Mosul, and Tikrit within a matter of days. As ISIL forces advanced into the country, Iraqi security forces shed their uniforms and fled by the thousands; those who did not escape were lined up and executed. The Iraqi government attempted to declare a state of emergency on June 10, but the parliament, with active dissent from Kurds and Sunnis, blocked the Shia-dominated executive branch from taking action and eventually forced the prime minster to resign.

On June 29 ISIL declared a caliphate in the territory it held in Syria and Iraq, allowing the leadership to impose what they claimed was the most complete and perfect form of Sharia law on the planet. Morality police, the Hizbah, began enforcing strict dress codes for women and men, outlawing smoking, and punishing the population for a range of minor offenses. ISIL forces slaughtered Shias by the thousands, accusing them of being apostates. They also killed Yazidis, Christians, Sufis (mystical Muslims), and Sunnis who did not adhere to their radical form of Salafi Islam. In addition to imposing its interpretation of sharia, ISIL also began taxing the population and providing basic resources, including food, road improvements, and electricity.

Despite ISIL's brutality Iraq's Sunni population largely welcomed its rapid advance into the country, and local Sunnis were photographed cheering its arrival into Mosul, Tikrit, and other cities. Moreover, the firebrand image of ISIL attracted tens of thousands of foreign fighters to Syria and Iraq with the hopes of living under "perfect" sharia, waging jihad, and becoming part of a historically transformative movement. In addition to individuals backing ISIL, Islamic movements in Libya, Egypt, Afghanistan, the Philippines, and Nigeria all pledged the *bayat* (oath of fealty) to the Islamic State, recognizing it as the caliphate.

The rapid advance of ISIL, the collapse of the Iraqi government and dissolution of its armed forces, along with the tacit and active support of its Sunni population, unequivocally revealed the failure of U.S.-led efforts to "nation build" in Iraq following the overthrow of Saddam Hussein in 2003. This strategy of nation-building included creating a stable democracy in Iraq that would be both domestically and internationally responsible, developing a functioning economy based largely on its oil production, establishing responsible and competent security forces, and providing key social services to keep the population loyal and happy to its government. Clearly, something went wrong in the U.S.-led efforts to build the Iraqi state after ousting Saddam Hussein.

In essence ISIL created a direct challenge to U.S.-led efforts to state build in Iraq and the Western state system more broadly, ignoring internationally recognized borders and offering an alternative to liberal democracy, freedom of religion and speech, and equality of citizens. Moreover, ISIL provided an identity, a sense of common purpose and destiny rooted in perceptions of divine justice and claims of the true path of Islam.

Anthropologist Scott Atran, in a 2015 testimony before the UN Security Council, called ISIL and groups like it "the world's most dynamic countercultural movement, one whose values run counter to the nation-state system."[1] To compete with this movement, Atran proposes three conditions that governments and communities need to provide young people: "offer youth something that makes them dream, of a life of significance through struggle and sacrifice in comradeship . . . which gives them a sense of special destiny and the will to fight; offer youth a positive personal dream, with a concrete chance of realization; and offer youth the chance to create their own local initiatives." Atran further asserts: "What dreams may come from most current government policies that offer little beyond promises of comfort and security? Young people will *not* choose to sacrifice everything, including their lives—the totality of their self-interests—just for material rewards."[2]

Atran's comments suggest that the U.S. approach did little to inspire the population, particular the youth, and to give them a vision for their lives, a sense of purpose, and a vested interest in the destiny of the country. Rather, the U.S. approach focused on developing the structure of the state and, by building the trappings of a state, the population would have its most basic needs met, would be allowed to choose its government, and would be peaceful with one another and loyal to the state. The appeal of ISIL suggests that something is missing from these basic provisions.

A similarly troubling trajectory is visible in Afghanistan, where the United States began its nation-building efforts in the wake of the September 11 attacks on the U.S. homeland. The United States invaded Afghanistan with the aim of deposing the Taliban and denying al-Qaeda and other transnational terrorists a safe haven from which to plan and execute operations. Although U.S. forces failed to capture Osama bin Laden, Mullah Omar, and other key leaders, the Taliban government was toppled in a matter of weeks. However, what began as a military campaign with specific goals quickly morphed into a massive state-building effort. A December 2001 meeting of Afghans and international leaders in Bonn, Germany—followed by a massive donor's conference in Tokyo, Japan a month later—aimed to transform the country from one of the poorest and least developed to a modern democratic state with complementary social, political, legal, security, and economic institutions. However, despite billions invested in these efforts and thousands of U.S. and NATO troops' lives lost along with countless civilian casualties, Afghanistan still faces insurgent threats from the Taliban and other groups, a fragile government, widespread poverty, and a booming illicit opium industry.

Understanding what went wrong in U.S.-led efforts to nation build in Iraq and Afghanistan has taken on new importance in light of ISIL's success as a counterforce to Western nation states. The current global security environment will most likely draw the United States into efforts to strengthen fragile states in the future, although perhaps not on as massive a scale as the operations in Iraq and Afghanistan. Weak and failing states create a security risk for the United States and its interests, especially if they provide spaces in which violent nonstate actors can reside, recruit fighters, and plan operations. Furthermore, weak and failing states are regionally destabilizing; internal wars rarely remain within the borders of a state and often produce refugees, weapons trafficking, and transborder skirmishes. Moreover, with the collapse of the Iraqi military and government in 2014, the United States finds itself being pulled back into the country by its commitment to train the Iraqi military and other initiatives. Therefore, understanding what went wrong in Iraq and Afghanistan and how best to aid failing states and put them on the path to long-term stability is imperative in this current security environment.

The Need for Population-Centric State-Building and National Unity

This book proposes that state-building efforts in the modern world require two key factors that were missing from U.S.-led operations to build viable states in Iraq and Afghanistan: popular involvement in the process of rebuilding the state that gives the population "ownership" of the process and its results; and efforts to foster and strengthen what will be called *national unity*.

State-building needs to start with the population for several reasons. First, now more than ever, a state's sovereignty rests with its people, and without their buy-in, states are unlikely to thrive or governments to succeed over the long haul. Sovereignty has undergone a series of shifts from the time of the creation of modern states in seventeenth-century Europe to the twenty-first century. No longer is a state's sovereignty defined by monarchies, or territory and borders, or just the monopoly on the legitimate use of force. The birth of modern-day democracies, the creation of security through the *levee en masse*, the rise of private property, the increase in levels of literacy and education, the emergence of the public sphere, the ideas of the Enlightenment, and the revolution in information technologies have shifted sovereignty from governments and territories to the people. Perhaps unlike ever before in history, people have the power to determine the viability of the state in which they reside, and excluding them from the process of state-building—including the development of its government, law, security forces, economic viability, and social well-being—is likely to undermine the long-term stability of the state. Efforts to state build, therefore, need to start with the people.

State-building efforts also need to start with and include populations in order to create programs that resonate with the population and give it ownership of the effort in the here and now, which will pave the way for a population that supports the state and its various institutions. As will be described, intervening powers in Iraq and Afghanistan largely predetermined how the state would look and what should be built and why. This approach, while expedient, did not start by trying to understand the populations' vulnerabilities, needs, or hopes, nor did it understand their perceptions of security or leadership. In many cases efforts taken by intervening powers actually worked against the populations' needs and fueled perceptions of mistrust and insecurity. For example, decisions made by U.S. civilian leaders to disband the Iraqi army and punish members of the Baath Party effectively excluded Sunnis from the state-building process and sent a strong signal that they would not be part of the new Iraq. These decisions have been credited with fueling the rise of some of the insurgent groups that emerged in the country. Within this top-down approach to state-building, the United States and its allies missed valuable opportunities to partner with the population, foster leadership and decision making, and put the country to work after decades of dictatorship and war. Ultimately, the population needs to have ownership of the state-building process and see the state as its future for the endeavor to succeed.

Starting with the population in state-building is also important because, if properly structured, this approach can be a powerful tool for building unity among the people. In Iraq and Afghanistan, U.S. efforts at state-building focused on establishing unity through power sharing in government and by creating multiethnic security forces. This approach, however, did more to enshrine ethnic differences in these countries than work toward social harmony and national unity. As will be argued, state-building can be structured in a way that helps to build a sense of common destiny among the people and between the people and the state.

Building on these points, the second key ingredient missing from U.S.-led efforts to create viable states in Iraq and Afghanistan is *national-unity building.* Despite calling its operations "nation-building," the United States really engaged in state-building. It developed the structure of the state, including its security, political, legal, economic, and social services sectors, or what the U.S. Institute of Peace calls the five desired end states of stabilization and state reconstruction.[3] However, building or rebuilding a state requires more than developing the capacity of its government or security forces. State-building programs also need to foster and strengthen the population's sense of common destiny and the need for its various factions to work together to build a healthy, prosperous state. In other words a state needs a population that coheres and supports the government and other state institutions for it to flourish. This is national-unity building.

As will be discussed, efforts at building national unity were all but missing from U.S.-led operations to create viable states in Iraq and Afghanistan. This may be for several reasons. First, U.S. state-building efforts rested on the assumption that building the capacity of the state and providing people with security, public utilities, and other resources would result in a peaceful population that supported the state. This dynamic, which is known as the social contract, assumes a purely utilitarian approach to states: governments provide security, consistency, and resources, and the population supports these initiatives through taxes and by giving up some of their liberties (such as taking the law into their own hands).

This utilitarian approach to state-building, however, misses a critical, necessary component of a viable state: the emotional attachment citizens feel toward one another and to their state. States, in other words, are not just structural, rational, utilitarian entities; they also provide a sense of identity, purpose, and destiny among their people. People need to identify with their country on a personal level, share its norms, and believe in their common destiny—this is national unity. Rebuilding states, therefore, should be more than just establishing or reestablishing the social contract; it should also include cultivating this sense of national unity.

Programs of national unity include identifying and fostering shared symbols, myths, and rituals, common values and norms, a shared understanding of history, and—most importantly—a sense of common destiny. It is creating what anthropologist Benedict Anderson calls "an imagined political community." "It is *imagined*," he asserts, "because the members of even the smallest nation will never know most of their fellow-members, meet them or even hear of them, yet in the minds of each lives the image of their communion."[4] Without the emotional attachment that being part of an imagined community creates, states are unlikely to cohere and citizens will find their identity and emotional attachment in other, competing sub- or super-states, a role that ISIL fulfilled in Iraq.

Furthermore, programs to rebuild Iraq and Afghanistan likely did not address fostering national unity because a commonly held perception is that nations build states, not the other way around, and therefore nations and national unity are not built but simply "are." For example, economist Francis Fukuyama argues in his 2004 book on state-building that "only states can be deliberately constructed" and "if a nation arises from [state-building], it is more a matter of luck than design."[5]

However, as will be described in chapters 2 and 3, nations are in fact created and the product of what will be called *national entrepreneurs*—artists, authors, socialites, philanthropists, politicians, businesspeople, and other members of society who develop and foster a sense of national unity through a range of initiatives. In seventeenth-, eighteenth-, and nineteenth-century Europe and the United States, for example, states were built first, and *then* nations were fostered thereafter. In Europe languages were formalized and became symbols of the nation, grand capital cities were built, national literature and art were cultivated, and monuments arose to document and reinforce the nation. In the United States, national-unity building included the creation of national parks, the founding of museums, and the construction of national myths that reinforced the United States' destiny as a great and pioneering nation. As will be shown, national entre- preneurs continue to play an indispensable role in shaping the nation within state borders, including in the United States and Europe countries. When they do this well, it is virtually imper- ceptible; the nation simply "is."

Finally, programs for building national unity were likely miss- ing in Iraq and Afghanistan because the prevailing wisdom about these countries is that their ethnic and religious diversity pre- cluded any efforts to build national unity. However, as will be dis- cussed, evidence from both of these countries in the early days of U.S.-led operations reveals that the overwhelming majority of Iraqi and Afghan citizens wanted their countries to remain unified, including Kurds and Sunnis in Iraq, and Pashtuns in Afghanistan.[6] The people, in other words, wanted to move for- ward together, and the United States and its allies missed valuable opportunities to seize on these desires and build national unity.

Ultimately, national-unity building may be *the* priority in twenty-first-century efforts to stabilize states and make them viable. Starting with the people and working through them to build and take ownership of the state, while recognizing their common destiny as citizens, may be the pathway to creating sta- ble and prosperous states. Although nations can survive without states (as the Kurds, the Palestinians, and others have shown), states cannot endure without a population that sees its future in the state and all its people; national-unity building is a critical place to begin fostering this necessary component of the state.

Organization of the Book

The book begins by recognizing that considerable confusion exists over what a nation is and how it differs from a state. Chapter 2, therefore, provides working definitions of key terms used in the book, including *nations, states, nationalism,* and *national unity,* basing these definitions on a review of the literature of nation-building and state-building. It proposes that states involve, at a minimum, legally recognized territory and a population; however, *healthy* functioning states also include a form of government that provides some goods and services for its population in exchange for the people's loyalty and support, what is known as the social contract, and that have civil societies, or interest groups and organizations independent of government. Nations, by contrast, are constructed groups that draw on the past to assert a common purpose and destiny that are both practical, often claiming rights to sovereignty and territory, and emotional. Nations that align with states reinforce their borders and institutions; nations that do not align with states can challenge states' viability. Furthermore, nations are created by what will be called national entrepreneurs—artists, authors, socialites, politicians, businesspeople, and other members of society who develop and foster a sense of nation through a range of initiatives. The chapter concludes by highlighting three forms of nationalism—ethnic, civic, and religious—and discussing their limits in building viable states and proposes a near-term goal for fostering cohesion among citizens of a state, national unity. National unity emphasizes the common destiny of a state's people and their need to work together to build a healthy, prosperous state.

Chapter 3 offers a look back in history at some of the most successful examples of state-building and nation-building: Western Europe and the United States, particularly in the seventeenth, eighteenth, and nineteenth centuries. While often dismissed as irrelevant for state-building and nation-building in the modern era, particularly for non-Western cultures and in developing countries, these cases offer important clues for how both states and nations were created. Specifically, chapter 3 investigates how national entrepreneurs along with governments developed and fostered a sense of national unity through the construction of the state—especially military forces, education systems, and bureaucracies—but also through national myths and rituals, flags and anthems, museums of national art and history, national parks and forests, literature, and the creation of grand capital cities. These programs created shared experiences among citizens and instilled a sense of common purpose and destiny. When done well, nation-building reinforced the state and appeared organic, not constructed.

Chapter 4 investigates literature on state-building and nation-building in the post–September 11 security environment. Specifically, it focuses on what are commonly recognized as the five pillars or end states of stabilization and state reconstruction—security, governance, economic development, rule of law, and social well-being—and proposes using these five end states as the framework for analyzing state-building in Iraq and Afghanistan. The chapter further proposes a new pillar, national unity, or emphasizing the common destiny of a state's people and their need to work together to build a healthy, prosperous state. Ultimately, chapter 4 emphasizes that states cannot prosper without some degree of unity and popular buy-in from the population. National unity, in other words, is a necessary component of a functioning state.

Chapter 5 traces the conditions under which the United States and its coalition invaded Iraq and the programs they initiated with the aim of "nation-building," which was actually a program of building the structure of the state. Using the five goals of stabilization and state reconstruction as an analytical framework—security, governance, economic development, rule of law, and social well-being—it asserts that state-building in Iraq focused almost exclusively on rapidly creating macro-level instruments of the state, such as conventional military forces, a democratic system, and public utilities, overlooking programs and initiatives aimed at working with and through the population to stabilize the country. Moreover, the United States and its allies missed key opportunities to build national unity and, in some cases, reinforced sectarianism, which contributed to the state's collapse in 2014.

Chapter 6 offers a hypothetical look at how the United States and coalition powers could have created programs designed to foster and reinforce national unity as part of their efforts to develop a viable and prosperous state in Iraq, using the five pillars of state-building, in addition to the proposed sixth pillar of national unity. Ultimately, in their attempts at state-building and nation-building, the United States and coalition powers should have understood and focused more on the population and less on the macro-level structures of the state to foster programs of building national unity and state-building. In the case of Iraq, the lack of national-unity building coupled with ineffective state-building programs paved the way for other nation-building entrepreneurs—ISIL—to divide the country along sectarian lines and capture the state.

Chapter 7 traces U.S., NATO, and UN efforts to develop Afghanistan in the wake of the 2001 invasion that deposed the Taliban. It highlights initiatives aimed at building the state along the five pillars of stabilization and reconstruction: security, governance, rule of law, economics, and social well-being. As in Iraq virtually no efforts were made to build national unity beyond creating power-sharing arrangements in the government and military and, by and large, the population was left out of the process. Ultimately, after more than a decade of international intervention and billions of dollars invested in Afghanistan, statistics suggest that the lives of average Afghans have improved only marginally, and poverty remains a perennial challenge, particularly in rural areas. Furthermore, the 2014 drawdown of ISAF forces and the persistence of insurgent threats have placed Afghanistan on a precarious road to the future.

Chapter 8 offers a hypothetical look at how the United States and coalition powers could have created programs designed to foster and reinforce the Afghan nation as part of their efforts to develop a viable state, focusing specifically on the five end goals of state-building, in addition to what a sixth pillar of national-unity building would have looked like. Ultimately the United States and coalition powers should have focused more on the population, pushing authority and resources out from Kabul, and less on the macro-level structures of the state. Moreover, given the predominantly rural nature of Afghanistan, building the Afghan state and nation should have focused more on two broad goals: better connecting people physically and virtually and addressing the everyday issues of poverty within the rural population.

The book concludes by proposing a program for state-building and nation-building in the twenty-first century, stressing that such undertakings are as much about *how* they are done as they are about specific tasks or programs. In particular the book's conclusion proposes six principles: start with the population; identify and incorporate local leaders into state-building and nation-building; allow the necessary time for change; stabilize the top and focus on change occurring at the local level; emphasize national unity in all efforts; and remember that building the state and the nation never end. The book further concludes with a discussion of state-building and nation-building responsibilities, noting that militaries will most likely be tasked to head-up these complex operations given their resources and abilities to perform in unsafe and austere environments; militaries should therefore be educated on the tasks of state-building and nation-building. The conclusion also calls for a "whole of nation" approach to build states and national unity, as opposed to a whole of government approach, and encourages leveraging U.S. society and businesses to build partnerships with affected countries and help with state- and nation-building efforts.

The book draws from a variety of sources to build these arguments. First, it consults literature from anthropology, philosophy, sociology, and history to consider the origins and purpose of states and nations, and how nations, states, and the notion of sovereignty have changed over time. It also capitalizes on the rich repository of academic literature on state-building and nation-building to construct a framework for state-building and nation-building in the twenty-first century. The book gathers further insights from primary sources, including reports, memos, briefings, and after action reports from the wars in Iraq and Afghanistan to investigate what was done, and not done, to build viable states in these countries. In addition to these primary sources, the book gleans insights from interviews with U.S. forces, primarily Special Operations Forces, who deployed to Iraq and

Afghanistan, and who experimented with projects aimed at building stability in their areas of operation.[7] Finally, the book echoes many of the conversations and debates that occurred in classes at the Naval Postgraduate School from 2006 to 2015, in which U.S. and international officers and noncommissioned officers wrestled with these and other topics. The contributions of these classes are duly noted throughout the book. Ultimately, most of the ideas presented here are not original; they are a compilation of projects implemented ad hoc and in one-off occurrences but that should be preserved as examples of how to work through the population to build states and foster national unity.

Given the likelihood that the United States and other countries will engage in state-building efforts in the future, although not perhaps on the magnitude of Iraq and Afghanistan, it is imperative to understand what went wrong and how to do better. Academics and policy makers owe it to U.S. taxpayers, who have footed the bill; U.S. troops, who have paid with their time, their health, and their lives; and the people in the countries they aim to help.

2

STATES, NATIONS, NATIONALISM, AND NATIONAL UNITY

The terms *state* and *nation* are frequently conflated in media and even academic literature. For example anthropologist Jack David Eller notes, "*Ethnic group* and *nation* are often used synonymously, and *nation* and *state* are often used synonymously, which is not only empirically wrong but leads to the logical conclusion that ethnic group is synonymous with state, which is absurd. In fact, not all ethnic groups are nations, but some are; not all ethnic groups or nations have or want states, but some do. Terminological sloppiness leads to muddled thinking and mental and political mistakes."[1] Conflating nations and states, therefore, is not just a matter of academic importance; it also has practical implications for policy, especially initiatives aimed at "nation-building" in the post–September 11 security environment. Any conversation on "nation-building" should begin with definitions so that the participants clearly understand what the policy goal should be in these initiatives.

This chapter provides working definitions of the book's key terms: *states, nations, nationalism,* and *national unity.* It begins by, first, highlighting key definitions of states, noting in particular that states involve, at a minimum, legally recognized territory and a population. However, *healthy* functioning states also include a form of government that provides some goods and services for its population in exchange for its loyalty and support, what is known as the social contract. Healthy states also include civil society, independent associations that allow individuals to organize for a variety of reasons and that help citizens recognize their commonalities. The chapter then touches on debates surrounding definition of nations in the modern world, stressing that the term has gone through several transformations in its history; ultimately, modern nations are constructed, not spontaneous and timeless. Furthermore, it proposes that nations are the product of *national entrepreneurs*—artists, authors, socialites, politicians, businesspeople, and other members of society who develop and foster a spirit of nation through a range of initiatives. The chapter then describes three forms of nationalism—ethnic, civic, and religious—discussing each of their limitations for modern-day state-building and nation-building. Finally, it concludes by proposing a near-term goal for fostering cohesion among citizens of a state and building a sense of loyalty—national unity. National unity emphasizes the common destiny of a population, and their need to work together to build a healthy prosperous state. Ultimately, national-unity building will pave the way for civic nationalism, but it also provides the necessary time for rule of law and other institutions to develop over the long haul.

States

Despite the confusion over the application of the terms *state* and *nation*, definitions of what makes a state are relatively straightforward. A common starting point for the definition of a state comes from the Treaties of Westphalia, signed by major European powers in 1648, following decades of war and bloodshed on the Continent. The treaties established the political norm of state sovereignty and noninterference in states' domestic affairs. These treaties created, in effect, a new political order based on states as the principal unit of political organization. The norms of state sovereignty and nonintervention in states' domestic affairs became lasting legacies of the treaties.[2]

Another often-cited definition of a state comes from nineteenth-century sociologist Max Weber, who defines a state as a "human community that (successfully) claims the monopoly of the legitimate use of physical force within a given territory." For Weber states are defined by their territory, by what he calls "a compulsory political organization," by what it does (specifically its use of force), and by the people who make up the state. Weber also describes the importance of creating state bureaucracies to maintain consistent authority within the state.[3] Another definition of a state comes from Charles Tilly's edited volume on the formation of nations and states in Western Europe. Tilly draws from Strayer to simply define the state as "durability, spatial fixity, permanent and impersonal institutions, final authority, and loyalty."[4] Of particular importance to Tilly's definition is the role that loyalty of the population plays in state formation, a point that will be elaborated on later.

Jack David Eller offers a more nuanced but still straightforward definition of the state. When discussing states versus ethnic groups or nations, he claims that a state is "the simplest of these terms to grasp, since the political entities that are the principle legitimate actors on the world stage are states; when one looks at a map, what one sees is states, not ethnic groups, not nations, and not any other form of political and social collectivity." Eller goes on to say, "States, even when they are real, are not 'natural' or 'given' but are generally products of a historical and political (often a military or colonial) process," and finally, "There are various kinds of states, of course, ordinarily distinguished by how they distribute political power through the population (e.g. monarchy, constitutional monarchy, republic, etc. and many permutations thereof—totalitarian, democratic, fascist, communist and so on)."[5] Eller's definition of a state, therefore, is the territory that makes up a state and the political system that governs it. Ultimately, states and the politics that govern them are constructed; they are the product of human agency.

Ashraf Ghani, Clare Lockhart, and Michael Carnahan define a state by two components, what they call de jure sovereignty (its legal, international recognition) and de facto sovereignty (the functions it performs). They assert that "legal recognition alone . . . does not suffice to define the sovereignty of a state," and that the gap between legal recognition of a state and the governing functions it performs creates state insecurity and instability. They call this the sovereignty gap.[6] Therefore, for Ghani and his colleagues, states are not only defined by their legal recognition but also by what they do and, particularly, what they provide their citizens. This definition builds on the concept of the social contract, the idea that citizens give up certain liberties, such as total freedom, and state sovereigns provide certain resources to citizens in return, such as security and other public goods. The philosophical origins of the social contract and its practical implications for modern-day states will be discussed further in chapter 3.

Similarly, Robert Rotberg defines states along a spectrum of strong on one end and collapsed on the other, focusing on the state's functions as the measurements. He contends that states "exist to provide a decentralized method of delivering political (public) goods to persons living within designated parameters (borders). . . . Modern states focus and answer the concerns and demands of citizenries. . . . They buffer or manipulate external forces and influences, champion the local or particular concerns of their adherents, and mediate between the constraints and challenges of the international realm and the dynamism of their own internal economic, political, and social realities."[7] Of particular importance to this definition of states is that in the post–World War II era, failing and even collapsed states do not cease to exist; rather they persist as internationally and legally recognized territory that lack a functioning or legitimate government that can provide basic services throughout the country.

More recently, Barry Buzan's *People, States and Fear* argues that a sovereign state consists of three variables: the physical base, which is the territory and its population; the institutions that govern the state; and the idea of the state in the minds of its people. In other words a state cannot be sovereign without the recognition of its existence and importance from its citizens. Buzan's observations are particularly important because they suggest that a state will succeed in the long run only if the concept of the state is embraced by the people.[8]

Finally, a healthy state includes vibrant civil society, independent associations that allow individuals to organize for a variety of reasons and help citizens recognize their commonalities. Political scientist Daniel Posner describes two broad types of civil society: those that provide advocacy, that lobby on behalf of citizens to the government for specific policies or resources; and those that provide substitution, or that offer a resource in lieu of the government, such as charities.[9] Alexis de Tocqueville's nineteenth-century study of democracy in America also notes that free associations exist for a range of activities, small and large, serious and fun: "[Americans] have not only commercial and industrial associations, in which all take part, but associations of a thousand other kinds: religious, moral, serious, futile, very general and very particular, immense and very small; Americans use associations to give entertainments, to found seminaries, to build inns, to construct churches, to diffuse books, to send missionaries to the antipodes; in this manner they found hospitals, prisons, schools."[10] Thus Tocqueville adds an important third type of collective to civil society, those that organize around recreation, fun, and frivolity. The conditions that foster civil society will be considered throughout these chapters, along with the role that free associations play, including those focused on fun and recreation, in helping citizens of a state recognize their common destiny.

States, therefore, at a minimum consist of internationally recognized borders, territory, and the people within that territory. In the modern era, states are further defined by the political system that runs them, as well as what states actually do, including the services they provide their populations. States are also defined by the presence or absence of civil society. Finally, states can be measured as strong or weak depending on their ability to govern their territory legitimately, provide goods and services to their populations, and ensure the health of its civil society.

Nations

Unlike definitions of the state, the term *nation* is fraught with unresolvable academic disagreement over its definition, including the origins of nations and their purpose. Charles Tilly's edited volume on the formation of nations and states in Western Europe eschews defining nations at all, describing the term as "one of the most puzzling and tendentious items in the political lexicon."[11] Walker Connor, in fact, calls it "terminological chaos."[12]

Despite the lack of consensus, some useful definitions of the term do exist. One of the more useful discussions on the nebulous meaning of the word *nation* comes from social historian Liah Greenfeld. She argues that, despite being an ancient word, *nation* has a modern meaning that is distinct from its ancient roots. Specifically, the term *nation* has gone through an evolutionary process in Europe that has, in turn, affected its meaning today. Its earliest meanings, in ancient Rome, referred to foreigners, and corresponded to the Greek *ethne*. In medieval Europe groups of students studying theology at the University of Paris were organized by ecclesiastical communities of opinion, which were called nations. This use of the term then evolved into the social elite. Greenfeld further chronicles the evolution of nations to refer not only to elites but to a "people," first in early sixteenth-century England and then in emerging states in Europe, when it came to mean "a sovereign people." Finally, *nations* became synonymous with the concept of "a unique people," regardless of their sovereignty.[13]

Perhaps all scholars would agree that nations are a collective of people who share some sort of bond with one another. Connor, for example, simply defines a nation as "a belief in or an intuitive conviction of common descent."[14] He notes that, according to this definition, most self-proclaimed nations are not truly nations, including the United States, which does not share a sense of common ancestry.[15] Anthony Smith offers a more detailed definition of nations, focusing on specific characteristics: "a named human population sharing a historic territory, common myths and historical memories, a mass public culture, a common economy, and common legal rights and duties for its members."[16]

Other scholars define nations by their inherent political nature, specifically their desire for self-rule. John Stuart Mill, for example, offers this definition of a nation:

A portion of mankind may be said to constitute a Nationality if they are united among themselves by common sympathies which do not exist between them and any others—which make them co-operate with each other more willingly than with other people, desire to be under the same government, and desire that it should be government [*sic*] by themselves or a portion of themselves exclusively. This feeling of nationality may have been generated by various causes. Sometimes it is the effect of identity of race and descent. Community of language, and community of religion, greatly contribute to it. Geographical limits are one of its causes. But the strongest of all is identity of political antecedents; the possession of a national history, and consequent community of recollections; collective pride and humiliation, pleasure and regret, connected with the same incidents in the past.[17]

For Mill, therefore, the political ambition of nations is paramount, and what gives nations a sense of common belonging is of secondary importance.

Another academic debate over nations concerns their origins, specifically whether nations are ancient and organic or more modern and constructed. Primordialists contend that nations are premodern, natural, and represent an almost collective social DNA. Primordial explanations of nations, therefore, suggest that they existed well before the creation of modern states in the sixteenth and seventeenth centuries.[18] Constructivists, on the other hand, argue that nations, while drawing from the past, are created and the result of social and political circumstances; as such, nations change over time and in relation to specific contexts.[19]

Perhaps one of the first scholars of the constructivist school, although he predates it, is the nineteenth-century French scholar Ernest Renan. In his 1882 speech at the Sorbonne, Renan explores several common assumptions about what makes a nation, including dynastic conquest, race, language, and geography. Within each of these factors, he carefully points out examples of nations that exist despite these primordial claims. Renan wholeheartedly rejects the notion of race and its role in nation-building, citing the constructed nature of race based on blood. "The truth of the matter," he asserts, "is that there are no pure races." Renan contends that defining nations based on race "is a great error, one which, should it become dominant, [would] result in the destruction of the European civilization."[20] Similarly, Renan notes that basing a nation solely on language would be equally problematic: "Languages are historically formations that imply nothing in regards to those who speak them. Nor should languages in any way shackle human liberty when it comes to determining the family with which one unites one's self in life and death."[21] When suggesting that nations can be defined by geography, Renan contends: "I know no more arbitrary or disastrous doctrine."[22]

Rather than focus on presumably fixed criteria to define a nation, Renan instead argues, first, that "a nation is a soul, a spiritual principle," and that it comprises two broad factors: "one is the past, the other is the present."[23] With regard to the past, he notes: "The nation, like the individual, is the outcome of a long past of efforts, sacrifices, and devotions. . . . A heroic past with great men and glory (I mean true glory) is the social capital upon which the national idea rests." He further asserts: "Having suffered, rejoiced and hoped together is worth more than common taxes or frontiers that conform to strategic ideas and is independent of racial or linguistic consideration."[24]

Renan further asserts that equally important to the creation and sustainment of a nation is its sense of future and common destiny. He contends that a nation "presupposes a past but is reiterated in the present by a tangible fact: consent, the clearly expressed desire to continue a common life." Nations, in other words, are defined by their common understanding of the past and what that struggle means for a common future together. Renan further describes a nation as "a moral conscience" and states, "As long as this moral conscience proofs [sic] its strength by sacrifices that require the subordination of the individual to the communal good, it is legitimate and has the right to exist. If doubts are raised along the frontiers, consult the disputed populations. They certainly have a right to express their views on the matter."[25]

In a similar vein to Renan, several scholars argue that the content of nations matter less than what they do and the perceptions they create. Connor, for example, argues: "The issue of when a nation came into being is not of key significance: while in factual/chronological history a nation may be of recent vintage, in the popular perception of its members, it is 'eternal,' 'beyond time,' 'timeless.' And it is not facts but perceptions of facts that shape attitudes and behavior."[26] Nations, in other words, are perceived as timeless, despite the fact that they are relatively modern constructions.

Similarly, Benedict Anderson argues that nations are in fact "an imagined political community—and imagined as both inherently limited and sovereign. It is *imagined* because the members of even the smallest nation will never know most of their fellow-members, meet them or even hear of them, yet in the minds of each lives the image of their communion."[27] Rogers Brubaker asserts that it is essential to consider nations not as "real collectives" but rather as a "practical category" and thus ask, "How is nationhood as a political and cultural form institutionalized within and among states?"[28]

Finally, Max Weber notes the emotional and irrational nature of nations. In *Economy and Society*, Weber asserts, "The fervor of [the nation's] emotional influence does not, in the main, have an economic origin. It is based upon prestige, which often extends deep down to the petty-bourgeois masses of states rich in the historical attainment of power-positions." Weber goes on to claim that "they comprise especially all those who think of themselves as being the specific 'partners' of a specific 'culture' diffused among the members of the polity. Under the influence of these circles, the naked prestige of 'power' is unavoidably transformed into other special forms of prestige and especially into the idea of the 'nation.'" Weber concludes that "the concept undoubtedly means, above all, that *it is proper* to expect from certain groups a specific sentiment of solidarity in the face of other groups."[29] Weber adds the critical dimension of emotional attachment to the creation of nations; in other words, nations are not purely rational and instrumental.

From this conglomerate discussion of what makes a nation, the following key components will be used to create a working definition of the term: nations are constructed groups that draw on the past to assert a common purpose and destiny that is both practical, often claiming rights to sovereignty and territory, and emotional. Furthermore, nations are created by what will be called *national entrepreneurs*: artists, authors, socialites, politicians, businesspeople, and other members of society who develop and foster a sense of nation through a range of initiatives. National entrepreneurs and the national unity they create will be a central focus of subsequent chapters.

Nationalism

In addition to disagreements over the definition of nations, the connection between nations and nationalism is also hotly debated within academia. At its most basic definition, nationalism is the creation of an ideology based on a group's perceived unique, common ties. Ernest Gellner, for example, defines nationalism as "primarily a principle which holds that the political and national unit should be congruent," a definition to which Eric Hobsbawm concurs and uses in his own work.[30] Greenfeld contends that, with the creation of nation-states in Europe, the idea of nations evolved from "a sovereign people" to what she calls "particularistic nationalism," or the fusion of political rights to unique attributes that entitle a group to self-rule.[31] Under these circumstances, states are no longer defined by territory, sovereignty, and subjects or citizens but rather are coherent collectives—nations—that make and are made by states.

Gellner argues that nationalism has its roots in economic development, specifically industrialization. He particularly looks at the interplay of three variables: power, and its centralization under greater industrialization; mass education, and the creation of a workforce with generalized skills, especially literacy and basic mathematics; and the spread of a common, standardized "high culture" through education. From the presence and absence of these three variables, he develops a typology of the evolution of nationalism and industrialization. Ultimately, Gellner concludes that nationalism, as a political ideology, created nations and not the other way around.[32]

Anderson's seminal work *Imagined Communities* contends that the development of nationalism was the process of specific historic circumstances but, "once created it became . . . 'modular', capable of being transplanted, with varying degrees of self-consciousness, to a great variety of social terrains, to merge and be merged with a correspondingly wide variety of political and ideological constellations." Anderson chronicles the spread of nationalism to colonial states through print media, the development of written history, racial hierarchies, census taking, map-making, and the creation of museums.[33] Similarly, John Breuilly investigates the development of nationalism and its spread from Europe to regions around the world, categorizing different forms of nationalism that emerged in regions ranging from Africa to the Middle East to Japan.[34]

As a political ideology, different types of nationalism are derived from the underpinning of the sense of community and the right to self-rule. Variations of nationalism run the gamut from ones rooted in ethnic legitimacy to legally based civic legitimacy to religion.[35] Ethnic, civic, and religious nationalism are three common and important forms of nationalism that deserve special attention because they tend to be the forms most commonly present in the modern era. As this discussion will show, each of these forms of nationalism has its own limitations for creating unity among a population within a state, especially in the wake of civil conflict.

ETHNIC NATIONALISM

Ethnic nationalism derives its moral underpinnings from a perceived sense of common ancestry among its members. Perhaps the most commonly cited definition of ethnic nationalism comes from Anthony Smith, who defines ethnic groups and nationalism largely by the characteristics they possess. According to Smith, ethnic groups are "a named human population with a myth of common ancestry, shared memories, and cultural elements; a link with historic territory or homeland; and a measure of solidarity."[36] As previously noted, ethnic groups become ethnic nations when they meet the following criteria: "[have] a named human population occupying a historic territory, and sharing myths, memories, a single public culture and common rights and duties for all members." Smith is quick to point out that the use of history and common ancestry need not be empirically accurate, but that nations are built on premodern origins.[37]

Connor defines ethnic nationalism as the politicization of a group's sense of common ancestry for the purpose of seeking self-rule and territorial sovereignty.[38] For Connor ethnic nations perceive themselves to be of common ancestry, but it is possible that these perceptions are not rooted in fact. Furthermore, nations are more than a list of characteristics; they also affect the behavior of its members. Ethnic nationalism, therefore, is not merely a set of attributes but also shared perceptions that shape reality and, in turn, affect members' behavior. In these cases nations make states; groups awaken to their sense of uniqueness and demand political and territorial sovereignty as a seemingly natural result of this awakening.

One of the more important tools of ethnic nationalism, and all forms of nationalism, is myth. The term *myth* today carries a pejorative connotation as something fictitious or untrue, and the term *national myth* is equally negative, suggesting a statewide cover-up or collective denial of some egregious wrongdoing.[39] Myths are also commonly understood as make-believe or in sharp contrast to history and science. Myths, however, are an important form of didactic storytelling that could be some of the oldest tales known to humanity, and national myths are particularly important for understanding the emotional attachments of its members.[40]

Mircea Eliade offers a useful definition of myths and their importance to nations and nationalism. He claims that a myth "narrates a sacred history; it relates an event that took place in primordial Time, the fabled time of the 'beginnings.' In other words a myth tells how, through the deeds of Supernatural Beings, a reality came into existence, be it the whole of reality, the Cosmos, or only a fragment of reality." Eliade further argues that a myth has five properties: "It constitutes the history of the acts of the founders, the Supernaturals; it is considered to be true; it tells how an institution came into existence; in performing the ritual associated with the myth, one 'experiences knowledge of the origin' and claims one's patriarchy; thus one 'lives' the myth, as a religion."[41] In other words myths tell groups where they came from, the heroic and supernatural nature of their founding fathers, and that they are active participants in the destiny of the group. Karen Armstrong echoes Eliade and notes that humans are "meaning seeking creatures," and that "a myth is not a story for its own sake. It shows us how we should behave." She further states: "Mythology is an art form that points beyond history to what is timeless in human existence, helping us to get beyond the chaotic flux of random events, and glimpse the core of reality."[42] Claude Levi-Strauss describes myth as "a form of language, and language itself predisposes us to attempt to understand ourselves and our world."[43] Robert A. Segal contends that social myths in fact serve to unify groups and are "indispensable to all societies."[44] Armstrong asserts that "a myth, therefore, is true because it is effective, not because it gives us factual information."[45]

Alongside myths are rites and rituals that reinforce and spread myths. Rites and rituals require individuals and groups to participate in acts that reinforce myths and personalize them. Literature on the study of myth tends to agree that myths are not complete without rites and rituals, which are also bound to the myths that give them meaning. Segal notes, "According to the myth and ritual, or myth-ritualist theory, myth does not stand by itself but is tied to ritual. Myth is not just a statement but an action." He further summarizes: "Ritual is the *application* not the *subject* of myth."[46]

In ethnic nationalism myths tend to focus on common ancestry or blood. Rarely are these claims true, but such myths unify people by making a claim about the group's origin. Furthermore, ethnic nationalist myths determine who is in the group and, in so doing, who is not in the group. Finally, myths of common ancestry are often invoked (or created) to make claims to territory and for self-determination. As noted, Anderson asserts that these claims have their origins in Europe, although once the concept of ethnic nationalism spread throughout the world, the myths based on common ancestry became a source of state-building and self-determination.

The spread of nationalism throughout the world created nations that, in turn, aspired to be states based on their common and unique history. Greenfeld notes that democracy and nationalism developed simultaneously in some European cases where being a nation was dependent on being democratic. But the idea of a unique people spread to other parts of the world independent from democracy, creating nations based solely on ethnic particularism.[47]

Ethnic nationalism has been one of the most persistent forms of national ideology in the history of modern states. It shaped the rise of nationalism in Europe, particularly in the nineteenth century, and continued to inspire self-determination following World War I and the decline of colonialism.[48] Ethnic nationalism abated somewhat during the Cold War, although nations demanding states based on their unique ancestry continued to exist throughout the world, including in the Middle East (Palestine), Asia (Tibet), and Africa (Eritrea). With the demise of Communism and the dissolution of the Soviet Union, ethnic nationalism reemerged with a vengeance, accompanied by conflict and bloodshed.

Post–Cold War literature on ethnic nationalism focuses heavily on the causes of ethnic conflict and the unique challenges associated with shoring up countries after ethnic atrocities have occurred within their borders.[49] Whereas ethnic nationalism had developed in seventeenth-, eighteenth-, and nineteenth-century Europe as a means of creating the perception of common ancestry largely within a state's borders, ethnic nationalism of the late twentieth century emerged *within* state borders, rending those states into subgroups demanding autonomy. Ethnic nationalism within borders continues to be a challenge for states around the globe.

Ethnic nationalism, therefore, is predicated on the belief in a perceived common ancestry and is often accompanied by a common language and unifying symbols, rituals, and narratives. It includes and excludes based on these constructs, which, although created, appear to be ancient and organic. As chapter 3 will describe, although many European states developed myths of common ancestry *after* the creation of sovereign territories with the aim of unifying subjects within their borders, ethnic nationalism became "modular"—to paraphrase Anderson—and its program spread to colonial states that developed their own ethnic nationalisms. Once created these nations demanded the right to self-rule and independence. In the post–Cold War era, ethnic nationalism emerged within existing states, tearing at their unity and leading, in many cases, to conflict, bloodshed, and even genocide. Ethnic nationalism, while once a program to create state unity, now leads more to disunity and conflict.

Finally, it is worth noting that the seventeenth-, eighteenth-, and nineteenth-century programs of European ethnic nationalism have begun to erode as non-European groups migrate to and settle in these countries. Turkish *Gastarbeiter* in Germany who never returned home, the migration of former colonial subjects to Europe, and the spread of non-European refugees into the Continent have presented new challenges for nations that are defined by language, religion, and blood myths. These developments suggest that, even when successful, ethnic nationalism is difficult to maintain in a globalized, cosmopolitan world where people are highly mobile.

RELIGIOUS NATIONALISM

In the twentieth century, another form of nationalism emerged, what sociologist Mark Juergensmeyer calls religious nationalism. Juergensmeyer argues that religious nationalism formed as a direct challenge to what he calls secular nationalism, which includes liberalism (civic nationalism), Communism, and ethnic nationalism, such as pan-Arabism. Religious nationalists aim to create an authentic ideology that is free of secular corruption and upholds orthodoxy, or right practices of the faith, by making religion the guiding principle of the state. Juergensmeyer argues that secular and religious nationalism are both ideologies of "order" that aim to minimize "disorder," which is barbarism, social chaos, and death. They are complex systems of beliefs that aspire to shape political and social action. As such secular and religious nationalism are in direct competition with each other.[50]

Religious nationalism shares many similarities with ethnic nationalism, but it also has some unique attributes. Like ethnic nationalism it is exclusive; in order to be part of the nation, one needs to be a member of that particular religious group and, perhaps more specifically, adhere to the specific interpretation of that group. Those who are not members of the religious group or do not adhere to its understanding of the faith cannot be members of the nation. Religious nationalism differs from ethnic nationalism in that it often transcends a myth of common ancestry. For example proponents of Islamic-based religious nationalism, often called Islamism, seek to unite Muslims and uphold what its leaders believe to be the correct understanding of the faith. Islamism aims to create a Muslim nation that transcends and eradicates other differences, such as secular nationalism or Communism, which its entrepreneurs consider Western constructs.

Finally, religious nationalism, like ethnic nationalism, capitalizes on emotional claims. As Weber discusses, nationalism gets its power from its emotional content, not from "economic" or pragmatic appeals. Religious nationalism derives its power and appeal from purported connections to the divine and attempts to guide citizens in the earthly struggle to live one's life righteously. As will be discussed in the case studies, while these claims are perhaps noble in their pursuits, religious nationalism is often accompanied by intolerance of other religions and even different interpretations within a religion, making national cohesion and state viability difficult.

It is important to note that religious nationalism is not just a Muslim phenomenon. Juergensmeyer is quick to point out that religious nationalism has been on the rise *across* religions, particularly in the postcolonial era. Hindu nationalism began to challenge the secular policies of India in the 1980s, leading to increased interreligious conflict. Also in the 1980s, Sikhs rose up in India demanding their own state based on religious principles. Israel also saw a rise in debates over the moral underpinnings of the state, including groups that believe that Israel should be a religious state, governed by the Torah and religious law. Sri Lanka and Myanmar have experienced tensions between their Buddhist majorities, who feel that the government should give them preferential treatment over the countries' non-Buddhist minorities. And a small but vocal minority of Christians in the United States has agitated for a greater inclusion of religious principles in government, including at its most extreme the creation of a Christian theocracy in the United States.[51]

Religious nationalism faces several challenges for the successful management of a state. First, similar to ethnic nationalism, what to do with those outside the religion becomes an important question for the stability of the state. For example the creation of the Islamic Republic of Iran in 1979, in which Shia Islam was named the official religion and became the principle source of law and governance, placed a significant minority of non-Shia, such as Sunni Muslims, Baha'is, and Jews, under Shia religious authority. The creation of the Islamic Republic of Iran also raised the questions of who interprets the religion and what to do with those who disagree with the state-driven interpretation of the faith. The Islamic Republic of Iran has had to confront both of these challenges. The 2009 "Green Revolution," in which thousands of protesters were imprisoned and abused after calling for the creation of a more just democratic system and fair elections, demonstrates that creating a state ideology around religion is fraught with challenges.

CIVIC NATIONALISM

Alongside ethnic and religious nationalism, civic nationalism emerged as another path to creating unity among people in a territory. Whereas ethnic nationalism built itself around concepts of common ancestry, language, and perceived shared history, civic nationalism is based on the ideals of the state, particularly the rule of law, and the shared trust it creates among its citizens. In theory states based on civic nationalism are open to anyone so long as he or she agrees to the rules of the state. Sidney Verba is quick to point out that civic culture, which undergirds civic nationalism, is not a new political concept and in fact dates back to some of the oldest political thinkers known to history, such as Plato and Aristotle, and to the political philosophers of the Enlightenment.[52]

Verba defines civic culture as "a substantial consensus on the legitimacy of political institutions and the direction and content of a public policy, a widespread tolerance of a plurality of interests and belief in their reconcilability, and a widely distributed sense of political competence and mutual trust in the citizenry."[53] His definition of civic culture includes several reinforcing components. First, civic culture is based on popularly held support of the rules of the state and the policies that are based on those rules. Second, it upholds a widespread belief in and support of plurality, which suggests tolerance of groups with different histories, ancestry, language, and religion. In theory, therefore, civic culture and the nationalism it produces could provide an overarching political and social framework in which multiple ethnic and linguist groups could share a state. Third, his definition stresses a necessary trust in fellow citizens. Civic culture, in other words, is not just about the rules or the constitution of the state; it is also about citizens and their relationship to and trust of one another and the state; civic culture needs to live in the people, or it will not be effective.

Civic culture becomes civic nationalism when it is absorbed into the psyche of most, if not all, of the nation's citizens and becomes the governing principle of the state. Civic nationalism is closely paired with democracy and the principle that the people of a state have the right to choose their leaders, but it is also intrinsically tied to liberalism, or the values that undergird democracy, such as freedom of speech and assembly, minority rights, and checks and balances on governmental authority.[54] Civic nationalism also requires state instruments to create and maintain this culture, including a healthy bureaucracy, military, and economy. The social contract, in other words, plays a crucial role in developing and maintaining civic nationalism. Finally, mass education is important for indoctrinating the population in its rights and responsibilities in civic nationalism. These organizational and institutional aspects are necessary but not sufficient to create civic nationalism.

Civic nationalism relies heavily on the participation of citizens in a state. Tocqueville's nineteenth-century study of democracy in the United States, for example, stresses the importance of citizen support and participation in social and state institutions for successful democracy building and state cohesion. He cites tools that support and reinforce citizen participation, ranging from national monuments to newspapers as necessary for creating a national sense of association.[55] Civic nationalism, in other words, is not just ideas but actions.

Tocqueville further notes the importance of volunteerism to establish and maintain civic nationalism, which includes activities connected both to the state (political organizations) and to free associations independent of the state, such as sports leagues, churches, and professional associations. Tocqueville asserts: "Among democratic nations . . . all the citizens are independent and feeble; they can hardly do anything by themselves, and none of them can oblige his fellow men to lend him their assistance. They all, therefore, become powerless if they do not learn voluntarily to help one another."[56] He further claims: "Americans of all ages, all conditions, and all dispositions constantly form associations," and "in democratic countries the science of association is the mother of science; the progress of all the rest depends upon the progress it has made. . . . If men are to remain civilized or become so, the art of associating together must grow and improve in the same ratio in which the equality of conditions is increased."[57] This voluntary participation helps create "cross cutting cleavages," or formal and informal ties to different segments of society that strengthen social cohesion of the wider society and prevent democracies from becoming a tyranny of the majority.[58]

Despite these very pragmatic and rational aspects of civic nationalism, its culture and political institutions are also dependent on myths, symbols, and rituals to educate and unify citizens in a state. As with ethnic nationalism, myths and symbols connect the past to the present in civic nationalism, but a greater emphasis rests on imagining a common destiny of its people. As will be described in chapter 3, the United States embodies this agenda. National symbols, like the Statue of Liberty, Washington DC, and the Golden Gate Bridge, are emblematic of the common destiny of the nation.

National myths also teach the common destiny of citizens. The American Dream, which echoes the Declaration of Independence, purports that liberty and prosperity are open to all who are willing to work for it, regardless of ethnic origins. The American dream, therefore, teaches the work ethic and the responsibility of individuals for achieving their own success. The American dream is accompanied by other idioms such as "pulling yourself up by your bootstraps," the idea that success depends on individual effort. Manifest Destiny, another American myth, asserts that it was divinely ordained for the United States to expand westward, eventually holding territory from coast to coast. In addition to the right to occupy land, Manifest Destiny has also been interpreted to identify the United States' role as a world power. Michael T. Lubragge's essay on Manifest Destiny, for example, ends by insisting on its timeless agenda: "Manifest Destiny has no end. It is perpetual and everlasting. Without Manifest Destiny the world would be flat and the earth would be the center of the solar system. Whether divinely ordained or not, expansion is inevitable and without limit. Yes, land is a finite commodity . . . on earth."[59]

As several scholars argue, each state produces its own unique blend of civic culture, drawing from the society's history, values, and myths. For example Verba notes that Rousseau defines political culture as "morality, custom, and opinion," and that these laws are "engraved on the hearts of the citizens. This forms the real constitution of the State, and takes on every day new power, when other laws decay or die out . . . keeps a people in the ways it was meant to go and insensibly replaces authority by the force of habit."[60] Civic culture and civic nationalism, therefore, are united by popularly held support of the rules of the state and the policies based on those rules, the institutional support of plurality, and trust in fellow citizens. There is a moral underpinning that unites people and allows for their common destiny.

Developing civic culture and nationalism, however, comes with certain challenges. First it requires civic entrepreneurs to shape and promote civic culture. European countries and the United States had the political philosophers of the Enlightenment—such as Hobbes, Locke, Rousseau, Montesquieu, and Jefferson—who drew from scholars of the classics, the moral roots of Christianity, and their social and political contexts to develop the philosophical and pragmatic underpinnings of civic culture in these countries. This observation suggests that political and philosophical entrepreneurs are required in other regions to develop civic nationalist agendas, and they need to draw from their own social and cultural milieus for civic nationalism to be rooted in specific contexts.

Second, civic culture and nationalism take time to develop and instill in the people. Particularly, evidence suggests that fostering civic nationalism takes longer and is more difficult than programs of ethnic or religious nationalism. Ethnic nationalism and religious nationalism capitalize on aspects of a group the people identify with easily, such as language, race, a history of persecution, or religion, and mobilize and build political agendas around these traits. Ethnic entrepreneurs, in particular, construct the past as a weapon to create circles of inclusion and exclusion, or as Jack David Eller puts it, "the ethnic group defines 'what we really are' in terms of 'what we were.'"[61] These narratives capitalize on highly emotionalized claims that, when coupled with the perception of a threat, produce conflict, panic, and even violence. Civic nationalism, by contrast, roots its agenda in establishing shared norms, rules and laws that help produce trust among citizens and between citizens and the state. This process requires time and education to "engrave on the hearts of the citizens."

Third, scholarship suggests that creating civic nationalism may be difficult—some say impossible—after ethnic discrimination, violence, and atrocities have occurred. Chaim Kaufmann, for example, argues that once ethnic conflict and bloodshed have occurred in a country, ethnic identities are hardened beyond repair and the only solution is to create "defensible enclaves" through partitioning or other programs aimed at detangling ethnic groups. Kaufmann asserts that attempts to create a civic culture will be fruitless under these conditions.[62] Jack Snyder lists several options for creating functioning states after ethnic-based conflict, including conflict driven by electoral competition. He identifies six options: "hegemonic control by the majority," ethnic partition, federalism, assimilation, political power sharing, and cross-ethnic alliances. Each of these arrangements presents challenges for state cohesion. Snyder does propose that cross-ethnic alliances, which include efforts "to depoliticize ethnicity by creating cross-ethnic alignments," could potentially create a viable state, but only if these alliances extend beyond mere voting and include impartial media and other "ethnically blind" institutions. He suggests that civic culture could in fact be created in the wake of ethnic conflict, but only with a holistic and comprehensive approach that includes both structural and perceptual changes aimed at creating cross-ethnic alliances.[63]

Finally, civic nationalism is constantly fraught with debate and nonviolent conflict over the rules and how to apply them within a given state. Civic nationalism may claim to be rooted in natural law or immutable Truth, but discerning these truths for each generation and in light of new social, political, and technological developments requires robust institutions that can find both the letter and the spirit of the law. In the United States, for example, each of the branches of government is responsible for this process. The United States Supreme Court is "the highest tribunal in the nation for all cases and controversies arising under the Constitution or the laws of the United States. The Court stands as the final arbiter of the law and guardian of constitutional liberties."[64] Civic nationalism is realized not merely through this process of discernment but also in the population, which agrees to work through the system for change and ultimately accepts the outcome of the rulings; the system is only as strong as the population's buy-in and support of the values that undergird civic nationalism.

Bridging the Gap—National Unity

If ethnic and religious nationalism are prone to create divisions and conflict within a state, and civic nationalism requires time and education to develop and foster, a more modest and near-term objective for creating a sense of cohesion among the members of a state's population and introducing their rights and responsibilities as citizens is required in modern-day state-building and nation-building. A program of national-unity building is designed to fill that gap.

National-unity building aims to do two broad things. First, and most importantly, it seeks to create a sense of cohesion among the factions of a state's population. This cohesion is centered not on perceptions of common ancestry or religion but on a common destiny. As members of a state, citizens need to recognize that they hold the power to make, or destroy, their own future. They are in the same boat, so to speak, and need one another not only to survive but to thrive. As citizens, as the true sovereignty of the state, they hold the power of the state and can make it prosper. National-unity building aims, therefore, to make this reality apparent to all citizens.

Within this sense of common destiny, national unity cannot deny the past, as Renan and others suggest. However, *how* the past is regarded becomes vital for national-unity building. A past that has included suffering, warfare, and harm to one another cannot be ignored, but nor should it be the defining element of the future. Rather, as Renan notes, it is the recognition of suffering through which people can find their common purpose and destiny. The past needs to be understood in terms of the present and the future together.

As an immediate and practical goal, national unity should work on building social capital among the people, that is, the informal norms and rules that are based on reciprocity and develop trust among the members of a population.[65] Social capital is often dysfunctional or destroyed in post–civil conflict environments; it must be rebuilt and the circle of trust widened and refashioned, as well as the conditions for fostering a wide array of free associations and civil society. As will be discussed in chapter 4, the way in which the core components of a state are built or rebuilt—including its physical infrastructure, economy, rule of law, security forces, government, and social services—needs to start with the people and include them throughout the process in order to help build social capital, give the population ownership and control of the state, and encourage them to build a future together.

Second, national unity aims to create a popular sense of rights, responsibilities, and loyalty to the state. This relationship between citizens and the state is fostered, in part, by the social contract, the idea that citizens give up certain liberties, such as total freedom, and governments provide certain resources to citizens in return, such as security or other services, like education, roads, potable water, and health care. National unity is realizing that the state—its government, military, rule of law, economy—are the responsibility of the population. People are the sovereign, and the state starts with them. However, building loyalty toward the state is more than just a rational quid pro quo; it is also involves emotional content. Myths, symbols, rituals, and other trappings of nations are equally important in efforts to build national unity. National unity is recognizing and identifying with the common destiny of both the people and the state. It is building an imaginary community based on these two principles.

Ultimately, a program of national-unity building should feed into civic nationalism. National-unity building should provide the necessary time and space to allow for the rule of law to be developed and institutionalized as a held belief among the members of the population. National-unity building should also begin to educate the people about their rights and responsibilities as citizens of a state and of a potential democracy. These underpinnings of civic nationalism, while the most inclusive form of nationalism, take time to develop and instill in the population. National-unity building in the near term provides that necessary time. Aspects of ethnic, religious, and civic nationalism and national unity are summarized in table 1.

1. Ethnic, religious, and civic nationalism and national unity

	Ethnic nationalism	Religious nationalism	Civic nationalism	National unity
Moral foundation	Nation formed by myth of common ancestry	Nation subject to divine rule, faith-based principles	Nation formed around norms, rules, and laws	Nation formed around common destiny
Focus	The past as justification for the present	Timeless upholding of "right" religious tenets	The present and the future	The present and the future
Membership	Inclusion limited to perceived blood or ancestral ties	Inclusion limited to those within the religion or specific interpretation	Inclusion based on agreeing and adhering to rules and norms—in theory anyone can join	Inclusion based on citizenship to state
Construction	Based on exploiting past to justify current agendas	Based on religious principles and laws	Rooted in philosophical and moral teachings	Based on the necessity of community and the state
Mobilization	Largely fear based	Fear based	Opportunity based	Opportunity based
Time to construct	Can be relatively quick	Can be relatively quick	Takes time to develop and foster	Interim step to civic nationalism

National unity, therefore, is aimed at recognizing common destiny among the members of a state's population and its vital role in the future of the state. National unity starts with the people to build or rebuild the state, develops social capital among them, and begins to create a sense of nation through them. National unity builds hope for the future.

Defining and distinguishing states from nations is an important first step in analyzing programs aimed at "nation-building." States—including strong, weak, failing, and failed—consist of internationally recognized borders, territory, and populations. Healthy states are further defined by the government that runs them, as well as what governments actually do, particularly the services they provide their populations, in addition to the health of the state's civil society. Nations, most broadly, are a collective of people who share some sort of bond with one another—be it a belief in common descent, shared rules and norms, or religious laws and values—and seek political goals based on these perceived common bonds. They are what Anderson calls "an imagined [political] community."

Nationalism—or the political ideology that fuses nations with the moral underpinnings of a state's laws, services, and government—is another important component of building a viable state. The three most common forms of nationalism today, ethic, religious and civil, all present challenges for state-building, particularly in a postconflict environment. Ethnic nationalism and religious nationalism are, by definition, exclusive in their membership. Civic nationalism, with its emphasis on rules, norms, and laws, takes time to develop and instill in the population.

A program of national-unity building bridges the gap between near-term requirements for creating cohesion among the members of the population and providing the time for civic nationalism to develop and take hold. National unity is recognizing and identifying with the common destiny of both the population and the state. It is building an imaginary community based on these two principles.

Chapter 3 will build on this discussion by examining state-building and nation-building in Europe and the United States, particularly in the seventeenth, eighteenth, and nineteenth centuries. This investigation will highlight the types of programs undertaken by national entrepreneurs aimed at constructing ethnic and civic nationalism in these countries and offer insights into what a nation-building program in the twenty-first century may include.

3

STATE-BUILDING AND NATION-BUILDING
IN EUROPE AND THE UNITED STATES

As described in chapter 2, the terms *state* and *nation* are not interchangeable and require distinct definitions in order for one to better understand how they are constructed and maintained. States are defined by territory, their populations, and international recognition, with more robust states including governance that provides services to their population and the presence of a vibrant civil society. Nations, by contrast, are defined most broadly as large groups that draw on the past to assert a common purpose and destiny that is political, often claiming rights to sovereignty and territory, and emotional, invoking attachment and some degree of loyalty to fellow members of the nation.

This chapter looks at what are perhaps the most successful examples of state-building and nation-building in history: Western Europe and the United States, particularly in the seventeenth, eighteenth, and nineteenth centuries. While often dismissed as irrelevant for state-building and nation-building in the modern era, particularly for non-Western cultures and developing countries, these cases offer important clues to how both states and nations are constructed. Arguably, Europe and the United States became the template for building the state and the nation throughout the world, both historically and today. Therefore, understanding the conditions that led to state creation in Europe and the United States, and how nations were forged from these states, is useful for understanding state-building and nation-building today.

Specifically, this chapter asserts that the creation of states in Europe and the founding of the United States preceded the development of nations. National entrepreneurs—artists, authors, socialites, politicians, businesspeople, and other members of society—along with governments developed and fostered a sense of nation through a range of initiatives in these countries. This chapter highlights two sets of nation-building tools in particular: specific state resources that political elites used to help forge nations within state boundaries, including militaries, education systems, and bureaucracies; and the construction of symbols and myths that created national unity within state borders. In both Europe and the United States, nation-building, once begun, was as much an initiative of private citizens as it was a state-led enterprise. When done well, nation-building reinforced the state and appeared organic, not constructed.

This discussion will suggest that modern-day efforts at both state-building and national-unity building are not doomed to failure if states are multiethnic, poly-linguistic, or have other potentially divisive subgroups. But as with the examples that will be given, political and social elites need to consciously create programs aimed at developing a sense of national unity in order for people to cohere into citizens and support the state.

State Creation in Europe and the United States

Conventional wisdom holds that nations build states. Certain groups awaken to their sense of nation-ness, which is organic and ancient, and demand territorial and political sovereignty. In other words the nation exists, it awakens, and then it creates the state. While support for this causal argument can certainly be found, particularly in twentieth-century examples of self-determination described in chapter 2, this was not the causal path for Europe or the United States. In both cases states preceded nations and were the product of specific historical circumstances that produced the need for new forms of sovereignty and the transformation of populations from subjects to citizens; these changes required state leaders to respond to their citizens in new ways. This causal path makes studying state-building and nation-building in Europe and the United States particularly useful for modern-day efforts at stabilizing preexisting states. In such cases states exist but the nation may not be fully developed and requires conscious programs initiated by state leaders, private citizens, and civil society to help foster a sense of national unity.

STATE-BUILDING IN EUROPE AND THE UNITED STATES

The creation of modern-day states in Europe and the United States is the product of a complex confluence of historic factors, including economic matters, intellectual thought, religion, war, language, class, the creation of public space, treaties, and technological innovations. Within this conglomeration of circumstances, the definition of sovereignty underwent a transformation from monarchs and Christendom, to kings and territory, to governments, people, and territory. Furthermore, the role of people evolved from mere subjects to citizens who play an active role in the state's overall viability.

Perhaps some of the earliest states in Europe were formed around economic interests. Independent city-states emerged in Italy between the ninth to the fifteenth centuries following the fall of the Holy Roman Empire. British economist S. R. Epstein describes a city-state as "a special kind of *universitas* that, in addition to municipal self-rule, practiced its own foreign policy, was fiscally independent, could raise an army and impose the death penalty, and could mint coins, sign commercial charters with other independent states, and requisition foreign merchants' goods."[1] City-states such as Venice, Milan, Florence, and Genoa became thriving centers of commerce, trade, and early capitalism. Some of these city-states retained elements of republicanism, and its members were more like citizens than mere subjects.[2]

Alongside newly emerging commercial interests, citizens began to assert their rights in new ways. One of the first and most important examples of this dynamic is the thirteenth-century Magna Carta, drafted by the archbishop of Canterbury to settle conflicts between the king of England and his noblemen, including economic interests. The Magna Carta delineated the role and limits of the king vis-à-vis his subjects and enshrined barons' rights. It is one of the earliest documents to limit leadership and safeguard the rights of subjects.

Similar economic interests were visible in the Dutch Republic, founded in the late sixteenth century. Jan Luiten van Zanden and Maarten Prak posit that "the Dutch Republic is arguably the best example of a small state playing a disproportionately large role in the European state system in this period."[3] They note the republic's influential role in commerce and the development of citizens' rights vis-à-vis the state as examples of its state-like functions during this time.

Another factor that contributed to the creation of modern states in Europe was an intellectual revival, the Renaissance, which was rooted in classic social and political thought. Not only were art, music, and architecture subjects of interest during the Renaissance, but so too were classical philosophical discussions about political organization and the concept of the ideal state. For example in the early 1500s Machiavelli penned *Discourses on Livy*, which describes Rome's republic around the third century BCE.[4] Philosophical discussions of republicanism also emerged among Dutch thinkers as well as among Poles and Lithuanians. These works questioned the role of common people in the political realm and the right to determine leadership. This trend in political thought became known as "early modern republicanism" or "early humanism" and shaped the transformation of Europe into modern states.[5]

Religion also played a crucial role in the creation of modern states. European states were, in fact, the accidental by-product of the Christian Reformation and inter-Christian struggles that emerged from the birth of Protestantism. Martin Luther's series of challenges to the papacy on doctrine and the interpretation of scriptures were not intended to forever rend Western Christendom; however, Luther's attempts at papal reform ended in an irreversible split within European Christianity and the end of Christendom anchored in the pope.

Technological innovations also led to the creation of modern states in Europe. The spread of Luther's controversial religious ideas accelerated with the advent of the printing press; an early press was located in Wittenberg a short distance from the seminary where Luther taught. One of the first books published on the Gutenberg press was the Bible translated into vernacular languages, not Latin, which gave these languages new prominence. The printing press sparked not only a religious revolution within Europe but also created a new level of consciousness that spread around the world. Books and the literacy they required, therefore, further changed the social and political order and helped foster the creation of states.

War also produced modern states in Europe. The Thirty Years' War, which began after Luther's attempts at reform and was largely a conflict between Catholic and several Protestant entities, expanded to include political battles for power. Ultimately the war engulfed the bulk of Europe in one of its bloodiest conflicts. Germany, for example, is believed to have lost between 15 and 20 percent of its population from fighting, disease, and famine by the war's end.[6]

The violence unhinged from the Reformation produced two important treaties aimed at creating peace and stability in Europe. First, the Peace of Augsburg in 1555 forged an agreement between Catholic Charles V and the Schmalkaldic League of Lutheran princes that formalized the Catholic-Protestant split within Christendom. The agreement stipulated *"curius regio, eius religio,"* or "whose realm, his religion," giving each prince the right to determine the religion of his subjects. The 1648 Peace of Westphalia, which ended the war between some, but not all, fighting factions of the Thirty Years' War, created the conditions for territorial and political sovereignty within Central Europe and marked a fundamental change in international relations. The treaties in the Peace of Westphalia, therefore, effectively created the conditions for the modern state system.

The Reformation also played a critical role in redefining the relationship between citizens and their governments. Jürgen Habermas notes that the Reformation, along with burgeoning capitalist markets and the creation of a new class, the bourgeois, helped create what he calls "the public sphere" and public authority, or the collectivization of citizens and their development of public opinion through debate and other mediums. According to Habermas, "The institutions of public authority, along with the bureaucracy and the military, and in part also with the legal institutions, asserted their independence from the privatized sphere of the princely court." From this process individuals became collective citizens and could assert their authority, compelling leaders to respond to their interests and demands.[7]

The Industrial Revolution was another important development that changed the social fabric of Europe and the relationship between governments and people. The birth of factories rapidly drew together individual laborers from towns and villages in a phenomenon that became known as urbanization. Rapidly expanding city slums of workers required policies, regulations, and laws to manage these new collectives. Furthermore, urbanization created new forms of identity and even consciousness among the many people uprooted from their families, traditional social structures, and means of subsistence. The Industrial Revolution also transformed the economic and military might of states, creating new levels of competition between states based on the ability to mass-produce weapons and raise capital.[8]

Concurrent with the Industrial Revolution, a second intellectual awakening, the Enlightenment, further developed the concept of citizens and their rights vis-à-vis rulers. In particular key concepts of the Enlightenment, such as the notions of equality, liberty, natural law, reason, and the roles and limits of government vis-à-vis its people, paved the way for modern states. Several philosophers of the Enlightenment also began to articulate what became known as the social contract between leaders and subjects. Thomas Hobbes (1588–1659), for example, argued that only a sovereign power could ensure security in a world where individuals are obsessed with self-preservation, are largely equal in strength, and cannot trust one another, a condition he called "the state of nature." In order for a sovereign to provide security, citizens must transfer some of their rights to that sovereign power, thus allowing it to impose order over its people in the form of a commonwealth.[9]

John Locke (1632–1704) contended that human nature is based on tolerance and reason, and that all have the right to defend what is theirs and seek reparation for what has been taken. Locke's social contract thus focused on the creation of civil society that mitigates and resolves disputes over property and a commonwealth that ensures impartiality and proportion.[10]

Jean-Jacques Rousseau (1712–78) concurred that all must relinquish some freedoms to create a social contract, but that it must be done not out of fear or coercion but from a point of active participation and common destiny. Rousseau thus divided his social contract into two parts. The first, what he calls "the sovereign," encompasses all people and their general will, which have the power to create laws. The second is the government, which applies the laws. Together these two halves of the social contract ensure liberty, equality, and self-preservation.[11]

The ideas of the Enlightenment, particularly the social contract, furthered the transition of people from mere subjects to citizens who had an active role to play in the destiny of their individual lives, their communities, and their countries. The 1689 English Bill of Rights enshrined the social contract, especially the ideas of Locke, to create rules and limits to government, rights of citizens, and the conditions under which royal succession occurred.[12]

The concepts of the Enlightenment received further validation in the American and French Revolutions. Both revolutions aimed to overthrow the monarchical system and the politically powerful churches under which their citizens lived. The 1776 U.S. Declaration of Independence drew from the English Bill of Rights and the ideas of Locke to declare both the rights of the people and the limits of government. The document's key phrase "life, liberty and the pursuit of happiness" is believed to have been derived from Locke's "life, health, liberty and possessions" described in his *Second Treatise of Government*, or possibly *An Essay concerning Human Understanding*, which deals extensively with human and public happiness.[13] The French Revolution added its own contributions to the discussion of the rights of citizens vis-à-vis their political leaders. The 1789 Rights of

Man and of the Citizen outlined universal rights of individuals and the collective, building largely off natural rights described by Rousseau and Montesquieu's discussion of the need for separation of powers in government.[14]

The creation of the United States, in particular, built on many of the ideas developed in Europe and became an important political experiment in designing a country where rights rested with its citizens, the government was limited in its authority, and states were given primacy over the federal system. The American Revolutionary War was fought not only for independence from British rule but also to forge a new kind of state rooted in the rights of the citizens. These ideals are clearly stated in the 1776 Declaration of Independence:

> We hold these truths to be self-evident, that all men are created equal, that they are endowed by their Creator with certain unalienable Rights, that among these are Life, Liberty and the pursuit of Happiness. That to secure these rights, Governments are instituted among Men, deriving their just powers from the consent of the governed,—That whenever any Form of Government becomes destructive of these ends, it is the Right of the People to alter or to abolish it, and to institute new Government, laying its foundation on such principles and organizing its powers in such form, as to them shall seem most likely to effect their Safety and Happiness.[15]

Following the Declaration of Independence, the states formed a loose alliance under the Articles of Confederation, which was drafted in 1777 and formally ratified in 1781. After the former colonies successfully achieved independence, the Articles of Confederation along with the Continental Congress were dissolved, and considerable debate broke out between the federalists, who believed the thirteen states should remain connected under some form of central authority, and the anti-federalists, who advocated for independence of each state.

In 1787 state representatives met in Philadelphia to draft the U.S. Constitution, which outlined laws for a federal government and its authority vis-à-vis states. Article 10 of the U.S. Constitution established the principle of federalism, which gave states and the people authority over the government, while the Supremacy Clause (article 6, clause 2) made the Constitution the supreme law of the land. These provisions set the framework for creating a central government but also for limiting its powers.

The U.S. Constitution also established a form of governance whereby a system of checks and balances further limited government powers. Articles 1, 2, and 3 of the Constitution call for the federal government to be divided into three bodies, the executive, the judicial, and the legislative branches, ensuring that no one body would hold too much power or be able to concentrate power in the head of state.

Along with limiting the power of the government through checks and balances, another key point of forging the United States was the creation of a bill of rights within the U.S. Constitution. The Bill of Rights, like the Magna Carta and the Rights of Man, upholds the rights of all citizens to specific liberties and restricts the power of the government to infringe on those rights. The First Amendment enshrines perhaps the most important liberties: the freedom of religion, speech, press, and assembly, legally preserving public space—freedom to collect, to organize groups, to debate, and to check the power of the government. The other amendments in the Bill Rights also protect the rights of citizens to defend themselves, to prevent unlawful trials and imprisonment, and even to prevent the government from compelling citizens to house soldiers, something that colonials were required to do during several wars on the North American continent. The Bill of Rights, in other words, simultaneously gave rights to citizens and restricted the power of the government.

In an effort to sway public opinion toward supporting ratification of the Constitution, Alexander Hamilton, James Madison, and John Jay drafted *The Federalist Papers*, which consisted of eighty-five articles published in journals and distributed throughout the states. *The Federalist Papers* stressed the practical and philosophical underpinnings of forming a central government, including the importance of one central authority to provide a common defense and the ability to collect taxes to pay for the common defense, to name but two key points.[16] In essence, *The Federalist Papers* became a massive marketing campaign aimed at selling the necessity of some form of central authority for the survival of the newly liberated United States.

The changed relationships between leaders and their people in Europe brought about by the ideas of the Enlightenment, the creation of public space, the concept of the social contract, and the American and French Revolutions created a new power among the people and the need for state leaders to instill a sense of belonging to and support of the state.

The Tools of Nation-Building

The creation of sovereign states, along with intellectual developments in the concepts of governance and the rights of common people, placed new demands on leaders in Europe and the United States. No longer mere subjects, citizens began to be active participants in the life of states and to see themselves as part of new collectives that were intrinsically bound to the state and in which sovereignty resided. This awakening led not only to a new level of consciousness concerning the relationship between citizens and their rulers but also to a new sense of belonging among citizens. In other words citizens began to see themselves as unique collectives defined, in part, by their affiliation with one another and with the states in which they resided. This awakening conforms to Greenfeld's discussion of the evolution of nations from elites to a "people," discussed in chapter 2.

However, the emergence of national consciousness in Europe and the United States was not an accidental by-product of history; rather, it was a deliberate program created by national entrepreneurs, elites who used a variety of programs to create a sense of common destiny among citizens and with the state. These entrepreneurs drew on two broad resources to build national unity within Europe and the United States. First, governments used resources of the state, such as education, state media, law, militaries, and bureaucracies, to develop and foster programs aimed at building national unity. Second, but equally important, private citizens along with governments developed programs aimed at creating a sense of national unity, including symbols, myths, literature, art, capital cities, museums, and national parks. Taken together these government tools and private initiatives forged national unity within these emerging states.

National entrepreneurs drew on several government services, programs, and resources to meld citizen into nations. In the European experience, perhaps one of the most important institutions of nation-building was the creation of a common, official language. This program was so successful that today it is rarely considered a deliberate creation. However, historians note that the construction of national languages was a process of conscious consolidation and even language "creation," beginning in the sixteenth century. Hobsbawm, for example, describes the process whereby various languages and dialects were deliberately melded into a common tongue, often constructed, by nation-building entrepreneurs. He notes that prior to the creation of common languages and their perpetuation through education, common people spoke different languages but did not perceive that as a sign of different entities or nations.[17] He further claims, "Languages, while not absent, came last. National languages are therefore almost always semi-artificial constructs and occasionally, like modern Hebrew, virtually invented. They are the opposite of what nationalist mythology supposes them to be, namely the primordial foundations of national culture and the matrices of the national mind. They are usually attempts to devise a standardized idiom out of a multiplicity of actually spoken idioms, which are thereafter downgraded to dialects."[18]

The process of language consolidation and education was the responsibility of national entrepreneurs, who had the intellectual tools to craft national languages, and of governments, which spread these common languages and instilled them in populations.[19] However, once constructed and adopted, language became a symbol of national unity and was perceived as organic, as will be described further below.

Alongside the creation of common and official languages of

the state, the development of mass education—which can be defined as universal (applying to all citizens), standardized, and rationalized, with one of its purposes being the socialization of individuals into the collective—helped build national unity.[20] Mass education served several important purposes for national consolidation. First and foremost, mass education spread literacy, which reinforced emerging national languages. Gellner summarizes the process: "Nationalism is essentially the transfer of the focus of man's identity to a culture which is mediated by literacy and an extensive, formal educational system."[21]

Common literacy and language, in turn, provided a skill for mass communication through print media, which became a powerful tool for forging, spreading, and consolidating national consciousness. Tocqueville notes in his seminal work, *Democracy in America*, that "nothing but a newspaper can drop the same thought into a thousand minds at the same moment."[22] Furthermore, according to Anderson the creation of print media would later make the concept of nationalism mobile and allow it to spread from Europe to its colonies and beyond, sparking nationalist sentiment and self-determination around the world.[23] In America prior to the revolution, for example, citizens created the first American newspapers, such as the *New England Courant*, founded by James Franklin; his brother Benjamin Franklin's *Pennsylvania Gazette*; the *Virginia Gazette*; and the *Massachusetts Spy*, which bound people together through not only information but also satire and humor.[24]

Mass education further formed national identities through the propagation of history in schools. These written histories built on and supplanted group narratives to create a common story of national origin and development. Historian Charles Beard notes that history making is intrinsically bound to and shaped by the historian's current circumstances. He describes the process: "History as record embraces the monuments, documents, and symbols which provide such knowledge as we have or can find respecting past actuality. But it is history as thought, not as actuality, record, or specific knowledge, that is really meant when the term history is used in its widest and most general significance."[25] In other words history says as much about the present needs and realities of those who create it as it does about the past.

Mass education also provided the skills necessary for economic development, particularly industrialization and the technological skills that mass production required. Gellner, in particular, stresses the role that mass education plays in developing basic skills for mass economic development: "[Mass education] refers to that complex of skills which makes a man competent to occupy most of the ordinary positions in a modern society. . . . Literacy is no doubt central to it. . . . The same goes for elementary numeracy and a modicum of technical competence." Gellner also asserts that mass education, beyond its role of providing individuals with skills for employment, was advanced by and perpetuates what he calls "high (literate training-sustained) culture"; all other cultures have become less significant in the industrial age.[26]

The creation of conscripted, mass-based militaries was another tool governments used to consolidate nations in Europe. Samuel Finer outlines the role of militaries in European nation-state-building. He argues that conscripted militaries were essential in functionally providing security for states and defending territory while, at the same time, becoming instruments of national consolidation. Finer contends that "the sense of nationhood is popular participation in matters affecting the whole population on the one side, and on the other, an identity of benefits received from this association."[27] Militaries, according to Finer, provide just such a function and purpose.

Napoléon's use of the *levee en masse* is particularly illustrative of the role that militaries played in national consolidation. Napoléon instituted the *levee en masse* on August 23, 1793, with the intent of defending France from invasion and stemming a civil war within its domain.[28] Article 1 of the decree states:

> From this moment until that in which the enemy shall have been driven from the soil of the Republic, all Frenchmen are in permanent requisition for the service of the armies. The young men shall go to battle; the married men shall forge arms and

transport provisions; the women shall make tents and clothing and shall serve in the hospitals; the children shall turn old
linen into lint; the aged shall betake themselves to the public
places in order to arouse the courage of the warriors and preach
the hatred of kings and the unity of the Republic.[29]

The *levee en masse* is believed to have raised a force of eight
hundred thousand for Napoléon's military campaigns.[30] Finer
describes the Napoleonic era as a time in which "state-building
received a new emphasis while the concept of a nation and of
the nation-state became full blown."[31]

The *levee en masse*, and later mass armies throughout Europe,
further allowed for a new level of popular participation, one that
created a political shift from subjects of a monarchy to citizens
loyal to the state. Not only did wars offer a means for citizens to
participate in the security and prosperity of the state, but such
participation also became the ultimate form of loyalty—the will-
ingness to risk one's life and to die for the nation. Participation
in mass armies also affected group cohesion, mixing people
together from across the state and giving them common purpose. In turn mass armies provided the state with security and
a means of territorial consolidation.[32]

The creation of mass armies in Europe, however, was not
without negative consequences. States had to create and maintain mass armies in order to successfully compete with one
another. Entire generations of men were conscripted and trained
in military arts and logic. Alfred Vagts calls this process "militarism;" a "vast array of customs, interests, prestige, actions and
thoughts associated with armies and wars and yet transcending
true military purpose . . . its influence is unlimited in scope."[33]
Countries defined by militarism used war as diplomacy, were
expansionist, and (ironically) unable to reach a secure relationship with their neighbors. Europe's use of militaries as tools of
state and national consolidation ended with the birth of the totalitarian regime, typified by Hitler, Mussolini, and Stalin, where
the principal purpose of the state was to condition people for
military ends.[34]

The creation of state bureaucracies was another important tool of both state and nation consolidation. Nineteenth- and twentieth-century German scholar Max Weber offers key insights into the construction and purpose of government bureaucracies and how they helped effect both state and national consolidation. Weber identifies several key components of a functioning bureaucracy: "the regular activities" of bureaucracy are fixed in rules, regulations, and official duties; the authority of the bureaucracy is a hierarchy that stabilizes the system and orders and executes duties in a consistent fashion that limits coercion and corruption; and qualified people are employed to perform these duties.[35] Weber also identifies the importance of civil servants to bureaucracies, noting that they differ from private employees because their task is wholly committed to public life, and the money and property in which they deal are not private. Weber further adds, "When the office is fully developed, official activity demands the full working capacity of the official, irrespective of the fact that his obligatory time in the bureau may be firmly delimited."[36]

State bureaucracies became the mechanisms through which the social contract was developed and realized. Governments collected taxes and, in turn, provided services to the people, ranging from security, to mass education, to public works such as roads, bridges, water, and sewage systems. As Rudolph Braun puts it, "Taxes are regularly paid compulsory levies on private units to produce revenues to be spent for public purposes."[37] Several scholars note that taxation did not begin with the modern state; the monarchies and local leaders preceding them had also collected money and resources from the population in times of war.[38] Charles Tilly, in particular, goes so far as to equate "war making and state making [with] organized crime."[39] Nevertheless, Braun asserts that while war may have led to greater taxation and the creation of bureaucracies, "common opinion gradually acquiesced in the permanent character of compulsory levies; it came to accept taxation as a permanent institution and as the 'inseparable twin of the modern state.'"[40] Taxation also created certain expectations among citizens, particularly for public goods—basic necessities provided by governments for their people.

Nation-building entrepreneurs drew from more than just the services of a functioning state to unify its population. They also used symbols, myths, and rituals to create national identities built around state institutions and a sense of emotional attachment among citizens and between citizens and the state. Once created perhaps the most visible symbol of the nation was language. Gellner asserts that the fusion of language with nationalism was successful when its adherents took for granted the two as intrinsically bound: "Language seems to them almost a biological inheritance, and its association with ethnic paternity strikes them as frequently powerful. They think it is 'acquired with the mother's milk.'"[41] Hobsbawm notes that today several countries go to pains to prevent other languages from seeping into the official language of the nation, thus keeping the country's language a symbol of national purity.[42]

States created other symbols that helped to build and reinforce national identities. Argyris Kyridis and his colleagues note that national symbols cover a wide range of items, including national holidays, stamps, national currencies, city and street names, and statues, to name a few, and that they play a critical role in defining national identity.[43] Sociologist Karen Cerulo asserts that "national symbols project a message. That message is purposively, meticulously constructed, with leaders of national governments consciously picking and choosing its elements."[44]

Cerulo argues, in particular, that national flags and anthems became important symbols of modern nations and the states they inhabit: "National symbols—in particular, national anthems and flags—provide perhaps the strongest, clearest statement of national identity. In essence, they serve as modern totems (in the Durkheimian sense)—signs that bear a special relationship to the nations they represent, distinguishing them from one another and reaffirming their identity boundaries. Since the inception of nations, national leaders have embraced and adopted national flags and anthems, using them to create bonds, motivate patriotic action, honor the efforts of citizens, and legitimate formal authority."[45] National flags and anthems, in other words, became important symbols not only of the state but of citizens and their nations as well.[46] Flags were originally used to denote specific militaries and navies. The first modern national flag was created in 1606 following the consolidation of England, Scotland, and Ireland under James I. Known as the "Union Jack," the flag combined elements of the three crowns to symbolically denote their union.[47] Similarly, the creation of a U.S. flag became an important symbol of independence during the American Revolution. Cerulo notes that "the American flag was carefully constructed by revolutionary leaders as a graphic manifestation of a new political program. The flag was to outline the structure of the governed, with stars and stripes representing the distinctiveness yet unity of the states."[48] David Madden, discussing the U.S. Confederate flag, notes that flags can simultaneously be symbols of triumph and persecution, unity and division, love and hate. He goes so far as to say that "a flag flying in the wind can look so awesome that it has the power almost of flesh and blood, like a living organism that thrives on air and sunlight."[49]

Alongside national flags and often in conjunction with rituals of flying the flag, national anthems also became important symbols of the nation and the state. The Dutch anthem, "Wilhelmus," believed to be the oldest national song, dates to the sixteenth century, although it did not become the official anthem of the Netherlands until 1932, when it replaced the anthem "Wien Neêrlands Bloed." The British anthem, "God Save the King/Queen," was first performed in 1745. Francis Scott Keyes penned "The Star-Spangled Banner" in 1814, although it was not officially adopted as the national anthem until 1931.[50]

National monuments also became important symbols of unity. Marvin Trachtenberg describes monuments as "public, permanent visual structures—traditionally sculpture, architecture, or both and sometimes paintings—that intend to symbolize something generally shared by a group or even an entire society." He also notes that the word stems from Latin and means "things that remind."[51] Hans Pohlsander notes that "no century, since antiquity, has built monuments more enthusiastically than the nineteenth century."[52] He chronicles, in particular, the creation of national monuments in nineteenth-century Germany. Pohlsander defines a national monument as "one which honors a revered leader or hero of a nation, keeps alive the memory of a significant event in the history of a nation, or expresses the ideals of a nation." He goes on to assert that "a national monument must transcend local or regional significance, must speak to the nation as a whole," for "monuments, like written documents, provide a historical record, but not necessarily a complete or objective record."[53] Pohlsander also notes that, despite being products of their time, national monuments can be reinterpreted in light of modern circumstances.

In the eighteenth and nineteenth centuries, virtually all modern states in Europe and the United States created national monuments that symbolized the spirit and ethos of their people. In the United States, private donations and federal support helped fund the base of the Statue of Liberty, which was a gift from France to help commemorate the centennial of the Declaration of Independence. The statue offered a modern rendering of the goddess of liberty, symbolizing the two countries' connection to this democratic principle.[54] The statue and a plaque engraved with Emma Lazarus's poem "The New Colossus" (referencing the ancient Colossus of Rhodes), proclaiming, "Give me your tired, your poor, your huddled masses, yearning to be free," were placed in New York harbor as symbols of the United States as the new carrier of the ancient torch of liberty.

Europe and the United States also undertook extensive programs aimed at creating capital cities that would stand as symbols of the nation. David Cannidine proposes that the construction of these new capitals was a form of public diplomacy: "This growing international competitiveness was mirrored in the large-scale rebuilding of capital cities, as the great powers bolstered their self-esteem in the most visible, ostentatious, manner."[55] In London George III hired John Nash in 1812 to redevelop Trafalgar Square, making it "a cultural space, open to the public."[56] His son, George IV, also hired Nash to update and enlarge Buckingham Palace, which was eventually finished by Edward Blore, and which placed the monarchy's residence near the city center. This change of residence eventually paved the way for the creation of the Mall, which connects the two iconic spaces.[57] In Paris Napoléon III hired Georges-Eugène Haussmann to transform Paris through the construction of grand boulevards, uniform buildings, public works, grand parks, the Paris opera house, and national monuments designed to create an awe-inspiring capital that could also accommodate its growing population.[58] Cannidine further cites Rome, Vienna, Berlin, and Washington DC as examples of capital cities that underwent grand renovation in the nineteenth century.[59]

In addition to the creation of capital cities, states founded national museums to document and display art, history, and natural science. Following the French Revolution, the Louvre was opened in 1793, offering free admission to citizens with the goal of making an aristocratic art collection accessible to the people.[60] Britain created its National Gallery on the edge of Trafalgar Square in 1832, and the monarchy set about purchasing art and commissioning portraits of national leaders. Also in the mid-1800s, the United States began to collect artifacts from around its expanding territories. In 1835 British natural scientist James Smithson bequeathed his inheritance to the U.S. federal government to "found an establishment for the increase and diffusion of knowledge."[61] Smithson's donation, which created the Smithsonian Institution, helped spawn federal interest in collecting cultural and natural artifacts from across the country and around the world, eventually leading to the first U.S. National Museum in 1881. Alongside these efforts, private citizens created the American Historical Association in 1884, which "networked with members of Congress and worked to archive the core documents in the history of the federal government."[62]

In addition to cities and museums, parks and forests became important symbols of the nation. France and Britain both created national parks in their capital cities aimed at developing public places that offered recreation and relaxation.[63] In the United States, women's associations began to purchase and preserve historic sites, transforming them into public parks. The Mount Vernon Ladies Association, for example, purchased George Washington's house at Mount Vernon in 1859 and restored it as a national heritage site.[64] In 1892 wildlife activist John Muir founded the Sierra Club with the aim of preserving wilderness in the United States, including sites like Yosemite and Yellowstone, and to raise public awareness of conservation.[65] These efforts helped designate large swaths of land as national parks and forests and to create the National Parks Service in the United States.[66]

Literature, poetry, and music also became important symbols of the nation, particularly in the nineteenth century. Pohlsander chronicles the construction of German nationalism through the creation of a "consciously German literature." He specifically credits Johann Gottfried Herder as "the founder of German nationalism" through philosophy, poetry, and literature that became a cornerstone of the Romantic era.[67] He further notes the collection of folk tales by the Grimm brothers as an example of intellectual efforts to create national sentiment through literature.[68] Similar examples of national literature can be found in France, where Victor Hugo became one of the most beloved poets and novelists of his time, particularly through *Les Miserables* and *The Hunchback of Notre Dame*. In the United States, Mark Twain gained celebrity status through his novels about life in America, particularly *Huckleberry Finn*. Later U.S. writers have emphasized Twain's lasting impact on American literature. William Faulkner asserted, "[Twain was] the first truly American writer, and all of us are since his heirs"; Ernest Hemmingway proclaimed, "All modern American literature comes from one book by Mark Twain. All American writing comes from that. There was nothing before. There has been nothing as good since."[69]

European monarchies were even transformed to become symbols of the modern nation. Eric Hobsbawm and Terrence Ranger's seminal volume, *The Invention of Tradition*, traces the creation of rituals and customs in the modern nation-state. Hobsbawm begins the volume by observing: "Nothing appears more ancient, and linked to an immemorial past, than the pageantry which surrounds the British monarchy in its public ceremonial manifestations. Yet . . . in its modern form it is the product of the late nineteenth and twentieth centuries. 'Traditions' which appear or claim to be old are often quite recent in origin and sometimes invented."[70] In an essay in this volume, David Cannidine describes in great detail the milieu in which "the ceremonial image of the British monarchy" was constructed in the later third of the nineteenth century, as the Crown receded from politics and became a national symbol. As Cannidine puts it, "power was exchanged for popularity," and the royal family became "patriarchal figures for the whole of the nation."[71] Cannidine further asserts that the rapid social and political changes brought about by industrialization fueled this transformation: "In such an age of change, crisis and dislocation, the 'preservation of anachronism,' the deliberate, ceremonial presentation of an impotent but venerated monarch as a unifying symbol of permanence and national community became both possible and necessary."[72] Cannidine is quick to point out that transforming the monarchy into a national symbol was common throughout Europe in the nineteenth century, and similar processes were visible in Prussian Germany and France, although with differing levels of monarchical power.

Alongside various symbols, national myths also became important tools for consolidating people into nations and distinguishing one group from another. Often these myths are organized around days of national awakening or independence. The United States, for example, has a myth of origin based on religious persecution, divine ordination, and common destiny. This myth is typified in the first Thanksgiving narrative. Virtually all Americans are infused with this story from childhood, one in which pilgrims, exiled from Europe for their devout Christian beliefs, journeyed to the United States, miraculously landed at Plymouth Rock, endured a harsh winter, and were saved by the grace of God and with the help of welcoming Indians. The original meal was meant to give thanks for God's providence, the bounty of the land, and the new friendships formed with the

Indians. Most primary school students spend their Novembers reenacting the first Thanksgiving in a school pageant and drawing pictures depicting the event.

The first Thanksgiving is a myth, a tale based very loosely on a few facts (and a significant amount of fiction) designed to tell Americans where they came from, how they ought to behave, and what their common destiny is. This national myth is taught in schools and reinforced every year through Thanksgiving meals served in homes throughout the country. Sociologist James Loewen has researched the perpetuation of the first Thanksgiving story in eighteen U.S. high school history books. He finds that this myth is presented as history, leaving out numerous historical facts such as the presence of settlers well before the arrival of the pilgrims and European immigrants' negative impact on Native Americans, notably the mass spread of disease and the slaughter of native populations. He also notes that Thanksgiving was designated a national holiday not in the early days of American history but in 1863, in the midst of the American Civil War.[73]

The Thanksgiving myth and the yearly ritual that accompanies it are a foundational institution for the American nation. They teach Americans where they came from; describe their heroic forefathers, the principles for which they were willing to risk everything, and the foundations of democracy (through the Mayflower Compact); and emphasize the importance of religious freedom, giving thanks, and welcoming all to the table. The myth also suggests that the land was waiting for the pilgrims, that it was uninhabited and flourished at the hands of its destined occupants. These values are transmitted and shared each year through the Thanksgiving holiday.

National myths, despite the powerful role they play in binding people together, are not without cautionary tales. Loewen and others point to the danger of national myths and "heroification," especially when they are confused with historical facts. One need only look to the horrors of World War II and the Holocaust to see the power and potential dangers that can come from myths that set one group over another and call for discrimination,

2. Resources of national-unity building in Europe and the United States

State services	Emotional programs
Creation of common language	**Common language**
Practical for commerce, bureaucracy, and military	Once established, a symbol of the nation
Promotes mass communication	
Mass education	**Symbols**
Literacy/common language	National flag
Tools for industrialization	National anthem
Official history/high culture	Monarchies
	Capital cities
National media	**Myths**
Inform citizens of countrywide events	National origin
Reinforce language and literacy	Heroes
	Destiny
National militaries	**Rituals**
Mix segments of the population	National holidays
Defend the state/the constitution	Parades
	Funerals
State bureaucracies	**National monuments**
Create consistency/predictability	National heroes
Implement social contract	Parks
	Museums
Official law	**National arts**
Rules and norms	Architecture
Enforcement	Poetry/literature
Protection of public space, free speech	Art

disenfranchisement, and violence. Ultimately, national myths need to be constructed in a way that is inclusive in order for them to build stability in states. The tools of nation-building are summarized in table 2.

The creation of states in Europe and the United States, coupled with philosophical thinking about the rights of citizens vis-à-vis their rulers, paved the way for the creation of nations in Europe and the United States, collections of people with a perceived sense of belonging and common destiny. National entrepreneurs used state services to help meld populations into nations, including variations on the social contract and the delineations of rights, rules, and citizen responsibilities. In addition and equally important, national entrepreneurs also engaged in programs aimed at developing a common identity through myths of ancestry, history, and destiny. The end result was nations that appear to be organic.

Expanding on these observations, chapter 4 will look at literature surrounding current efforts at state-building. Within these initiatives, the chapter will propose a more holistic program that includes not only developing key state functions but also instilling a sense of identity and purpose within its population.

4

STATE-BUILDING PROGRAMS POST 9/11

The terms *state-building* and *nation-building*, just like *state* and *nation*, are used interchangeably in media and even academic literature. For example, the RAND Corporation has published a series of books on what it calls nation-building, including the role of the United States, the United Nations, and Europe in the process, in addition to a beginner's guide to the topic.[1] However, these books focus on what should be called state-building: efforts to develop the structure and services of a state, such as governance, rule of law, security forces, a viable economy, and a healthy bureaucracy to support these services.

Alongside these attempts at state-building, virtually no effort has gone into nation-building, or helping to foster a sense of common destiny within the state's population and creating a popular sense of rights, responsibilities, and loyalty to the state that is both practical and emotional. As will be shown, international efforts aimed at fixing weak or failed states appear to rest on the assumption that developing state services and institutions is sufficient for creating a viable state and that fostering national unity within state borders is either unnecessary for state stability or that national unity will develop as a by-product of delivering these services.

However, as the previous chapters have argued, nations are a necessary component of viable states. Without a sense of emotional connectedness among fellow citizens and a degree of public loyalty to the state, the state is unlikely to cohere and succeed in the long run. This chapter will further argue that building state services, such as education and health care, are necessary for stabilizing weak or failing states, but these services alone will not produce national unity. Rather, as illustrated in chapter 3, national-unity building is a conscious process that involves a host of actors, including the government, academics, artists, social groups, and private citizens. These "national entrepreneurs" work within public space to craft monuments, stories, art, public opinion, histories, and symbols that provide a sense of "nation-ness" and common destiny among citizens of a state. Creating national unity, therefore, is neither organic nor the accidental by-product of state-building; it is its own conscious effort. Moreover, as argued, states cannot survive without some degree of unity and popular buy-in from the population. National unity, in other words, is a necessary component of a functioning state, and conscious efforts should be taken to promote its creation.

This chapter investigates efforts at state-building in the post–September 11 security environment. It begins by summarizing literature on stabilizing and building a state's capacity as well as the few investigations of what can truly be called nation-building. The chapter then proposes a program for building nation unity, including the types of assets useful for creating such a program. It further considers how building national unity could be incorporated into state-building with the aim of producing both the structure of a state *and* a sense of common purpose and destiny among its citizens. Ultimately, state-building and national-unity building are two distinct yet reinforcing components of creating viable states; efforts should be made to develop both when attempting to fix weak or failing states.

State-Building and Nation-Building Post 9/11

Considerable literature exists on state-building programs in the post–September 11 world. Much of this literature was generated in response to the U.S. invasions of Afghanistan and Iraq and the state-building efforts that followed as a strategy of reducing terrorist safe havens and regional instability. This strategy rested on several key assumptions. First, stable states can police their own, thus reducing the chance of terrorist groups setting up recruitment and training centers within their borders. Second, governments that provide services for their populations—such as security, education, health care, and job opportunities—create happy citizens who will not resort to violent extremism. Third, the creation of democracies will allow citizens to choose their leaders, thus giving them a say in their political destiny and, in theory, providing an opportunity to address political grievances through the political system instead of with violence.[2]

Academics and practitioners have devised several formulas for creating stable and prosperous states. Virtually all these models focus almost exclusively on developing a state's capacity to govern, grow its economy, and provide services to its population. For example in 2007, the United States Institute of Peace (USIP) published the *Guide for Participants in Peace, Stability, and Relief Operations*, with the aim of creating a more unified effort among U.S. agencies, international actors, and nongovernmental organizations (NGOs) in stabilization efforts and state-building. The guide states: "While they may be listed in different order—or combined in different ways—we believe all recent international interventions can be described as having explicitly or implicitly five desired end states: a safe and secure environment, the rule of law, a stable democracy, a sustainable economy, and social well-being." The guidebook goes on to argue that there is a remarkable degree of consensus on these goals among actors that engage in state-building efforts.[3] This framework was further echoed in *Guiding Principles for Stabilization and Reconstruction*, a 2009 joint publication of the USIP and the U.S. Army Peacekeeping and Stability Operations Institute, except that the pillar "stable democracy" was replaced with "stable governance."[4]

This list of end goals and the intermediate objectives that accompany each are focused solely on the structure and function of the state. Even the pillar of "social well-being" focuses on items like access to food and water, health care, and education. The guidebook also includes "addressing legacies of past abuses" and the "peaceful coexistence" of citizens as part of social well-being, but it names mechanisms such as truth and reconciliation commissions as the path to achieving these objectives, not constructing a sense of national unity among the people.[5]

The U.S. military also drafted documents aimed at better understanding stabilization efforts and state-building post September 11. In 2008 the U.S. Army released FM 3-07, "Stability Operations," which it later amended in 2014.[6] FM 3-07 looks at the necessary services and institutions that a state should provide to create stability, particularly in the wake of violent conflict or the collapse of a government. The manual defines the goal of stability operations as "operations focused on stability that aim to stabilize the environment enough so the host nation can begin to resolve the root causes of conflict and state failure. These operations establish a safe, secure environment that facilitates reconciliation among local or regional adversaries. Operations focused on stability aim to establish conditions that support the transition to legitimate host-nation governance, a functioning civil society, and a viable market economy."[7] In particular FM 3-07 considers five core tasks for state stability: "establish civil security; establish civil control; restore essential services; support to governance; support to economic and infrastructure development."[8] Within these core tasks, the manual includes considerations such as "support war crimes courts and tribunals" and "support public outreach and community rebuilding programs," in addition to stressing the hazards produced by infighting among the people and the need to provide security. However, the manual does not address specific programs aimed at fostering a sense of national unity. As with the USIP guidebook, FM 3-07 focuses almost exclusively on state services and the role that services plays in stabilizing a state.

As previously mentioned, the RAND Corporation drafted a series of reports describing what it calls "nation-building" with the goal of informing efforts to create governance and stability in Iraq and Afghanistan following the U.S.-led invasions of these countries. One of the reports defines nation-building as "the use of armed forces as part of a broader effort to promote political and economic reforms, with the objective of transforming a society emerging from conflict into one at peace with itself and its neighbors."[9] The RAND monograph *America's Role in Nation-Building: From Germany to Iraq* considers historic case studies of U.S. involvement in state-building, including in Germany, Japan, Somalia, Haiti, and the Balkans, with the intent of gleaning lessons from each of these experiences. The book's analysis focuses almost exclusively on quantifiable data, specifically sums of money, the number of troops, and the amount of time put into building a state. It also considers four outputs: "the numbers of postconflict combat deaths among U.S. forces, time until the first elections after the conflict, return of refugees and IDPs, and growth in per capita GDP."[10] These data, in other words, are focused on state capacity to provide security and economic prosperity and the degree of cost-effectiveness in terms of money and troops. They do not consider building national unity.

This framework is largely replicated in the other RAND reports that consider the role that the size of troops, time, and money play in stabilizing a conflict-ridden state.[11] *The Beginner's Guide to Nation-Building*, for example, is broken down into the following topics: the military, police, rule of law, humanitarian relief, governance, economic stabilization, democratization, and development. As with the USIP *Guide for Participants in Peace, Stability, and Relief Operations*, postconflict reconciliation is proposed through truth commissions, noting that "they focus on the past." The guide also stresses the importance of linking tribunals to the overall legal system to improve accountability and the legitimacy of the rule of law within that country.[12] *The Beginner's Guide* further discusses the role that civil-society building plays in holding governments accountable, arguing that "resuscitating, fostering, and protecting [civil society] while dampening ethnic or religious tensions is one of the most difficult tasks facing the intervening authorities."[13] Within these chapters virtually no attention is paid to mending postconflict society by creating a sense of common destiny among citizens. Rather they consider the main point of connection between the successful working of the state and its citizens to be a common rule of law, voting, and taxes.

Economist and political scientist Francis Fukuyama has also

written several books aimed at improving efforts at state-building in the wake of September 11. He contends that "state-building is the creation of new government institutions and the strengthening of existing ones."[14] Fukuyama focuses on two aspects of state-building in particular: scope, which involves the "different functions and goals taken on by the government," and strength, what he calls the capacity of the state to "plan and execute policies and to enforce laws clearly and transparently."[15] Fukuyama includes state functions ranging from defense to property rights to education and social services as types of institutions that define both the scope and the strength of a state. In regard to nation-building, he argues: "If a nation arises from this, it is more a matter of luck than design."[16]

Separate from his discussion on state-building, Fukuyama also describes three stages of what he calls nation-building, focusing particularly on U.S. efforts post September 11. He describes the first stage of nation-building as outside powers stabilizing states by providing security, humanitarian aid, and "technical assistance." If the state stabilizes, the next task is building "self-sustaining state institutions that can survive the withdrawal of outside intervention." The final task involves strengthening a state's capacity to enforce laws and provide services evenly across the state.[17] This program for nation-building clearly focuses on developing the capacity of the government; there is no mention of programs aimed at fostering a sense of cooperation among citizens or loyalty to the state.

Another post–September 11 book, the edited volume *When States Fail*, offers several perspectives on rebuilding the capacity of states that have weakened through poor governance or violent conflict. Jens Meierhenrich's chapter, in particular, outlines a program for fixing states after failure and "how to form new states from scratch."[18] He argues, "In our conventional understanding, states exist not only because they are successful in generating positive payoffs for a majority of the citizens, but also because a degree of loyalty binds citizens to the state. In situations of state failure, this loyalty is frayed or entirely absent." He further observes, "State formation must recreate this tie by focusing on the utility of states. The rationality of the state, I submit, is *purely instrumental.*"[19]

Specifically, Meierhenrich focuses on the creation of a "usable state" that develops stakes by establishing a consistent legal code and a healthy bureaucracy. Together these state functions produce predictability and consistency that promote buy-in to the state. "Once legality and bureaucracy are established and relatively routine, secondary institutions can be introduced." Ultimately, Meierhenrich argues that a usable state should have six functions: "(1) encouraging predictability; (2) creating confidence; (3) lending credibility; (4) providing security; (5) displaying resolve; and (6) controlling resources."[20] He thus contends that creation of a usable state is bound by the functions it performs. He is quick to point out that this type of loyalty is entirely independent from the creation of identity: "The promotion of the idea of the state must not be confused with promotion of nations."[21] For Meierhenrich, therefore, the creation of state services, specifically law and bureaucracy, is the start of a functioning, usable state that provides services, and in turn, these services are what create loyalty among its citizens.

Ashraf Ghani and Clare Lockhart also devise a post–September 11 framework aimed at fixing weak or failed states. They list ten criteria that they believe are necessary for measuring a state's sovereignty: rule of law; a monopoly on the means of violence; administrative control; sound management of public finances; investment in human capital; creation of citizenship rights through social policy; provision of infrastructure services; formation of a market; management of public assets (including "fixed assets" such as land, "natural capital" such as the environment, and "intangible assets" like contracts and licenses); and effective public borrowing. The better the state is at managing and providing these resources, the greater its sovereignty.[22] Ghani and Lockhart's list, while more extensive than the pillars of reconstruction and containing several functions that focus on the population, such as investment in human capital and the creation of citizenship rights, still primarily concerns state-building and capacity.

Perhaps the most interesting of Ghani and Lockhart's state functions is the "creation of citizenship rights through social policy." The authors argue that the creation of effective social policy helps reduce or eliminate gender, ethnic, religious, or other forms of discrimination. They further contend: "When the state uses social policy as an instrument for the establishment of equal opportunities, the social fabric created can lead to a sense of national unity and a shared belief in common destiny."[23] While surely creating equality through the construction and enforcement of the law is necessary for a sense of national unity, this state function still does not completely address the emotional needs of citizens to feel a sense of belonging with one another and to the country in which they live. In other words social policy that creates equality is necessary but not sufficient for fostering a sense of nation-ness. In essence this approach to building national unity is still based on state services and resources, not specifically developing emotional sentiment toward fellow citizens and the country. It is an aspect of the social contract between states and citizens.

Counterinsurgency expert David Kilcullen develops his own program for stabilization in a postconflict environment. Specifically, he calls for eight best practices: "a political strategy that builds government effectiveness and legitimacy while marginalizing insurgents, winning over their sympathizers, and co-opting local allies"; a comprehensive approach that harmonizes civil and military efforts; continuity of policy; "population-centric security"; "cueing and synchronizing" development efforts; partnering with local actors; creating legitimate security forces; and a regional approach.[24] Kilcullen's program is important because it stresses the need to focus on the population through all aspects of stabilization, including the creation of security and legitimacy of state services and institutions. As with the other programs of stabilization, however, no specific emphasis is placed on developing national unity.

Within these arguments for building the structure and resources of the state, a few scholars underscore the importance of building social cohesion or national unity as well. Amitai Etzioni, for example, argues that nation-building post September 11 has focused on three trajectories: building communities, democratization, and economic development. In his observations on building communities within states, he notes that "a nation is widely understood to be a community invested in a state," and that this process involves "forming a community where none previously existed, or shoring up one that was not firmly or properly constructed, or whose existence has been undermined in many cases by war or inner strife." Etzioni stresses the importance of social movements in building communities within states, noting that large-scale, foreign interventions designed as "social engineering" tend to fail, as did such domestically undertaken projects in the Soviet Union and the "Great Society" initiative in the United States. Community building, in other words, needs to come from the people.[25]

Historian Toby Dodge outlines a program for state-building and nation-building in his work on the British occupation of Iraq in the 1920s and 1930s. He argues that the "model state is legitimized by its ability to deliver public goods to the population contained within its recognized borders through a differentiated set of centralized government institutions," and that the success of this effort is measured in the state's ability to maintain a monopoly on the use of force and "to impose and guarantee the rule of law, penetrate society, mobilize the population and extract resources."[26] Once this is accomplished, efforts at nation-building can begin via civil society. "Civil society can then become the vehicle for building a national, collective sense of identity that can rival or even replace substate, centrifugal political mobilization."[27]

While Dodge and Etzioni make important observations for state-building *and* nation-building, the present work will make two adjustments to their programs. First, it will argue that efforts to build the state should include nation-building programs; in other words, the nation and the state should be built simultaneously. Developing a state's capacity first and then focusing on national unity runs the risk of not bringing the people along in the state-building process and not developing their critical attachment to fellow citizens and loyalty to the state. Further-more, without the necessary ingredient of national cohesion, state-building efforts could be pulled apart by substate loyalties. Nation-building, therefore, needs to be addressed from the start. Second, civil society and social movements alone should not bear the burden of nation-building. Rather, national entrepreneurs from within the government should also play a role in nation-building and should leverage state resources such as universal education and military service to do so. This was how nations were forged in Europe and the United States, and their efforts offer important clues for nation-building programs.

Along these lines, political scientist Nicolas Lemay-Hébert offers a theoretical approach that stresses the need not only to build both the state and the nation but also to construct them simultaneously. He contends that post–September 11 state-building has focused heavily on a Weberian "institutional approach," which concentrates on building structures and bureau-cracies of the state. An alternative trajectory, what he calls the "legitimacy approach" rooted in Durkheimian logic, recog-nizes the need for building social cohesion and popular legit-imacy *through* state construction. In other words legitimacy, social cohesion, and state structures and institutions should be built simultaneously and in a way that is mutually reinforc-ing.[28] Lemay-Hébert's proposed approach to state-building and national-unity building, specifically the need to construct the state and national unity simultaneously and to use state-building as a vehicle for creating national unity, will be considered later in this book. However, in addition to this approach, a separate pil-lar of national-unity building is proposed to further strengthen and reinforce this necessary component of the state.

The idea of creating programs aimed specifically at building national unity is controversial at best. For example, within his discussion of state-building, Fukuyama flatly contends: "Euro-peans tend to be more aware of the distinction between state and nation and point out that nation-building in the sense of the creation of a community bound together by shared history and culture is well beyond the ability of any outside power to achieve. They are, of course, right; only states can be deliberately constructed."[29] Fukuyama's contentions emphasize the conventional wisdom that the deliberate creation of nations is impossible. However, as chapters 2 and 3 illustrated, the creation of nations in Europe and the United States and the spread of nationalism around the globe in the nineteenth century prompted elites and governments to create programs aimed at developing a sense of national unity. Nations, in other words, were constructed just as states were.

Despite the historical record, very little literature focuses exclusively on nation-building programs either before or after September 11. Perhaps one of the most comprehensive looks at what can truly be called nation-building comes from the 1931 book *The Making of Citizens*, by Charles E. Merriam. Merriam contends that there is a strong connection between what he calls "political" or "civic education"—instilling norms, values, and laws of the political system and developing a healthy sense of patriotism—and citizens' loyalty to the state. Furthermore, states must always constantly be educating their population on the values, laws, rights, and responsibilities of being a citizen, especially since laws are always changing.[30] Merriam also warns against competing loyalties to the state and argues that the state must always be working to minimize these other elements— such as ethnicity, tribe, clan, family, and religion—and promoting loyalty to the state.[31]

Through a comparative look at different political regimes— specifically, the United States, Britain, Germany, France, Russia, Switzerland, and the Austro-Hungarian Empire—Merriam identifies general trends of building citizens loyal to the state that include "schools, governmental service, political parties, special patriotic organizations, traditions, symbols, language, literature, press, and the love of special localities," what we might call regionalism.[32] While Merriam does not make one specific recommendation for building loyalty among citizens and to the state, he contends that these ingredients, when conscientiously employed in civic education and managed by the state, tend to produce citizens whose loyalties are to the nation and the state.[33]

Concurrent with Merriam's observations, chapter 3 noted several key programs aimed at fostering a sense of national cohesion, including the development of national languages; symbols, myths, and rituals aimed at fostering a sense of national destiny; the creation of national monuments, museums, capital cities, parks, and forests that offer public spaces in which people can interact; and national literature and art. In the cases of Western Europe and the United States, these programs were not developed from scratch but rather built on existing culture and history, refashioning them into national-level programs.

Furthermore, various actors played a role in developing these programs. Governments created flags and anthems as symbols of the nation. Elites fostered myths of origin, which were reinforced through public rituals. State leaders and private citizens created national monuments and museums that collected and housed natural and social history, as well as art. Intellectuals penned national literature and music. In the United States, women's groups bought historic homes of state leaders and restored them as national parks for all to see. Wildlife-preservation groups created parks and forests as symbols of national beauty. Throughout Europe state leaders hired architects and city planners to make grand capital cities. These programs helped to create national symbols that, among other things, aimed to inspire a sense of emotional connection among fellow citizens and encouraged them to identify with one another and the state. Within these programs state services and institutions were a vital and necessary part of developing both the state and a sense of unity among citizens, but state services alone did not create nations. Rather, elites from various circles of power in these countries fostered national programs; these initiatives created what Benedict Anderson calls "imagined communities."

Today, given the advances in information technology, particularly the internet and social media, as well as the emerging phenomenon of crowd sourcing, the number of actors and resources available to create programs aimed at national-unity building is much more extensive than in seventeenth-, eighteenth-, and nineteenth-century Europe and the United States.

These resources have been credited with helping to spark the Arab Spring in 2010 and 2011, which brought people together to topple regimes. Average people have more of a voice than perhaps ever before, and these technologies provide new and exciting opportunities to build imaginary communities.

As with their seventeenth-, eighteenth-, and nineteenth-century counterparts, and perhaps even more so today, the population needs to be an active player in this process and programs need to be rooted in culture and history (real or perceived) in order to resonate and be genuine contenders for fostering national cohesion. Many but not all of the nation-building programs in the nineteenth century are applicable to post–September 11 state-building.

Combining Nation-Building and State-Building Programs

Chapter 2 proposed national-unity building with a near-term goal of developing recognition of a common destiny among a state's population and its vital role in the future of the state. National unity starts with the people to build or rebuild the state, develop social capital among the population, create an awareness of the population's common destiny, foster hope for the future, and pave the way for civic nationalism.

This program of building the state and national unity proposes that, first, national-unity building, despite being analytically distinct, should not be developed independently of state-building efforts. In fact programs designed to build national unity are more persuasive and effective if combined with state-building initiatives, as Lemay-Hébert suggests. Furthermore, as will be demonstrated, state-building programs *require* national-unity programs to make sense of the effort within the population. Without popular support and buy in, states cannot endure over the long haul. States, therefore, need to foster programs that inspire their populations, promote national unity, and encourage loyalty toward the state.

The following discussion describes a hypothetical state- and nation-building program based loosely on the five end goals of state-building described above: security, law, governance, economics, and social well-being. Within each pillar nation-building initiatives are folded into efforts to develop state services and institutions that root both state- and nation-building efforts in the people and help make them active participants in the destiny of their countries. Finally, a program for developing a sixth pillar of national unity specifically aimed at fostering imaginary communities is proposed.

SECURITY

Creating security in a fragile state requires security forces, but it should neither begin nor end with their construction. Security forces are only as effective and legitimate as the population believes them to be, and without popular buy-in and support of security forces, they can actually become a source of insecurity. By the same token, security forces must be a source of support, and not a threat, to the population. Dictators, for example, often use security forces to squash opposition; under these conditions police and military forces can become a source of insecurity for the population. Security, therefore, is not just about the absence of violence but also about people *feeling* safe; it is as much a perception as a measurable effect.

Ultimately, the goal of security should be a sense of safety derived from the population. This goal includes security forces but is much broader. Security should be presented as a corporate phenomenon; it is every citizen's right and duty to safeguard his or her local community and the country. Furthermore, security should be based not on fear of the enemy but on love—love for fellow citizens, for communities, for nations, and for a particular way of life. To paraphrase counterinsurgency expert David Kilcullen, citizens should know what they are fighting *for*, not just what they are fighting against.[34]

To ensure this sense of population-centric security, security forces should be largely, if not wholly, composed of volunteers. The construction of security forces needs to mirror the population. This could include the representation of different ethnic groups in security forces' ranks and the presence of men and women. But the construction of security forces needs to go much further than this. Hy Rothstein notes that the United States created security forces in Iraq as part of Operation Iraqi Freedom in the image of the United States, not Iraq, including its organization, composition, and rank structure.[35] This artificial grafting of the United States' understanding of how security forces should be constructed has arguably led to their demise in Iraq, a point that will be discussed further in chapter 5.

Moreover, security forces should expand beyond just police and the military to include firefighters, search and rescue personnel, first responders, and other services committed to providing a sense of security within the population. Stabilizing forces should also work at the local level to facilitate the creation of neighborhood watch programs, with an emphasis on knowing and supporting neighbors as a means of providing a sense of security. Those seeking to stabilize countries should also consider creating a civic corps in which high school or college graduates could enlist to give a year's service to their country in a variety of areas that, broadly, could promote a sense of security through projects like reforestation, countering urban and rural poverty, education, and a variety of other services to the country.

National programs that provide security, broadly defined, should create a sense of honor and duty centered on servings one's community and country. Within all state services, security forces and their broader programs should have an oath that participants take to defend, protect, and serve the nation, as opposed to the state or even the government. Security services and programs should require formal education that not only trains participants in skills specific to the job but also teaches them what these forces are fighting for and against, whom they are in service to, and what their greater purpose is. Furthermore, education should expand beyond just security forces and those providing public services to include the entire population, thereby ensuring that the people understand their responsibilities in providing security to the nation.

Finally, governments should create awards and ceremonies to honor those who volunteer and provide these services and remember those who die in the line of duty. Parades, national holidays, and other rituals should also be prominent programs aimed at publicizing national service and reminding citizens of their common duty to protect and serve. Monuments, including statues and national cemeteries, should also honor those who provide security in the broadest sense.

RULE OF LAW

Several scholars argue that law is one of the most important areas in which to begin state-building. Meierhenirch notes, for example, that law creates transparency and predictability, which manage the expectations of the population. However, as will be shown in the chapters on Iraq and Afghanistan, rule of law is the most difficult pillar to build because it requires tremendous planning, vision, and resources. Furthermore, law is closely aligned with security and forms the foundation on which security forces are allowed to act. Therefore, laws need to be in place and be institutionalized within the population and security forces in order for these forces to know their limits and the population its rights.

Equally important, laws need to resonate on some level with the population in order for the laws to have true legitimacy. In other words laws need to be rooted, at least in part, in the population's understanding of justice. Francis Fukuyama alludes to this point by drawing from nineteenth-century German scholar Ferdinand Tönnies's concept of *Gemeinschaft*, that is, the community and how it is governed by social capital, or unofficial norms, rules, and trust brought about by face-to-face interactions, and *Gesellschaft*, which is the societal level of order typified by formal rules and contracts. Fukuyama argues that all societies need both *Gemeinschaft* and *Gesellschaft* in order to function properly. Social capital reduces the need for laws and contracts to govern everything, and societal-level laws create consistency among and across large numbers of people.[36] These observations further imply that societal and state-level laws need to echo community norms and practices to some extent in order to take root with the population.

Establishing rule of law is particularly difficult in former dictatorships, where populations may have languished under unjust laws or their uneven application; it is entirely possible that the population's sense of justice has been skewed or weakened in such cases. Countries can also have more than one legal system, based on religion or ethnicity, which poses challenges for getting the population to agree to one rule of law for all. Furthermore, some local customs impose measures that are no longer considered just in the eyes of the international community and from a human rights perspective, such as stoning women for adultery or selling people like property. These local customs, while perhaps perceived as just by the community, come into direct conflict with international legal norms and codes. Therefore, establishing rule of law requires a delicate balance of resonating with the population but also rooting out unjust or discriminatory practices.

Finally, rule of law requires not only reaching agreement on the legal code but also the ability to enforce that code with trained police officers, lawyers, judges, jails, courts, and so on. These necessary human and material resources are typically atrophied or missing in weak states. All these issues make instilling respect for and enforcing law and order difficult as part of a program of state-building and nation-building. Laws that the population views as unjust or that are applied unevenly can lead to a sense of insecurity and lack of trust in local and state leadership; ultimately the law is only as effective as its adoption by the population.

Merriam proposes that education in the law is the way to address many of these challenges. He argues that "the establishment of civil rights, the enforcement of the laws, ensuring greater social justice, must be accompanied or even preceded by an intensive system of the re-education of the public." He also concurs that "it is impossible to legislate laws which have no popular support."[37] However, a mass education program on the rule of law requires significant planning and resources, including a legal code, schools and teachers, mass media outlets, and other resources that can teach these rights and responsibilities. These resources are also most likely atrophied or absent in a weak state or former dictatorship.

Nevertheless, the goal with rule of law is that it needs to be embraced by the population, to be institutionalized, in order to be effective over the long run. Not only should the construction of the law be perceived as fair and even but so should its application. The population needs to respect the law and recognize its importance for order and prosperity. Law should be understood as in service to the community and the nation.

Nation-building programs that promote the rule of law should include, first and foremost, education on the law at all levels and citizens' rights and responsibilities under the law. The law should be presented not as a dry set of rules but as an institution that requires citizen participation in order for it to be truly valid. Citizens should have the right to hold local law enforcement, politicians, and civil servants accountable to the law through independent watchdog groups like the American Civil Liberties Union in the United States. Popular participation in the law should also be reinforced through activities like jury duty.

Finally those developing rule of law as part of a state- and nation-building initiative should stress that the law is not fixed; it changes with time and in accordance with the population. In the United States, slavery used to be part of the law; it is no longer. Women did not have the right to vote; they do now. The law is not a set of fixed rules but rather is a living, breathing document that adapts to new developments, new realities, and new levels of consciousness. The purpose of the law and of lawmakers is to reflect and discern these changes and adjust the law accordingly.

GOVERNANCE

As discussed above, states can exist without functioning governments; these are failing or failed states. However, it is difficult for a state to be truly sovereign without some form of government. Furthermore, enduring sovereignty needs to be rooted in the people, and the people need to see their government as legitimate; otherwise they will ultimately challenge their leadership, either through violent means, such as insurgent movements, or through mass uprisings, which may or may not be violent.

The *Guide for Participants in Peace, Stability, and Relief Operations* names "stable democracy" as the objective of the governance pillar, including representative parties, a robust civil society, and a fair media.[38] The logic behind naming democracy as the long-term goal appears to hinge on the concept that popularly elected governments reflect the will of the people and therefore should be more stable. Furthermore, democracy as a system creates rotation of leadership and checks and balances on authority. It also offers the hope that those who do not win in one year's elections will have another chance in the next round of elections.

Naming a stable democracy as the goal of the governance pillar, however, comes with several important challenges. First, democracy may be a long-term solution for building stable governance, but the transition to democracy is fraught with peril. Edward D. Mansfield and Jack Snyder note, for example, that countries transitioning to democracy are 66 percent more likely to go to war than countries that are either dictatorships or mature democracies.[39] These findings, based on a large-N study, suggest that transitioning to democracy may result in both internal and transnational conflict. Furthermore, holding elections early on in a postconflict country, especially in countries riddled with ethnic conflict, could actually calcify the conflict, especially if parties are drawn along ethnic lines. In these circumstances voting becomes more of a "census taking exercise," with the majority ethnic group seizing power, than true representation of the entire population. As will be argued, this is what happened in Iraq following the overthrow of Saddam Hussein in 2003.

Second, democracy may not be the only form of legitimate rule in the eyes of the population. Max Weber's foundational look at leadership and loyalty names three broad sources of legitimate authority: rational, which is legally established and impersonal; traditional, which is based on "the person of the chief who occupies the traditionally sanctioned position of authority and who is (within its sphere) bound by tradition"; and charismatic, which is defined by a leader's "heroism or his exemplary qualities so far as they fall within the scope of the individual's belief in his charisma."[40] Weber is quick to point out that no legitimate lead-

STATE-BUILDING PROGRAMS POST 9/11

ership falls cleanly into one of these categories; in practice they are mixed. He also notes that these forms of leadership can be accompanied by their own forms of bureaucracy and routinization.[41] In order for governance to be truly legitimate and represent the people, those aiding in state-building and stabilization may need to acknowledge that democracy is neither practical nor culturally reflective, at least in the short run.

State-building programs aimed at creating governance need to begin with popular perceptions of leadership and its sources of legitimacy. In particular leadership should begin at the local levels, including civil-society building and examples of leadership rooted in the will and welfare of the people. Ghani and Lockhart identify national programs as a potential vehicle for civil-society building, leadership development, and popular participation that could help foster legitimate governance over time. They cite examples like the 1944 GI Bill for World War II veterans in the United States, the creation of the U.S. Interstate Highway System initiated by the Eisenhower administration in the 1950s, and the creation of the National Solidarity Program in Afghanistan as examples of state-building programs that linked the population to the government and worked within existing norms to foster good governance.[42]

National programs that teach and reinforce good governance should—like all the other pillars—focus on the role of the population in governance; specifically, it is the people who are the sovereign of a country, not the head of state or the territory, and popular-based rights and responsibilities accompany good governance. State-led programs that reinforce these points could include leadership building as a component of education through school councils, elections with goal setting, and accountability. Furthermore, the education system could emphasize historic examples of responsible and legitimate leadership; these examples could be further reinforced by national monuments that heroicize the nation's good leaders.

National myths are also an important tool that can teach good governance. Every American knows the story of Washington and the cherry tree, and his purported response, "I cannot tell a lie," when he was confronted over the tree's demise. This myth, while unlikely true, teaches that U.S. leaders, particularly the country's founding father, have been honest when confronted and have owned up to their mistakes. The myths surrounding Abraham Lincoln (humble beginnings, did not give up in the face of adversary) and Martin Luther King, Jr. (nonviolent change, moral legitimacy rooted in faith) provide further examples of national myths and their role in teaching good leadership.

The economic pillar of stabilization and state-building is arguably one of the most important pillars because, in theory, it affects average citizens' welfare and quality of life; if people are able to find consistent work and earn a decent living, they should be happy, productive, and cooperative citizens. Furthermore, if a population is gainfully employed, states can extract taxes from citizens that, in turn, will pay for key services, such as education, health care, defense, and physical infrastructure, which are part of the social contract. These services further allow for economic opportunity and prosperity, making citizens happy and productive. Economic stabilization, therefore, creates a virtuous cycle of prosperity through employment, taxes, and the social contract, outlined in chapters 2 and 3.

State-building programs aimed at stabilizing and growing the economic health of a country include improving physical infrastructure, such as roads, electrical grids, waterways, ports, and airports; instituting universal education; and even establishing universal health care as a means of ensuring a vibrant workforce. The *Guide for Participants in Peace, Stability, and Relief Operations* also names sound fiscal policies, including trade, and consistent rule of law as necessary for creating a sustainable economy. Both the *Guide* and *Fixing Failed States* stress the importance of managing natural resources—such as oil, minerals, and timber—as essential for economic development.[43]

Literature on state-building emphasizes certain metrics for evaluating economic stabilization. The RAND reports on nation-building stress gross domestic product (GDP) over time as a useful indicator of economic development and stabilization. Specifically, they consider GDP overall, GDP per capita, and aid as a percentage of total GDP as useful indicators of economic stabilization.[44] These metrics, however, have several shortcomings. Perhaps most important, they do not consider the distribution of wealth across regions in a country, nor do they look at the disparity between those who are prosperous and those who are poor, and issues of ethnicity and gender as correlates of wealth or poverty. The distribution of economic opportunity and wealth is clearly important for creating a stable state over the long haul. Developing these indicators is more difficult and requires regional and demographic knowledge of a state. Finally, measuring what Nobel laureate Mohammad Yunus describes as "hard core poverty"—those fighting for physical survival—is an important undertaking, particularly in fragile states that are on the road to recovery. Therefore macro-economic indicators, while easily accessible, do not present the entire picture of a country's economic stability or a population's economic opportunity.

Furthermore, in addition to state-building programs aimed at economic stabilization, nation-building programs provide added context that can help guide populations and provide hope. Ultimately, economic development and stability need to be about the nation as a whole prospering. The social contract, in which citizens give up some of their prosperity (in the form of paying taxes) or liberties (not taking the law into their own hands) to create security and stability for the greater good, should be a cornerstone of both nation-building and state-building for economic prosperity.

Nation-building programs aimed at improving economic stability should also stress the importance of equal access to and opportunity in the job market and career advancement. The system and the nation should provide the opportunity for all to participate in the economy and reap its benefits. If opportunity is available only to some, those shut out of the system are unlikely to buy into or support the state. However, the myth of prosperity should emphasize not only the opportunity that the system provides but also the importance of individual responsibility and accountability in seizing that opportunity. The myths of "the land of opportunity" and "pulling yourself up by your bootstraps" in the United States suggest that it is the state's job to safeguard opportunity but the individual's responsibility to capitalize on that opportunity and to prosper.

SOCIAL WELL-BEING

The *Guide for Participants in Peace, Stability, and Relief Operations* describes the objective of the social well-being pillar as ranging from "ensur[ing] population is fed," to "meet[ing] basic sanitation needs," to "promot[ing] peaceful co-existence."[45] This pillar, in other words, is a catchall for a variety of the population's needs, ranging from basic physical requirements to better social cohesion. Other scholars of state-building echo the importance of these provisions for creating a viable state. Fukuyama, for example, talks about the importance of developing healthy social capital, or the informal norms and rules that build trust and bind people together, as a necessary component of social cohesion.[46] This is also echoed in Jennifer Widner's work on rebuilding communities in Africa after conflict.[47]

Clearly state-building requires focusing on the population and its basic physical needs, including food, water, shelter, and sanitation. However, these basic physical needs are distinct from the emotional needs of conflict resolution and social cohesion, which deserve separate treatment in state-building. National unity and cohesion are unlikely to develop spontaneously as a result of people having clean drinking water or enough to eat. Furthermore, national unity should be included in this list of emotional needs, and efforts to develop it should include programs that promote a sense of nation-ness among citizens of a state. Therefore, these objectives are better understood as two distinct pillars: social well-being and national unity.

State-building programs designed to promote social well-being should include efforts aimed at establishing basic human services, such as potable water, sanitation, access to food, and proper shelter. Social well-being programs should also include universal education—which transects economics, security, law, and governance—and access to basic health care. Furthermore, depending on the population's expectations, state-building programs aimed at social well-being can also include child care and elder care as basic human needs.

National programs that seek to build on and reinforce state-building programs should stress that well-being is both a right and a responsibility of everyone; social well-being is only as strong as the communities that create and support it. As with the other pillars, a theme of volunteerism should be emphasized as a means of recognizing the interdependence of individuals and their need to support one another. Social well-being efforts should also involve recreation, including sports, and access to parks, forest, and other national lands; this is an often-overlooked aspect of civil-society building and social well-being. As proposed in chapter 2 and illustrated in chapter 3, recreation is an important component of modern society and can be a powerful symbol of the nation and the state.

NATIONAL UNITY

Analytically distinct from the provision of basic physical human needs is a pillar that focuses on creating national unity. This pillar includes elements of state programs named in the social well-being pillar, such as "address legacy of past abuses" and "promote peaceful coexistence," but also moves beyond these important efforts to develop a sense of national cohesion through a variety of state- and citizen-led initiatives. Ultimately, the goal of national unity, as described in chapter 2, should be to foster a sense of belonging and common destiny among a state's citizens. As discussed in chapter 3, these themes were omnipresent in the creation of nations in Europe and the United States through a variety of programs.

State programs aimed at fostering national unity can include the creation of national parks and forests, along with the preservation of heritage sites. These public spaces become not only places that individuals can visit and experience nature; they also can stand as important national symbols of pride, as the U.S. National Parks system has become. Other programs can include national museums that house art, natural artifacts, and key mementos of national history. These spaces can also serve to help citizens remember social injustices and the measures taken to correct these wrong-doings, such as the National Holocaust Museum, the National Museum of the American Indian, and the National Museum of African American History and Culture in Washington DC. Governments and civil-society groups can provide grants to develop these spaces, with the aim of recording history, nature, and art and thereby emphasizing the nation and its destiny.

National programs can also include government and private initiatives that aim to promote myths and symbols of national unity. Governments can create the space for civil society groups and philanthropists to focus on national heritage or the construction of monuments, such as the Statue of Liberty, described in chapter 3. These programs can also include state-led promotion of symbols, such as the national flag and anthem; rituals, like oaths of office and state burials; and even myths, such as Thanksgiving, that teach national values. The careful construction of national myths, symbols, rituals, and holidays can serve to promote a sense of national unity and teach values to citizens. Government-led initiatives aimed at promoting national unity should include programs that teach conflict resolution, particularly in schools, as a means of resolving grievances nonviolently and working through social and political channels to effect change. Alongside conflict resolution programs, equality in law and economic opportunity should be emphasized as state initiatives that aim to resolve social grievances and promote national unity.

Ultimately, national unity focuses on fostering a sense of common purpose and destiny among a state's citizens, and the role that the state plays in bettering citizens' lives. Building the state is a practical means of achieving this goal, but specific programs aimed at fostering this sense of national cohesion are also essential for reinforcing these norms in the near and long term. The six pillars of stabilization, including their state and national programs, are summarized in table 3.

3. Combined state- and nation-building programs

Pillar	Goal	State-building programs	Nation-building programs
Security	People's perception of safety. Security is a cooperative responsibility. Love of nation, over fear of enemy	Security forces Civilian corps Fire, emergency, search and rescue	Emphasis on volunteer forces Youth programs Awards and parades Honor fallen in national ceremonies, cemeteries
Law	Legitimacy rooted in and embraced by the people	Constitution Local laws Penal and civil codes Lawyers, judges, legislatures	Civic education in school about the law, citizens' rights and responsibilities Jury duty
Governance	Leadership rooted in popular perceptions of legitimacy. People are the sovereign	Allow civil-society Possible elections or other methods of choosing leaders Social contract	National myths of exemplary leadership Monuments to key leaders Education on responsible leadership in schools Junior leadership programs
Economics	Perception of opportunity, equal access to resources that will allow for job opportunities	Develop infrastructure Education Health care Taxes	Pride in prosperity and economic strength of the nation Create and enforce equal opportunity in economy
Social well-being	Right and responsibility of all to basic human necessities	Meet basic human services Meet popular expectations for social contract	Stress volunteerism with health and well-being of the nation

National unity	Inspire population to see common destiny	National parks National arts National museums Nationally funded grants for arts National protection of land and historic sites	National myths and symbols of unity history and unifying elements Teach conflict resolution Citizen-led nation-building programs Private national entrepreneurs

Domestic and international efforts aimed at state-building are likely to fail if they do not include initiatives that seek to create a sense of national unity. If the people do not have a sense of emotional connectedness to fellow citizens and a degree of identification with the state, the state is unlikely to succeed in the long run. State services such as education and health care, along with a viable economy and security, are necessary components of a healthy functioning state. Nation-building efforts, while analytically distinct in their programs and goals, are most successful when they are combined with constructing the services and institutions of the state. Together state institution building and nation-building create a viable state that provides good and services as well as national cohesion.

The next chapter will look at state-building efforts in Iraq following the U.S.-led invasion in 2003 that toppled Saddam Hussein's government. Building on these observations, it will highlight missed opportunities to build national cohesion during the eight-year occupation, missed opportunities that likely contributed to the rapid defeat of the country's military by ISIL in 2014 and lack of popular resistance to the group's occupation of large swaths of the country.

5

STATE-BUILDING IN IRAQ, 2003-2011

The United States, together with a small coalition of other countries, invaded Iraq with the aim of deposing Saddam Hussein, interdicting the country's alleged WMD (weapons of mass destruction) program, and severing purported ties to al-Qaeda. As part of the wider strategy to invade Iraq, the Bush administration launched a program of what it called "nation-building," which included establishing a stable democracy in Iraq that would be both domestically and internationally responsible, securing a functioning economy based largely on the country's oil production, creating responsible security forces that would not be a menace to its neighbors, and providing key social services to keep the population loyal and happy. Within this initiative of what should really be called state-building, Iraq's ethnic and sectarian tensions would be managed through democratic institutions, economic prosperity, and a multiethnic security force.

U.S. and international efforts at state-building in Iraq endured considerable challenges throughout the eight-year war, including multiple insurgencies against coalition forces and the fledgling government, a Sunni boycott of elections, high numbers of civilian casualties, and rampant political corruption. Despite these challenges, U.S. and coalition forces withdrew from Iraq in 2011, declaring operations and state-building efforts a success. In a speech marking the end of the war, President Obama proclaimed, "Everything that American troops have done in Iraq—all the fighting and all the dying, the bleeding and the building, and the training and the partnering—all of it has led to this moment of success. Now, Iraq is not a perfect place. It has many challenges ahead. But we're leaving behind a sovereign, stable and self-reliant Iraq, with a representative government that was elected by its people. We're building a new partnership between our nations. And we are ending a war not with a final battle, but with a final march toward home."[1]

In 2014, not three years after this speech, U.S.- and coalition-trained Iraqi security forces collapsed in a manner of days as officers abandoned their troops and thousands of enlisted were rounded up and killed by the rapidly advancing forces of the Islamic State in Iraq and the Levant (ISIL). The tacit and active support of the Sunni population during the onslaught of ISIL could not be ignored, nor could the reassertion of Kurdish troops, the Peshmerga, as the only viable force left to fight ISIL in Iraq. ISIL's successful capture of key cities in Iraq—including Mosul, the country's second largest city—and other key Sunni areas brought to conclusion eleven years of state-building in Iraq at a total cost estimated at just over $2 trillion.[2]

This chapter examines the conditions under which the United States and its coalition of supporters invaded Iraq and the programs they initiated with the aim of "nation-building." It argues that the focus was almost exclusively on creating macro-level instruments of the state, overlooking programs and initiatives aimed at working with and through the population to stabilize the country. Moreover, the United States and its allies missed key opportunities to build national unity and, in some cases, reinforced sectarianism, which contributed to the state's virtual collapse in 2014.

The chapter is divided into four sections. The first section outlines conditions in Iraq leading up to the U.S. invasion, considering briefly the creation of an Iraqi state in 1921, the declaration of a republic in 1958, and the social, political, and economic dynamics of the country under twenty-three years of Saddam Hussein's rule. The second section highlights the conditions for invasion, including the goals and the underlying assumptions that fed the U.S. invasion and stabilization plans. The third section looks at programs undertaken to build the state during the

U.S.-led occupation, arguing that virtually all efforts focused on a top-down approach to building the instruments of the state with virtually no efforts to engage the population or build national unity. Finally, the fourth section offers concluding thoughts.

Political, Social, and Economic Conditions of Pre-invasion Iraq

Although some claim that political and social tensions in Iraq date back to the seventh century split between Sunnis and Shias (the two main branches of Islam) and centuries-old animosities of Arabs toward the Kurds, the challenges to Iraqi cohesion that the United States inherited in 2003 stem largely from the management of territory under the Ottoman Empire, the way in which the modern state of Iraq was created during the British mandate period and, most importantly, the twenty-three-year rule of Saddam Hussein.

Prior to the creation of an Iraqi state in 1921, the territory that is now known as Iraq fell under the rule of the Ottoman Empire. Modern-day Iraq was divided into three provinces, Baghdad, Mosul and Basra, in which Mamluks, Sunni military leaders, ruled the provinces and provided a buffer zone between the Ottomans to the west and the Shias to the east. These Mamluks engaged in alliances with Sunni tribal leaders and created a system of social hierarchy within their respective domains, leaving Shias outside the system of patronage. The Ottoman Empire ended the Mamluks' rule through a series of military engagements culminating in 1869 followed by the establishment of the *vilyat* system, which set boundaries and created administrative control over the area, in addition to new systems of loyalty and patronage. As with the Mamluks, the *vilyat* system favored Sunnis and did not allow Shias positions of power.[3]

The dissolution of the Ottoman Empire following World War I and the rise of the British mandate era introduced new political systems to the region. Middle East historian Toby Dodge argues that the emergence of substate identities truly began with Britain's creation of the Iraqi state in 1920 and the political competition it introduced among groups inside the country. In his detailed account of the British occupation of Iraq from 1914 to 1932, Dodge highlights policies that helped create social and political friction in the emerging country, conditions that contributed to the 1920 uprising and the eventual creation of a dysfunctional but independent state in 1932. In particular the British installation of King Faisal as head of state, a foreign Sunni and Hashemite, and the creation of a government that greatly favored Sunnis and left the Shia majority largely outside the political system were important decisions that fostered political tensions between these groups.[4] British historian Charles Tripp notes that, following the creation of an Iraqi state and military, King Faisal was tasked with creating an independent state and unifying the population under his rule. While Faisal ultimately succeeded in establishing independence for Iraq in 1932, his efforts to create a unified Iraqi nation were undermined by a system of patronage in which "on all sides there was everything to play for," and key positions in the government and military were available only to Faisal's supporters.[5]

Despite this dysfunctional system of patronage within the Sunni monarchy, the creation of a state produced some notions of the Iraqi nation. The founding of the Iraqi Army in 1921 became a symbol of the Iraqi nation, a symbol that transcended British rule, a military coup in 1958, the birth of the republic, and the rise of the Baathist-led government. Tripp notes that, also during the 1920s, poetry emerged as a powerful medium that depicted hints of Iraqi unity. "It presented an articulate opposition to British control, characterized by telling criticisms both of British policies and of their prejudices in dealing with the Iraqis. Furthermore, it tried to encourage a sense of a distinctively Iraqi national community that would bridge the many particular identities of Iraq's inhabitants." Tripp goes on to note, "To some extent there was a conscious effort on the part of certain writers to construct a secular identity that would minimize sectarian differences between Sunnis and Shi'a." Tripp concludes by stating, however, that this identity was Arab and excluded Kurds.[6]

Alongside poetry, print media and literature also flourished during this era. One of the first Arabic newspapers, *Al-Zawraa*, was founded in Baghdad in 1869 under Ottoman ruler Midhat

Pasha; it ran for forty-eight years until the British closed it down during World War I along with other publications in the areas they occupied.[7] Following the creation of the Iraqi state under British mandate, new publications sprang up and helped foment the 1920 revolt. Historian Ahmed K. Al-Rawi argues that, "indeed, the mandate and the criticism published in the Iraqi press created a popular opinion against the British which ultimately led to the 1920 Iraqi Revolution."[8] He further contends that "the most liberal and democratic" stage of the Iraqi press occurred leading up to and following Iraq's independence from Britain, in which political parties created their own papers, and satirical publications emerged. This era of liberal press came to an end in 1941, following an attempted military coup.[9]

Iraq's status as a kingdom was relatively short lived. A group of officers inspired by growing pan-Arabism in the region overthrew the monarchy in 1958 in a military coup that declared Iraq a republic. A 1963 coup brought the Syrian-based secular, pan-Arab Baath Party to power. This coup was quickly followed by a countercoup and eventually a second Baathist coup that kept the party in power until the U.S. invasion in 2003. The Baathists' successful seizure of power in Iraq, however, eventually became linked to key Sunni tribes as a means of consolidating power, including Saddam Hussein's Albu Nasr tribe.[10]

In 1979 Saddam Hussein consolidated power as the head of the Baath Party and the Revolutionary Command Council, and he effectively seized control of the country. His rule is perhaps the most significant development in understanding political, social, and economic conditions in post-invasion Iraq. Politically, Saddam Hussein consolidated power by installing members of his tribe and others from his native city of Tikrit within the government and officer's corps. Once again Shias and Kurds were largely excluded from the positions of power.

Tripp argues that this approach to power consolidation took on new impetus with the 1980–88 Iran-Iraq war, which pitted a Shia-revolutionary state against Iraq. He argues that "the widespread purges of the party and the leadership underlined for those who survived the fact that they held their positions based on sufferance. Obedience to Saddam Hussein and proximity to him were now to be the criteria for promotion and indeed for political—and sometimes actual—survival."[11] During the war Shia leaders were either executed or driven into exile. For example the Ayatollah Mohammad Baqir al-Hakim, the leader of the Supreme Council for the Islamic Revolution in Iraq (SCIRI), fled to Iran, where he built a resistance movement that fought with Iran against Iraq, further driving a wedge between Sunnis loyal to Saddam and Shias.[12] The Daawa Party, another Shia group, largely stayed in Iraq and resisted the regime, which earned it the support of many Shias in the country.[13]

Saddam Hussein also targeted Kurds as a means of consolidating and retaining power during this period. Beginning in 1986 Operation Anfal targeted Kurdish communities believed to be sympathetic to Iran, culminating with Saddam's use of chemical weapons against the Kurdish city of Halabja in 1988. The attacks killed an estimated 3,200 to 5,000 and resulted in lasting health complications for survivors. Reliable estimates indicate that 100,000 Kurds lost their lives as a result of Operation Anfal and 80 percent of villages were destroyed.[14] Several countries condemned these acts as genocide, and the U.S. Congress proposed the Prevention of Genocide Act in 1988; the bill, however, was eventually blocked by the Reagan administration.

In August 1990, following a dispute over oil-drilling practices, Saddam marched Iraq's forces into Kuwait and occupied the country. The United States, along with a coalition of other countries, initiated Operation Desert Storm with the goal of driving Iraq's forces back over the border. Following the war, which lasted one hundred hours, Shias and Kurds revolted, believing that Saddam's authority had been weakened by the war and that the United States would support the rebellion. The uprisings resulted in a brutal crackdown by the regime, the slaughter of tens of thousands of Iraqis, and the displacement of millions.[15]

Following the revolt the Iraqi Shia grand ayatollah Mohammad Mohammad Sadiq al-Sadr, a long-standing critic of Saddam Hussein, helped to organize disenfranchised Shias in Iraq, in addition to providing basic services that the government was not giving these communities.[16] In 1999 he was gunned down along with two of his sons in Najaf, in an ambush believed to be orchestrated by the state. His sole surviving son, Moqtada, who was young and untrained as a religious leader, would later don his father's mantle of authority and become a key figure of resistance to U.S. occupation after 2003.

In addition to targeting Shia leadership, Saddam Hussein also punished the Shia population more broadly. At several points in his rule, but particularly following the failed 1991 uprising, Saddam deliberately targeted the Shia stronghold of the marshes of Maysan Province, diverting water from the Tigris River and turning the marshes into wastelands. This policy forced the resettlement of large numbers of Shias who had lived near and fished the marshes, driving them to the slums of Baghdad, particularly Sadr City, and to Iranian refugee camps.[17]

Following Operation Desert Storm and the failed uprisings of the Kurds, the United States and Great Britain created a no-fly zone in the north, allowing Kurds a considerable measure of autonomy and self-rule. These security measures gave Kurds the space to develop politically, including the consolidation of two main political parties, the Kurdistan Democratic Party and the Patriotic Union of Kurdistan. Key Kurdish leaders, such as Marsoud Barzani and Jalal Talibani (later to become the president of Iraq), also gained prominence during this time. And Kurdish resistance fighters, the Peshmerga, had the space to train and further hone their skills.

Economically, Saddam Hussein drove Iraq to the brink of collapse. Following the Gulf War, harsh and crippling economic sanctions were imposed on the country. The Central Intelligence Agency estimates that "before the Gulf War, oil accounted for more than 60 percent of the country's GDP and 95 percent of foreign currency earnings. Following Iraq's invasion of Kuwait in 1990 and the embargo on Iraqi oil exports, Iraqi oil production fell to 10 percent of its prewar level from 3.5 million barrels per day in July 1990 to around 350,000 barrels per day in July 1991."[18] The devastating results of sanctions were passed on to the population. The CIA reports that Iraq plummeted on the UN Human Development Index, which measures health, education, and per capita GDP, following sanctions. Although once near the top of the HDI, "by 1995, Iraq had declined to 106 out of 174 countries and by 2000 it had plummeted to 126, falling behind Bolivia, Egypt, Mongolia and Gabon and close to the bottom of the 'medium human development' category."[19] Iraq's infrastructure also suffered considerably as a result of sanctions and war. All these factors became a problem for U.S. efforts at state-building after 2003.

Iraq's political and economic arrangements further affected social dynamics in the country. Shias, the numerical majority in Iraq, had been repeatedly denied access to political power, which fostered tension and resentment between the Shia leaders and the Sunnis in power. Furthermore, Shias had organized resistance movements and parties, at home and in exile, with the aim of asserting a Shia agenda and caring for the downtrodden, particularly in the Shia slums of Baghdad. These organizations would later allow Shias to move quickly and mobilize for elections following the overthrow of Saddam Hussein.

All these factors affected U.S. efforts to stabilize and rebuild Iraq after the invasion: systems of patronage that favored some tribes and ethnic groups over others; the desire for revenge; economic devastation; crumbling infrastructure; a warped sense of justice; and an overall mistrust of the United States and its motives based, in part, on past experiences.

U.S. Planning for War and Its Aftermath

Scholars, journalists, and policy pundits have conducted numerous investigations aimed at better understanding the conditions that led to the United States invading Iraq in what most would now consider a huge policy blunder. Thomas Ricks's award-winning book *Fiasco*, for example, begins by arguing:

> President George W. Bush's decision to invade Iraq in 2003 ultimately may come to be seen as one of the most profligate actions in the history of American foreign-policy. The consequences of his choice won't be clear for decades, but it is already abundantly apparent in mid-2006 that the U.S. went

to war in Iraq with scant solid international support and on the basis of incorrect information—about weapons of mass destruction and a supposed nexus between Saddam Hussein and al Qaeda's terrorism—and then occupied the country negligently. Thousands of U.S. troops and an untold number of Iraqis have died. Hundreds of billions of dollars have been spent, many of them squandered. Democracy may yet come to Iraq and the region, but so too may civil war or a regional conflagration, which in turn could lead to spiraling oil prices and a global economic shock.[20]

Alongside calls for war based on the threat posed by Saddam Hussein's purported WMD program and his alleged connections to al-Qaeda—both of which have been proven in retrospect to be based on faulty intelligence and untrue—the Bush administration also aimed to depose Saddam Hussein, to end the decade-long containment strategy against the Iraqi regime, and to instill new leadership and a new system in its place. Ricks refers to this plan as the "neo-conservative" agenda, promoted by "essentially idealistic interventionists who believed in using American power to spread democracy."[21] Ricks contends that "'stability' wasn't their goal, it was their *target*. They [the neo-conservatives] saw it as synonymous with stagnation. They wanted radical change in the Middle East."[22]

Despite calls for Saddam Hussein's removal from power in the 1990s, the September 11 attacks on New York and Washington DC gave new impetus to regime change in Iraq. Leading up to September 11, the United States' strategy of containing Saddam's power had focused on two primary approaches: crippling economic and diplomatic sanctions; and Operation Northern Watch, which imposed a no-fly zone over northern Iraq with the aim of protecting the Kurdish autonomous areas established under Operation Provide Comfort in 1991. Following September 11 the Bush administration argued that a strategy of containment was slow, risky, and not proactive enough; more aggressive action was needed.[23] Within days of the September 11 attacks, the White House called for actions aimed at deposing Saddam Hussein, and by November 2001, the Pentagon began drawing up new plans for invading Iraq.[24] A September 2002 National Intelligence Estimate further fueled the call for war, claiming that Iraq's WMD program was expanding.[25] These concerns were further echoed by a select group of Iraqi expatriates and a defector who reinforced claims of Saddam's thriving WMD program.[26] Leading up to war, the Bush administration justified the call for military action as one of "preemption," a plan to attack before threats were allowed to be fully formed.[27]

Ricks points out that a few voices within the Bush administration and the U.S. military expressed concern over going to war with Iraq and misgivings about the plans to stabilize the country after deposing Saddam Hussein. Ricks chronicles conferences held at the National Defense University and the Army War College—two military schools—where participants expressed concerns about the war and its aftermath, including the dangers of disbanding the Iraqi military for state and national stability.[28] He also notes that Major General Newbold, a Marine general on the Joint Chiefs of Staff, voiced concerns over going to war and chose to retire as war became imminent.[29]

Perhaps one of the strongest statements of concern about invading Iraq came from the U.S. Army's then chief of staff, General Eric Shinseki. On February 25, 2003, just weeks before the invasion, General Shinseki testified before the Senate Armed Services Committee; in his statement, he noted that "several hundred thousand soldiers" would be needed to secure the peace in Iraq following invasion. Shinseki stated, "We're talking about post-hostilities control over a piece of geography that's fairly significant, with the kinds of ethnic tensions that could lead to other problems. . . . It takes a significant ground force presence to maintain a safe and secure environment, to ensure that people are fed, that water is disturbed, all the normal responsibilities that go along with administering a situation like this."[30] General Shinseki's comments were a direct contradiction to the civilian leadership in the Pentagon, who called for no more than one hundred thousand troops to secure the country.[31]

Academics also expressed concern about national unity and the potential for ethnic and sectarian infighting in the midst of regime change. The Washington Institute for Near East Policy convened a conference in autumn of 2002 that culminated with an edited volume titled *How to Build a New Iraq after Saddam.*[32] The book includes topics ranging from stabilizing Iraq in the wake of the invasion to building an accountable government. The volume also contains a chapter on managing ethnic tensions, in which it argues that Shias and Kurds could take advantage of the power vacuum created by deposing Saddam Hussein, and that Shias could attempt to settle old scores of power exclusion. It further advises that U.S. forces needed to be prepared to manage these tensions in the wake of the invasion. The volume also notes that plans to create an Iraqi federation would be challenging because different ethnic groups had different visions of a federated state. Finally, the book argues that the regular Iraqi army could and should be salvaged post-invasion and used to secure the population.[33] All these observations became critical issues for the United States after invading Iraq.

Despite considerable efforts from inside the U.S. military and among academics, the Department of Defense conducted surprisingly little planning beyond the initial invasion. Shortly after September 11, the State Department began planning for the stabilization process following a U.S. invasion of Iraq. In total the State Department gathered "over 200 Iraqi engineers, lawyers, businesspeople, doctors and other experts into 17 working groups to strategize on topics including the following: public health and humanitarian needs, transparency and anti-corruption, oil and energy, defense policy and institutions, transitional justice, democratic principles and procedures, local government, civil society capacity building, education, free media, water, agriculture and environment and economy and infrastructure."[34] The working groups ultimately produced a 1,200-page, thirteen-volume report titled *The Future of Iraq*, designed to offer guidance for stabilizing the country. Among its many recommendations, *The Future of Iraq* raised the issue of looting as a concern following the fall of the regime. The project also stressed the importance of leaving the Iraqi military in place as a useful security force. Neither of these and many other recommendations were heeded.

The Department of Defense chose rather to take the lead on what it called "phase IV" of the war, which is postwar stabilization, and largely ignored *The Future of Iraq* and other efforts aimed at preparing for stabilizing the country. The department's plan, under the initial leadership of retired lieutenant general Jay Garner and the newly created Office of Reconstruction and Humanitarian Assistance (ORHA), focused heavily on rapidly transitioning the running of the state to interim leadership filled by Iraqi expatriates, followed by elections that would allow Iraqis to choose their leaders. In that time period, the U.S. military and government would ensure that basic humanitarian assistance and services were provided to the population.[35]

This postwar plan rested on several key assumptions that later proved to be unfounded. First, it hinged on the optimism that the Iraqi population would recognize expatriates as legitimate and accept their authority. In fact some of the Iraqi leaders handpicked by the U.S. administration were not only perceived as illegitimate but were actual criminals. This was the case with Ahmed Chalabi, who had been tried and convicted in absentia for bank fraud in Jordan. Ultimately, this approach to transitional governance did not resonate with Iraqis.

Furthermore, this plan for interim governance did not leverage local leaders who did have legitimacy with the population. Various groups inside and outside Iraq had begun to mobilize prior to the invasion with the aim of providing transitional leadership and helping Iraq move toward a more representative government. In 1991 "around 300 delegates from 20 opposition groups," consisting of exiled leaders from various Shia parties and Kurds, met in Beirut to discuss the creation of an interim government in the event of Saddam's demise; the conference, however, did not produce unity of effort or lasting results. This meeting was followed by a conference in Vienna in 1992, and a subsequent meeting in Salahuddin, in the Kurdish north, attended by a reported 234 delegates representing "90 percent of Iraqi opposition groups." Also from 2001 to 2002, Shias met in London to discuss governing Iraq following Saddam's overthrow and addressing anti-Shia biases in Iraq's history of governance, resulting in "the Declaration of Shia in Iraq." Among other things, the document stated its commitment to a unified Iraq, not the dissolution or Islamization of the country.[36]

Second, the Bush administration's approach to transitioning governance in Iraq appears to have rested on the assumption that creating a power-sharing government, a multiethnic military, and social services would make the population cohere. One of the first orders of business for the Coalition Provisional Authority (CPA), which succeeded ORHA, was to draft a constitution that would set the rules for democratic elections, including ethnic power-sharing arrangements, the creation of a multiethnic military, and the provision of basic services, especially electricity. This plan did not include measures aimed specifically at building national unity but rather aimed to use the democratic process and security forces to force integration among the different ethnic groups. As will be discussed, the United States and other actors that focused on stabilizing and reconstructing Iraq missed valued opportunities to foster a sense of national unity through the emphasis of symbols, myths, rituals, and other emotionally based programs. Their purely instrumentalist approach failed to produce a sense of nation-ness among Iraqis.

State-Building in Iraq

Chapter 4 outlined the pillars of reconstruction and stabilization often associated with efforts at state-building—rule of law, governance, a sustainable economy, a safe and secure environment, and social well-being—noting ways in which these pillars could be developed while simultaneously fostering a sense of national cohesion.

Using these five pillars of reconstruction, this section highlights actions taken by coalition authorities to rebuild the Iraqi state following the invasion and overthrow of Saddam Hussein in 2003. In particular it demonstrates that most efforts at state-building focused on a top-down approach of developing the structure of the state—actions that could be easily measured—and not engaging the population or giving it a sense of ownership of state-building efforts. Furthermore, initiatives to build national unity were almost nonexistent, and in some cases, efforts taken actually exacerbated ethnic tensions rather than build a sense of common destiny among the Iraqi people.

SECURITY

Academics, policy makers, and practitioners of state-building almost universally agree that a safe and secure environment— what the military calls security—is the first and most important pillar of state-building. Despite this consensus there is considerable debate over how to achieve and measure a safe and secure environment. The RAND report on U.S. nation-building, for example, names the absence of U.S. troop deaths as an indicator of a safe and secure environment.[37] This metric, however, fails to consider that civilian casualties are a significant factor in insurgencies and civil wars, as are deaths of indigenous forces; both civilian casualties and Iraqi troop deaths became important considerations for measuring Iraq's security as it slid into insurgency and civil war.[38] Furthermore, in a population-centric conflict, which the one in Iraq was, one could argue that security is as much about popular perceptions of security as actual metrics of violence or its absence. In other words whether or not people *feel* safe and secure may be more important than counting troop or civilian casualties.

The U.S.-led occupation made several critical blunders in the early days of the invasion that most likely cast the die for perceptual and actual security problems in the creation of a viable Iraqi state and nation. The chaotic environment following the first days of the invasion in 2003, particularly the massive looting in Baghdad, did little to instill confidence in the population that U.S. forces had come to establish a safe and secure environment. In addition to sending a negative message, the rampant looting also destroyed the bureaucratic foundation of the country and some of its infrastructure, requiring that these state instruments be rebuilt.[39]

Furthermore, the looting significantly damaged Iraq's national museum, destroying valuable documents and artifacts of Iraq's ancient history, and allowing over three thousand items to be stolen. U.S. Marine Colonel Matthew Bogdanos, who volunteered to help recover the stolen items while a member of a counterterrorism unit, noted in a 2007 article that "this failure to protect a rich heritage going back to the dawn of civilization has convinced many in Iraq and the Middle East that the U.S. does not care about any culture other than its own."[40] Equally devastating, the destruction of the museum and black market sale of Iraqi artifacts helped to undercut an opportunity to use Iraq's ancient history as a potential symbol of national cohesion that could have united different groups around this common point of pride.

The second major misstep in the U.S.-led occupation that caused a perceptual and literal deterioration in a safe and secure environment was CPA Order No. 2, which disbanded the Iraqi military and Ministry of Defense on May 23, 2003. Prior to the invasion, the National Security Council (NSC) had recommended that the Iraqi military be used to stabilize the country and help with reconstruction, echoing *The Future of Iraq* and academic voices.[41] The rationale given by the CPA for the order was to dismantle a destructive instrument of Saddam Hussein's power. CPA leader Paul Bremer stated in a May 20, 2003, memo to the president, "We must make it clear to everyone that we mean business: that Saddam and the Baathists are finished."[42]

The decision to dismantle the Iraqi Army had several problematic effects on a perceived and actual safe and secure environment. First, as suggested by the NSC and others, these forces could have been used to help secure the country in the days following the invasion. In the first days of the invasion, U.S. forces encouraged Iraqi security forces to surrender but stay in formation to allow for detention and demobilization by coalition forces, suggesting that they could have been used to secure the population. However, many Iraqi forces "self-demobilized"; they took off their uniforms, looted their barracks, and returned home with their weapons.[43] These forces, therefore, were largely unavailable to help secure the country in the wake of the invasion. Hypothetically, it may have been possible to recall forces for the purpose of securing the country in the weeks following the invasion. However, the CPA's May 2003 decision to disband the Iraqi army effectively eliminated this possibility.

Second, CPA Order No. 2 put roughly 350,000 Iraqi men out of work. This decision, in other words, had both security and economic implications. The CPA attempted to pay Iraqi conscripts in the first months of the invasion, and to encourage some emergency forces, such as firefighters, to return to work, but these payments did little to quell growing mistrust of and discontent with the occupying powers.[44] Disbanding the Iraqi Army therefore created a large number of idle, armed, angry men who would later help fuel the insurgencies in Iraq.[45]

The decision to disband the Iraqi Army also destroyed an important symbol of Iraqi pride. As previously mentioned the Iraqi army was created in 1921, well before Saddam Hussein's arrival on the political scene. It fought in several wars, including the Anglo-Iraqi war of 1941, the Arab Israeli war of 1948, and the 1967 and 1973 wars against Israel. Although it was not successful in these campaigns, Iraq's armed forces stood as one of the country's state and national symbols; it had transcended the British mandate period, the country's status as a kingdom, the Baathist coup, and the rise of Saddam Hussein as head of state. Following the CPA decision to disband the army, the *Washington Post* reported one member of the Iraqi Governing Council stating, "It's still in our minds and hearts that the Iraqi army was the best army in the Middle East." Regarding the CPA decision, another council member declared, "It stokes the fires of the officers and the enlisted men who served in that army, and I think that this is not a wise thing. . . . It's a gratuitous insult." A soldier claimed, "The Iraqi Army is an honest, good, strong, Muslim army and is willing to defend the whole Arab nation. . . . I feel betrayed."[46] Completely disbanding the army, as opposed to retraining existing forces, became another missed opportunity to draw from a historic symbol of Iraqi statehood and nationness, as well as leverage a preexisting instrument of the state.

Instead, the United States and its partners envisioned creating a safe and secure environment through a massive effort to rebuild Iraq's security forces virtually from scratch. Coalition forces began this initiative within the first months of the occupation. The goal was to create distinct internal security forces—

which would operate under the Ministry of Interior—and air, land, and sea forces that would defend Iraq from external aggression.

Unlike the military Iraq's internal security forces—primarily police forces, border police, and emergency response—had not been disbanded. After the CPA fired a reported seven thousand officers believed to have ties to Saddam Hussein and hired thousands of new individuals, the ninety-two-thousand-strong police force was put through a three-week retraining course for existing police and an eight-week course for new recruits, followed by a twenty-four-week on-the-job mentoring course led by U.S. contractors and international police.[47] Following national elections, in which Shias won the majority of seats and dominated the government, a Shia appointee, Baqir Jabr al-Zubeidi, took control of the Ministry of Interior and was later accused of using units as hit squads against Sunnis, particularly in Baghdad.[48] Iraq's internal security forces continued to be a problem for security and stability throughout the occupation.

The construction of Iraq's new military did not fare much better. Coalition forces planned to create a three-division-size force of around roughly forty thousand troops and support personnel, proportional to Iraq's ethnic makeup of Shias, Kurds, and Sunnis.[49] The goal was to have significant numbers of forces trained and operational at the time of the CPA's dissolution in June 2004. However, efforts at training the new Iraqi military were plagued with problems from the beginning. The first battalion graduated from training in the fall of 2003, but its members almost immediately began to desert in high numbers. Considerable criticism also fell on the contracting services, MPRI, responsible for training the forces.[50]

In 2004 the U.S. Army headed up the creation of training and advising teams initially called Army Support Teams and later renamed Military Transition Teams (MiTTs). MiTTs—typically made up of fifteen members—aimed to provide newly trained Iraqi forces with mentoring and guidance. A 2008 *Military Review* article on MiTTs argued that subsequent training focused heavily on advising in tactical proficiency, the planning process, and preparing Iraqi forces for the types of actions they would face in providing security for their country such as counterinsurgency operations.[51]

Within these advising efforts, little to no training was given on the greater purpose of security forces and what Iraqis were fighting for; in other words, MiTT teams did not instill in these fledgling troops a sense of responsibility to the Iraqi nation or their role in the country's destiny. This was a critical missed opportunity to help build Iraqi national unity. Without this education it is unclear that Iraqi troops understood their national obligation or what they were fighting for.[52]

Following several years of insurgency and growing insecurity throughout much of the country, Sunnis approached U.S. forces in 2006 with the hopes of forming an alliance to uproot al-Qaeda in Iraq (AQI) from Sunni areas in the country, especially in Anbar Province. These efforts resulted in the "Anbar Awakening," in which Sunni tribal sheiks began to fight AQI forces with the training and advising of U.S. forces. Part of this effort was the creation of community-based, ad hoc security forces tasked with defending their neighborhoods against AQI; these armed neighborhood watch groups became known as the Sons of Iraq (SOI).[53]

The SOI performed several important stabilizing roles. In addition to providing security against AQI, the SOI also employed men and gave them an income of around $300 a month.[54] Prior to the program, unemployment rates were astronomical in Anbar Province; some argued that participating in the insurgency was one of the few opportunities for employment, and individuals could receive quick cash for laying improvised explosive devices (IEDS) or performing other actions to aid insurgents.[55] The SOI also gave local men a sense of pride. Sunnis were hard hit by decisions made in the early stages of the war, including the disbanding of the Iraqi Army and de-Baathification, both of which disproportionately affected Sunnis. The SOI not only offered security and income, but the program restored honor. Coalition forces duplicated the SOI program elsewhere, including in Baghdad and Diyala Province to the north of the capital. At the height of the program, more than ninety-five thousand Iraqis had joined the SOI, an estimated 80 percent of whom were Sunni.[56]

The program also expanded to include "Daughters of Iraq," local women who helped screen other women at checkpoints.[57]

While the SOI was important for tipping the battle in favor of the Iraqi government and coalition forces, the program also came with problems that have undermined the long-term stability of the state. First, the SOI created problematic redundancies in Iraqi security forces. The SOI was established in addition to the Iraqi police forces and the military and outside the chain of command of the central government. Perhaps more importantly, however, these units were constructed along ethnic lines and created bands of Sunnis who, in some cases, turned against the Shia-led government. In March 2009 the Iraqi government, aided by U.S. forces, had to use force to put down a Sunni uprising of SOI members in Baghdad.[58]

Ultimately, U.S. and coalition efforts to create a safe and secure environment focused almost wholly on top-down, macro-level initiatives that could be easily measured, such as the training of security forces and the number of U.S. troop casualties. Moreover, Iraqi security forces were not instilled with a sense of what they were fighting for, which is critical for any national security force. Finally, one could argue that a safe and secure environment is as much about popular perceptions of security as actual metrics; not enough was done to engage the population and address its security needs.

GOVERNANCE AND DEMOCRACY

One of the principle goals the Bush administration gave for invading Iraq was the creation of a democracy in the heart of the Middle East. The logic of this goal appears to rest on "democratic peace theory," which postulates that mature democracies do not fight one another but rather resolve conflicts through a culture of compromise and negotiation, and that democracies are responsive to their populations, addressing grievances before they grow into violent actions against fellow citizens and the state. In a November 2003 speech to the National Endowment for Democracy, Bush argued: "This is a massive and difficult undertaking—it is worth our effort, it is worth our sacrifice, because we know the stakes. The failure of Iraqi democracy would embolden terrorists around the world, increase dangers to the American people, and extinguish the hopes of millions in the region. Iraqi democracy will succeed—and that success will send forth the news, from Damascus to Teheran—that freedom can be the future of every nation. The establishment of a free Iraq at the heart of the Middle East will be a watershed event in the global democratic revolution."[59]

Following the invasion, the Bush administration stated its vision for political transition, which was wholly a top-down installation of democracy. The administration aimed to establish a transitional government no later than May 2003 to manage "non-sensitive" ministries like education. A provisional government would follow this body between "six months to two years after the interim authority was created"; this polity would have more authority and be responsible for writing the constitution. Finally, national elections would complete the transition process and establish the government.[60]

The declassified *Future of Iraq* report stressed the importance of finding known and reputable leaders to help run the country in the wake of the invasion. For example, the document "The Future of Iraq: The Iraqi Component," called for a three- to five-person Sovereignty Council accompanied by a twenty-to-thirty-person advisory council designed to oversee the transition to democracy and would consist of members of "the highest integrity, widely respected inside Iraq." Furthermore, the interim governing bodies "must have *national* vision for the future democratic direction of the country—not sectarian or regional." And, finally, the council would be "the Iraqi face—they [would] become the face of the future Iraqi government to the world and to the Iraqi people." The document named several potential leaders including Adnan Pachachi (a Sunni), Sayyed Abdul Majid al-Kho'ei, who organized the 2003 London conference of Shias, and Sayyed Ibrahim Bar Aluloom of SCIRI; these were leaders known to Iraqis with a record of serving their country.[61]

However, despite these recommendations the CPA chose rather to work with several key expatriates who were well known in

Washington. On July 13, 2003, the CPA established the Iraqi Governing Council (IGC) and appointed Iraqi leaders to offer advice on governance matters prior to the creation of the Iraqi Interim Government. The IGC consisted of six major political parties: the INC (headed by the secular Shia Ahmed Chalabi, a controversial expatriate who had been convicted in absentia of bank fraud in Jordan); the INA, headed by secular Shia expatriate Ayad Allawi; the two main Kurdish parties, the KDP and the PUK; and the two main Shia parties, SCIRI and Daawa, in addition to minor parties and independent leaders.[62] The ICG had twenty-five members (including three women): thirteen Shia, eleven Sunnis (including five Kurds, five Arabs, and a Turkoman), and one Assyrian Christian, with a total of sixteen members who were either expats or from the Kurdish areas. Three months after the ICG's formation, a poll showed that the majority of Iraqis still did not know about the IGC or its members.[63]

Initially the CPA planned to select the IGC's replacement body; however the IGC along with a fatwa from Ayatollah Sistani, the leading Shia cleric in the country, called for elections to select the transitional authority. A compromise between the CPA, the IGC, and the UN produced the Iraqi Interim Government (IIG) in June 2004, headed by Ghazi Yawar, a forty-five-year-old Sunni tribal chief, with Iyal Alawi as the prime minister. The IIG together with UN special envoy Laktar Brahimi chose a thirty-two-member cabinet that had only six ministers connected to the main political parties—Foreign Affairs (KDP), Finance (SCIRI), Public Works (KDP), Communications (PUK), Youth and Sports (SCIRI), and Women (PUK). Significantly, none of the cabinet ministers was from Chalabi's Iraqi National Congress party. Sistani and the Organization of Islamic Conferences (OIC) formally recognized the IIG, which gave it regional legitimacy. Most importantly, however, average Iraqis supported the new interim government. Polling data showed that 68 percent of Iraqis knew about the IIC and had "confidence" in its leadership, and 84 percent approved of President Yawar.[64]

The IIG offered a degree of continuity as the CPA dissolved its authority at the end of June 2004, just over a year after its creation. Following the dissolution of the CPA, the IIG called for a national assembly in July 2004 and provincial elections at the end of the year, followed by national elections in 2005. The decision to hold elections within the first two years of the occupation created several problems for governance in Iraq. First, some political parties had formed well before the invasion and therefore had already mobilized, specifically the Kurds and some Shia parties, while other groups had to start from scratch. Early elections favored the more organized and mobilized parties.

Second, parties largely broke along identity lines, not along interests. Scholars note that parties based on identity tend to "calcify," meaning that only members of that particular ethnic group would vote for that party.[65] Under these conditions elections would favor the ethnic group with the greatest numbers, which in this case was the Shias. This problem was exacerbated by the Sunnis' decision to boycott the first elections, initially leaving them with little political representation. Iraq's first elections, followed by each subsequent election, did indeed break along ethnic lines and put Shias in control of key ministries, such as the Ministry of Interior, and gave Sunnis and other minorities lesser roles in governing the country.

Third, democratic culture was weak in Iraq following thirty years of dictatorial rule. Iraq held pseudo elections under Saddam Hussein, which did more to discredit the process than teach democratic principles. More importantly, the democratic values of division of power, compromise, tolerance, coalition building, respect for the rule of law, and rotation of leadership were not practice in Iraq under Saddam Hussein. Civil society had also atrophied under Saddam's rule; organizations that were permitted, such as labor unions, were highly regulated. Finally, potential leaders had been persecuted, killed, and driven into exile under Saddam Hussein, depleting this important resource.

Fourth, several examples of local governments self-organizing in the wake of the invasion also provided valuable opportunities to build on Iraqi initiatives; coalition forces worked with these initiatives in some cases and stopped them in others. The RAND report *After Saddam: Pre-War Planning and the Occupation of Iraq* notes, for example:

> In May, just one month after Saddam's government fell, several cities began to show signs of political development by electing governing councils and mayors. On May 5, 2003, Mosul, with support of U.S. military personnel, chose a 24-member interim government, which in turn selected a mayor. In the southern Shi'ite city of Amara, local resistance fighters overthrew Iraqi forces in the early days of the war and established a city council that included a body of 27 people picked to run local facilities. On May 15, British forces handed over the southern port city of Umm Qasr to a 12-member council, followed by the transfer of the port to Iraqi leaders on May 22. And on May 24, 300 Iraqi delegates elected a council in the northern city of Kirkuk. The U.S. military oversaw the election, which included all three of the city's major ethnic groups, Kurds, Arabs, and Turkomans. The council, in turn, elected a mayor on May 28.[66]

After Saddam further chronicles that coalition authorities also shut down local governance initiatives.

> In June 2003, citizens of Basra protested British forces' selection of leaders and technocrats for the city, particularly criticizing the absence of clergy in the appointed government. They demanded the right to run their own city. CPA halted elections in the southern Shi'ite city of Najaf, claiming that conditions were not appropriate for elections. Despite U.S. Marines having overseen the process, CPA appointed a former Iraqi military officer (who was later sacked on corruption charges) to the post of mayor. Similarly, U.S. forces halted elections in Samarra on June 28 and appointed a leader, angering citizens there. In total, CPA reportedly appointed mayors in a dozen cities.[67]

The Future of Iraq project stressed the importance of capitalizing on local governance and building civil society as key pillars for building good governance in Iraq. It specifically named "civic education" as necessary for Iraqi governance to develop, noting, "In the last four decades, [Iraqis] have been ruled by force, fear and humiliation. Considering these factors, unfortunately, there has been a degradation of moral ethics and values." To correct this, "Iraqis should be taught how to share responsibilities in serving the community and not to expect the government to be the sole provider for social welfare, services and other amenities. They have to be able to take initiatives and be active in making changes and creating a better nation."[68]

Ultimately, the U.S.-led approach to governance focused on a top-down approach to democracy, establishing first an interim and then elected body to hand off authority to Iraqis and to end the occupation. This approach focused on working with leaders known to Washington, rather than letting the population truly choose leaders who had popular legitimacy. When elections were held, voting broke along ethnic lines, which favored the Shias as the numerical majority.

RULE OF LAW

The United States placed considerable emphasis on the creation of rule of law, but as with the construction of security forces, this initiative focused heavily on the U.S. understanding of law and missed critical opportunities to create a system of justice that drew from moral leaders and non-Western sources of law. U.S. efforts to create law and order in Iraq were also hampered by its own missteps in the occupation.

One of the greatest mistakes for setting the tone of justice in Iraq was the U.S. military prison guards' actions at Abu Ghraib in the months following the invasion. The revelation of prisoner abuses—including sexual assault, torture, and other humiliating acts—destroyed U.S. credibility and Iraqi perceptions of motives for invading Iraq.[69] While U.S. officials took measures to prevent future atrocities and to hold some of its military leaders responsible, this incident became a watershed moment in the first year of the war.[70]

Alongside these disastrous actions, the CPA began drafting an Iraqi constitution, which would determine the role of the central government, set the rules for holding elections, and limit powers of the executive branch. These efforts, however, were almost immediately met with resistance from one of the leading Shia clerics in Iraq, the Ayatollah Ali Sistani, who issued a fatwa on June 28 calling for direct elections for those responsible for drafting a constitution. The fatwa proclaimed: "Those forces have no jurisdiction whatsoever to appoint members of the Constitution preparation assembly. Also there is no guarantee either that this assembly will prepare a constitution that serves the best interests of the Iraqi people or express their national identity whose backbone is sound Islamic religion and noble social values. The said plan is unacceptable from the outset."[71] In the same fatwa, Sistani called for general elections to select a body that would be responsible for drafting the Iraqi constitution.

Initially ignoring Sistani's influence in the creation of the rule of law and democracy in Iraq was a problematic oversight for the U.S. occupation. A 2007 U.S. Institute for Peace report describes Sistani as "one of the most powerful figures in Iraq" who "brings the Shi'is closer together across the greater Middle East."[72] The report further notes that Sistani's insistence on the inclusion of Islam in the Iraqi constitution was "not intended to make Iraq an Islamist state based on juridical *sharia* strictures, but rather to limit the *total* secularization of the constitution, which would deprive a Muslim country of an 'authentic' national identity based on its Islamic heritage."[73]

Eventually, the CPA had to yield to his request and held a referendum for the drafting of the constitution. In the interim the IGC and the CPA drafted and ratified the Transitional Administrative Law (TAL), in March 2004, including a thirteen-article bill of rights that named Islam as "a source" of law. The TAL also created a quota of 25 percent of parliament's seats for women and called for elections in January 2005 for a 275-member transitional assembly. Finally, the TAL gave Kurds "broad autonomy," which upheld the current political arrangement with the North.[74]

The final constitution was approved on October 15, 2005. Article 1 of the constitution states: "The Republic of Iraq is a single federal, independent and fully sovereign state in which the system of government is republican, representative, parliamentary, and democratic, and this Constitution is a guarantor of the unity of Iraq."[75]

Article 2 adds:

First: Islam is the official religion of the State and is a foundation source of legislation:

A. No law may be enacted that contradicts the established provisions of Islam

B. No law may be enacted that contradicts the principles of democracy

C. No law may be enacted that contradicts the rights and basic freedoms stipulated in this Constitution.

Second: This Constitution guarantees the Islamic identity of the majority of the Iraqi people and guarantees the full religious rights to freedom of religious belief and practice of all individuals such as Christians, Yazidis, and Mandean Sabeans.[76]

Although the constitution did not contain the same separation of religious and state powers as is in the U.S. Constitution, drafting the document ultimately involved both Iraqi leaders and the general population, which gave it an important degree of credibility.

In addition to drafting a constitution, Iraqis called for the creation of a tribunal to try Saddam Hussein and his inner circle for crimes against his own citizens. A January 2004 *London Times* report estimated that the total number of Iraqis killed by Saddam to be around three hundred thousand and that hundreds of mass graves existed throughout the country.[77] Similarly, a 2004 *Chicago Tribune* article reported that 282 mass graves had been identified since the fall of Saddam and that one of the sites had as many as fifteen thousand bodies in it.[78] On October 1, 2003, the IGC announced the three types of crimes that would be tried in the Iraqi Special Tribunal (IST)—genocide, war crimes, and crimes against humanity—and that the tribunal would be an Iraqi-run court with international support. International legal experts raised concerns about using only Iraqi judges, claiming that Iraq's legal system had weakened under Saddam's rule and its judges were not experienced in these types of criminal proceedings. These experts further noted that tribunals in

Rwanda, Bosnia, Cambodia, and Sierra Leone all involved international lawyers with specialization in war crimes.[79] Nevertheless, the IST began hearing cases, including Saddam Hussein's case; he was found guilty of crimes against humanity in 2004 and executed in 2006.

Ultimately, the U.S. and coalition powers' focus on creating a constitution as the first benchmark for law and order in Iraq following the overthrow of Saddam Hussein failed to include local leaders and the population, which derailed their efforts and forced them to include voices in the process. The final document, while not reflecting the U.S. Constitution, did appear to have the population's support and that of key leaders.

ECONOMIC DEVELOPMENT

Coalition efforts aimed at developing Iraq's economy focused heavily on its most profitable natural resource: oil. Part of the United States' plan for Iraq's postwar reconstruction hinged on bringing its oil production back up to presanction levels and using its profits to pay for the development of infrastructure and the creation of capital.[80] However the coalition, especially the CPA, took measures that hindered Iraq's economic development and—more importantly—helped reinforce sectarian strife within the country. As with the other pillars of stabilization and reconstruction, this top-down, macro-level approach missed critical opportunities to foster a sense of Iraqiness and to work with and through the population to build the state.

The U.S.-led occupation focused heavily on restoring Iraq's oil production, often to the detriment of other sources of economic development. Following the fall of Baghdad in April 2003, rampant looting broke out in the city, allowing the population to strip the city of resources and destroy infrastructure. U.S. forces, however, guarded Iraq's Ministry of Oil and prevented it from being destroyed. One Baghdadi was reported as saying, "They came from the other side of the world. Do you believe they're going to do much for me? They've just come for the oil."[81] Ten years after the invasion, most major U.S. and European oil firms and their supporting companies had a presence in Iraq.[82]

Focusing on Iraq's oil wealth, in addition to spurring conspiracy theories about the intentions of the war, involved several challenges for national unity. First, Iraq's oil fields are concentrated in the south, which is Shia dominated, and in the north near Kurdish regions. The city of Kirkuk, for example, holds important oil reserves and is contested by several ethnic groups. The heavy emphasis on oil, coupled with major shifts in political power that favored the Shias and the Kurds, sent powerful signals to the Sunni minority that they were being cut out of Iraq's economic future.

To address this concern, coalition powers, in coordination with the fledgling Iraqi government, attempted to create a hydrocarbon law that would establish rules and regulations for oil extraction, exploration, and sales that would benefit all Iraqis. A policy was proposed in 2007; however, it bogged down over issues of federal versus regional authorities, particularly the Kurdistan Regional Government (KRG), and the rights to export oil directly to Turkey and develop new oil fields.[83] Despite the inability to pass a hydrocarbon law, Iraq and the KRG began taking bids for oil extraction in 2009.[84]

Revenue sharing of Iraq's oil wealth remains one of the most important macroeconomic decisions of the country. Article 112 of the Iraqi constitution stipulates: "The federal government, with the producing governorates and regional governments, shall undertake the management of oil and gas extracted from present fields, provided that it distributes its revenues in a fair manner in proportion to the population distribution in all parts of the country, specifying an allotment for a specified period for the damaged regions which were unjustly deprived of them by the former regime, and the regions that were damaged afterwards in a way that ensures balanced development in different areas of the country, and this shall be regulated by a law."[85] Despite this article, realizing the best means of distributing oil wealth following the fall of Saddam Hussein has remained unresolved.[86]

Efforts to seize Iraq's oil profits and use them to reconstruct the country also fell short. The United States created the Iraq Relief and Reconstruction Fund in November 2003 and allocated $18.4 billion to reconstruction efforts. In addition to these funds, numerous countries pledged amounts to help rebuild Iraq in a 2003 conference in Madrid, totaling over $13 billion. The United States also help establish the Development Fund for Iraq, which aimed to seize wealth from Saddam Hussein and his family, and to capture oil wealth and use it for the betterment of the Iraqi people. Lack of transparency and accurate accounting led to strong criticisms of the CPA and its use of all these funds. By one report $9 billion went missing in the first year of the war alone.[87] A 2013 investigation of spending in Iraq concluded that over $60 billion in U.S. taxpayer money was spent in the course of the war.[88] In other words Iraqi oil did not fund reconstruction efforts.

Furthermore, early efforts aimed at restoring Iraq's economy did not put the same emphasis on other sectors of its economy, including agriculture, industry, and the services sector. Iraq has a history of robust agriculture and industry. However, USAID—the U.S. government's development agency—did not begin major efforts to reinvigorate Iraq's agricultural sector until 2007. Prior to the rise of ISIL in 2014, USAID boasted "the generation of $142 million in direct sales of agricultural commodities since 2007, helping the agricultural sector rebuild and begin to meet local demands," and "the creation of 14,711 jobs for Iraqis since 2007, helping to generate rural employment and private sector growth in this industry," in addition to training programs, and initiatives aimed at teaching sustainable farming to youth and widows. Prior to 2014 agriculture was the third largest sector in Iraq after oil and government jobs.[89]

Iraq's service sector was also promising and an area that did not receive due attention in the aftermath of the coalition forces' invasion. Iraq's potential as a tourist destination, in particular, is exceptional, given that it boasts the ancient cities of Babylon and Ur, with still-extant ancient buildings and sites such as the ziggurat. Helping to develop Iraq's tourism sector was a particularly valuable missed opportunity because it could have helped instill a sense of national pride and potential national unity around these symbols of Iraq's great history.

Finally, Iraq's unemployment rate remained a problem throughout the occupation. The CPA's decision to disband the Iraqi military, as previously mentioned, not only created security problems in the months following the fall of Saddam Hussein and helped fuel the insurgency against coalition forces, but it also had economic implications for the country. The decision to put an estimated 350,000 men out of work sent a powerful message that the day-to-day lives of these Iraqis and their families were not a priority for the occupation. Unemployment was a particularly serious problem in the Sunni stronghold of Anbar Province, which became the seat of AQI. As previously mentioned, the Sunni insurgency was fueled in part by economic opportunity, and individuals could make money from tasks ranging from offering intelligence to planting IEDs. Reducing Iraq's unemployment rate and providing jobs for Iraqi citizens, especially men, could have helped reduce bitterness about the occupation and the need to find employment through nefarious means.

SOCIAL WELL-BEING

The U.S.-led occupation's efforts to improve social well-being in Iraq focused heavily on easily measurable effects, especially electrical output, education, and other basic necessities. However, occupying forces failed to provide perhaps the most important basic necessity of social well-being: security, particularly after the rise of sectarian and insurgent violence that caused the death of thousands of civilians.

Beginning in the months following the invasion, the Brookings Institution in Washington DC began compiling "economic, public opinion and security data," in what it called the "Iraq Index." The index's creators argued that it was "designed to quantify the rebuilding efforts and offer an objective set of criteria for benchmarking performance." The first reports focused heavily on coalition troop casualties, but as the reports continued, they emphasized the availability of basic resources like sewage management, water, electricity, telecommunications, and fuel, based roughly on the U.S. military's SWEAT acronym (sewage, water, electricity, academics [sometimes agriculture], and telecommunications or trash).[90] The assumption appears to be that these variables, which are easily measurable, would provide social well-being.

Focusing on basic utilities presented several problems for the occupying powers and their troops. First, Iraq's infrastructure—particularly its electrical, water, and sewage systems—were outdated and in need of significant improvements. It appears that the U.S. Department of Defense did not anticipate the amount of work required to actually deliver these utilities across the country on a consistent level. As a case in point, providing electricity to Baghdad was a major challenge in the first years of the occupation and became a near obsession of the CPA, which reported megawatt outputs on a daily basis.[91] Second, these benchmarks for social well-being were based on the occupying powers' assumption of what was needed to keep the population happy and show prosperity. It is unclear that these expectations were shared by the Iraqi population on the same level. In other words the occupying powers may have created these expectations within the population instead of responding to what their priorities were for well-being. If that was the case, coalition forces could have focused their efforts on factors that mattered more to the population.

Of particular importance for understanding the average Iraqi's sense of well-being throughout the occupation, the Iraq Index also began compiling polling data on Iraqis' perceptions of progress in the country. Virtually from the beginning of the invasion, Iraqis felt that their personal security was at risk. For example a November 2003 Iraq Index report notes that, while 67 percent of Iraqis polled believe that their future would be better because of Saddam's removal, 60 percent also were afraid at times to go outside their home. The perception of personal security remained poor throughout most of the occupation.[92]

Interestingly, while much of the U.S.-led occupation's efforts focused on creating Iraqi security forces, this endeavor did not result in greater personal security for average Iraqis, particularly in the capital and other major cities. As the insurgencies grew in Iraq, and elections resulted in Sunnis losing control of political power, Sunni-Shia violence erupted in several major cities, resulting in thousands of deaths. The 2005 attack on the Shia Al-Askaria Shrine in Samarra, for which Sunni-led AQI claimed responsibility, further exacerbated Sunni-Shia tensions and violence. Coalition forces were slow to respond but eventually initiated the "surge" in 2006, which placed a greater number of troops in the cities and cordoned off neighborhoods with the goal of reducing sectarian violence.

Perhaps one of the biggest missed opportunities for creating social well-being was to recognize and build on national unity already existing in the country, which could have reinforced national cohesion prior to insurgent attempts to drive a wedge between Sunnis and Shias. For example, one of the more significant overlooked examples of cross-ethnic collaboration occurred in the summer of 2002, prior to the outbreak of war. Shia leaders met in London to draft the "Declaration of Shia in Iraq," in which they chronicled a history of Shia oppression in Iraq dating back to the British. However, the declaration did not call for Shia secession; rather it proclaimed:

> The lessons drawn from Iraq's history are clear—the Shia have at no point sought to establish their own state or unique political entity. Rather, whenever the opportunity was afforded to them, they participated enthusiastically in nation-wide political movements and organisations, ever conscious of the need to maintain national unity and probably more so than other groups inside Iraq. . . . The Shia of Iraq, in spite of being constantly and maliciously tested as to the depth of their national loyalty, have proven, time and again, their commitment to Iraq even at the expense of their own sectarian interests. Their call for the restitution of their civil and political rights can in no way be seen as a threat to national unity, when they have indisputably proven that they have been its principal protectors in word and in deed.[93]

The declaration goes on to list three basic demands:

1. The abolition of dictatorship and its replacement with democracy.

2. The abolition of ethnic discrimination and its replacement with a federal structure for Kurdistan.

3. The abolition of the policy of discrimination against the Shia.[94]

The Declaration demonstrates that the Shia, the majority of Iraq's population, were well organized before the invasion and that they were supportive of a unified Iraq that ended sectarian and ethnic conflict and embraced democracy. The United States should have worked with this group to help secure the country and establish an interim government after invasion. This was a significant missed opportunity to develop national unity by leveraging leaders with legitimacy prior to and during the early days of the invasion. Building on this national momentum could have reduced ethnic and sectarian violence during the occupation. The summary of the coalition forces' state-building efforts appears in table 4.

The U.S.-led invasion of Iraq may have occurred under faulty intelligence about Saddam's WMD capability and connections to al-Qaeda. However, efforts to "nation build" in Iraq, which included top-down initiatives aimed at establishing a stable democracy, a functioning economy, responsible security, and key social services, missed numerous opportunities to work with and through the population for change and to stabilize the state. Furthermore, coalition efforts to build the Iraqi nation through unofficial quotas in the government and the military and to focus on oil wealth may have done more to drive wedges between the ethnic groups in Iraq than to unite them. Democracy expert Larry Diamond summarizes the flaws in U.S.-led efforts to state build in Iraq: "The obsession with control was an overarching flaw in the U.S. occupation from start to finish. In any postconflict international intervention, there is always a certain tension between legitimacy and control. Yet for most of the first year of [the Iraq] occupation, the U.S. administration opted for the latter whenever the tradeoff presented itself."[95] The next chapter will offer an ex post facto, hypothetical look at how the United States and its coalition could have engaged in fostering national unity while building a stable Iraq.

4. Coalition forces' state-building efforts in Iraq

Pillar	Coalition actions	Effect
Safe and secure environment	Did not stop looting	Fueled negative perceptions of coalition forces
	Disbanded Iraqi military	
	Trained Iraqi security forces	Destroyed Iraqi artifacts and symbols
	Created Sons of Iraq	Did not create a sense of Iraqiness in security training and service
Governance and democracy	Used expatriates as key political figures	Interim government not known to populous
	Established Iraqi interim governments	Left local leaders out of process
	Held elections	Exacerbated ethnic competition and divisions through elections
Rule of law	Prisoners abused at Abu Ghraib	Fueled negative perceptions of coalition forces' sense of justice
	Drafted a constitution	
	Helped create war crimes tribunal	Left key figures out of process
Economic development	Focused on oil production	Fueled conspiracy theories about the invasion
	Did not focus on other sectors	Uneven economic growth
	Did not focus on employment	Policy bogged down in regional/ethnic rights to oil
Social well-being	Focused on basic utilities (SWEAT)	Inability to provide basic utilities consistently
	Polled about popular perceptions	Perception of poor personal security
	Did not focus on providing personal security	Rampant sectarian violence

6

COUNTERFACTUAL STATE-BUILDING AND NATION-BUILDING IN IRAQ

The United States and its coalition missed valuable opportunities for building and strengthening national unity in post-Saddam Iraq. Despite calling their efforts "nation-building," occupying powers focused heavily on building the structure of the state. While important for stabilizing Iraq in the wake of the invasion, these state-building initiatives also missed critical opportunities to weave national unity into the reconstruction efforts, and in some cases, coalition powers' initiatives actually helped to perpetuate ethnic strife, rather than build unity. The result of these efforts was a Shia-dominated government and security forces, a lack of consensus on developing Iraq's oil industry and distributing its wealth, and the fall of significant portions of the country to the Sunni insurgent Islamic State in Iraq and the Levant (ISIL) in 2014, aided in part by the Sunni population, which saw no future in the current Iraq state.

This chapter offers an ex post facto, hypothetical look at how the United States and the coalition powers could have created a program designed to foster and reinforce Iraqi national unity as part of their efforts to develop a viable and prosperous state. It begins by discussing the conditions for national-unity building, noting evidence that the Iraqis themselves did not want a divided country in the wake of the war and that hints of national unity did exist in post-Saddam Iraq. It then considers how U.S. and coalition powers could have fostered national unity within their state-building programs, focusing specifically on the five pillars of stabilization and reconstruction—security, governance, economic development, rule of law, and social well-being—in addition to what a sixth pillar of national-unity building would have looked like.

Ultimately in their efforts at state-building and nation-building, U.S. and coalition powers should have understood and focused more on the population and less on the macro-level structures of the state to foster a program of national-unity building and state-building. As the events in 2014 have demonstrated, if intervening powers do not help to foster national unity among a country's citizens, another national entrepreneur is likely to step in and do so. In the case of Iraq, the lack of initiative to foster the Iraqi nation, coupled largely with ineffective state-building programs that perpetuated ethnic conflict, paved the way for other nation-building entrepreneurs—ISIL—to divide the country along sectarian lines and capture the state.

Conditions for Initiating a Program to Build National Unity in Iraq

Perhaps the first place to begin in a program to build national unity in Iraq is to ask if any semblance of a nation existed within the country leading up to the invasion. Along with this question, it is necessary to consider whether the Iraqis themselves believed in the possibility of an Iraqi nation at the time of the invasion in 2003.

First, polling data suggest that the Iraqi people overwhelmingly wanted their country to remain united. For example, the Brookings Institution's Iraq Index chronicles questions regarding whether Iraqis felt the state should remain unified. In February 2004, just prior to the first anniversary of the invasion, 79 percent of Iraqis, drawn from across ethnic groups, answered that the Iraqi state should remain unified. Even in 2007, after years of insurgency and sectarian violence, 58 percent believed the country should remain whole, as opposed to 28 percent who favored some form of partition.[1]

However, within this overall support of a unified Iraq, when asked how likely Iraq will be a single state in five years, 80 percent of Shias answered favorably, 65 percent of Kurds, and only 56 percent of Sunnis.[2] Of considerable importance, Kurds consistently answered in favor of Iraqi unity in the first few years following the overthrow of Saddam Hussein. However, with time and the collapse of the Iraqi government in 2014, Kurds abandoned their preference for a unified Iraq and eventually voted for secession in 2017. Perhaps equally important, Sunnis saw themselves less and less as full members of the Iraqi state and were the least optimistic about Iraq's future over time. This lack of optimism came to a destructive conclusion with the arrival of ISIL in 2014. In other words these data show a squandered opportunity to build on Iraqis' desire to keep the country unified and build national unity from the time of the invasion. Instead, the United States' erroneous assumptions about Iraqi disunity appeared to drive state-building initiatives.

In addition to polling data, chapter 5 highlighted the past and present moments of national unity that could have been seized on and nurtured as examples of the Iraqi nation. Iraq had examples of national unity since the British created the state in 1920. As described in chapter 5, the founding of the Iraqi Army in 1921 became a symbol of the Iraqi state. Also during the 1920s, poetry emerged as a powerful medium that depicted hints of Iraqi unity, particularly in its criticism of British policies. Alongside poetry Arabic newspapers played an important role in unifying Iraqis, including satirical publications that criticized the British and local politics. These moments of national unity were followed by spurts of disunity and ethnic strife, driven by elites and their efforts to unify and divide the population in response to specific political opportunities. These fits and starts of the Iraqi nation suggest that, given the right leadership and incentives, national unity could have been fostered in post-Saddam Iraq as well.

In addition to recognizing these historic examples of national unity, the coalition powers needed to believe in the possibility of Iraqi unity and take actions aimed at realizing this goal. The prevailing wisdom in efforts to stabilize a state, discussed in chapter 4, was that establishing a functioning, representative democracy, developing a secure environment and prosperous economy, and ensuring social well-being would stabilize the country. In other words state services and the social contract—the informal and formal agreement between citizens and the state whereby citizens give up some of their liberties and resources in return for security and services—would make citizens happy and loyal to the state.

However, loyalty to the state is not achieved by purely utilitarian means and includes an emotional component as well. Individuals support the state and are loyal to it not just because of what it gives them but also because of the deep, emotional sense of belonging and identity that states help create in the minds and hearts of its citizens. Without this emotional attachment and the "imagined community" of citizens of the state, social cohesion of the state is unlikely to endure, particularly during the inevitable times of national questioning and struggle.

Chapter 2 proposed a near-term objective for developing the nation in postconflict and weak states: national unity. National-unity building aims to do two broad things. First, and most importantly, it seeks to create a sense of cohesion among a state's citizens. This cohesion is centered not on perceptions of common ancestry or religion but on a common destiny. As members of a state, citizens need to recognize that they hold the power to make, or destroy, their own future. As citizens, as the true sovereignty of the state, they hold the power of the state and can make it prosper. Within this sense of common destiny, however, national unity cannot deny the past. A past that has included suffering, warfare, and harm to one another cannot be ignored, but nor should it be the defining element of the future. The past needs to be understood in terms of the present and the future together. In other words *how* the past is regarded becomes vital for national-unity building.

As an immediate and practical goal, national-unity efforts should work on building social capital among the people, or the informal norms and rules that are based on reciprocity and develop trust among a people. The way in which the core components of a state are built or rebuilt—including its physical infrastructure, economy, rule of law, security forces, government, and social services—needs to start with the people and include them throughout the process in order to build social capital, give the population ownership and control of the state, and foster a future together.

Second, national unity aims to create a popular sense of rights, responsibilities, and loyalty to the state. This relationship between citizens and the state is fostered, in part, by the social contract, the idea that citizens give up certain liberties, such as total freedom, and governments provide certain resources to citizens in return, such as security, education, roads, potable water, and health care. However, building loyalty to the state is more than just a rational quid pro quo; it also includes emotional content. National unity is realizing that the state—its government, military, rule of law, economy—are the responsibility of the population. People are the sovereign, and the state starts with them. Myths, symbols, rituals, and other trappings of nations are equally important in efforts to build national unity. National unity is recognizing and identifying with the common destiny of both the population and the state. It is building an imaginary community based on these two principles.

However, despite the false assumptions of the Iraqi people and their preferences coupled with the speed with which intervening forces aimed to transform Iraq, occupying powers still could have initiated programs that most likely would have quickly and positively affected the population and worked to rebuild both the Iraqi state and nation. Moreover, focusing on national-unity building could have prevented some of the bigger blunders the occupation committed, which actually help pull the country apart. The dissolution of Iraq, in other words, was not a foregone conclusion.

Hypothetical State-Building and National-Unity Building in Iraq

U.S. and coalition efforts to build the Iraqi state after 2003 focused on rapidly transitioning Iraq to democracy, building responsible security forces, and getting the country's oil industry up and running. These were all top-down-driven initiatives with easily measured outputs. The United States most likely did not start with the population because it had already decided what was important to Iraq and did not take the time to see if the population agreed. Moreover, assessing popular expectations and priorities requires "boots on the ground"—troops, scholars, aid workers, and others who can interact with the people to better understand their needs and vulnerabilities. This process of discernment, while valuable, takes time and is manpower intensive. However, starting with the population could have given the population buy-in to the process. Furthermore, as will be discussed below, U.S. and coalition forces could have structured their state-building initiatives in a way that would have promoted national unity.

POPULATION-DRIVEN SECURITY

Security was an immediate concern to the Iraqi population. As noted in chapter 5, polling data from the first months of the occupation show that, while Iraqis were optimistic that their lives would be better, they were afraid to leave their homes and security was a primary concern.[3] Lack of security continued to be a problem during the occupation of Iraq; looting and unrest gave way to an organized insurgency, which helped fuel sectarian conflict and civil war, all of which greatly impacted the population's sense of security. Ultimately, security in Iraq improved after years of violence and instability with a combination of "the surge"—which brought greater numbers of U.S. troops with better tactics, techniques, and procedures for creating security—and locally led security initiatives, such as the Sons of Iraq, described in chapter 5.

It is very likely that security could have been improved in the early stages of the occupation by leveraging population-driven initiatives at the local level. Under these conditions U.S. and coalition forces could have worked with local leaders to set up ad hoc security forces for villages and neighborhoods in cities. This approach would have accomplished several positive steps at once: it would have empowered local leaders; it could have given these leaders the opportunity to exercise decision-making skills and consensus building, thus fostering good governance; it would have held leaders accountable for bad events in their areas of authority; and in successful areas it would have reduced the need for U.S. and coalition forces, freeing them up to concentrate their efforts in problem areas.

Furthermore, occupying forces should have taken a more holistic approach to understanding security. Rather than focusing on attacks on coalition forces, Iraqi troops, or government sites— which is essentially government and security forces centric— the United States and its allies should have concentrated more on what is often called "human security," which is the focus on the population and its overall perception of security, including access to food and water, freedom of movement, and physical safety from a wide array of threats, ranging from disease to crime to sectarian violence.[4] This approach would have driven security down to the local level and better reflected the fears and perceptions of the population and the best ways to address the broad spectrum of security concerns.

Anecdotal evidence exists of Iraqi initiatives in the early days of the invasion that aimed to establish security at the local level. As discussed in chapter 5, in the days following the invasion ad hoc governance and security groups sprang up in numerous cities, including in Amara, Kirkuk, Mosul, and Sadr City, the Shia slum in Baghdad, which became a major security concern for coalition forces throughout the war. In many of these cases, U.S. and coalition forces worked with these locally led initiatives. In other cases, especially in the Shia-dominated south, coalition forces stifled efforts to create ad hoc governance and security. Ultimately, the occupying forces' efforts at leveraging and guiding these fledgling governance and security initiatives were jettisoned for top-down efforts to create Iraq's security forces virtually from scratch.

A locally led approach to security would not have been without its challenges. Specifically, coalition forces would have needed some means to judge the legitimacy of local leaders and mechanisms for dealing with corrupt or abusive leaders in a way that would be supported by the population. Furthermore, creating incentives and other mechanisms for including minority groups in areas that had ethnic strife, like Kirkuk, would have been important. Equally important a mechanism for transitioning ad hoc security teams (and their leaders) to some form of legitimate security forces and governance would have been necessary for stabilizing the state over the long haul.

Coalition forces did in fact leverage population-centric security as part of the 2006 Sunni "awakening," particularly through the creation of the Sons of Iraq. As described in chapter 5, this program helped forge an alliance between coalition forces and the disenfranchised Sunni population to drive out al-Qaeda in Iraq. While the short-term benefits of the Sons of Iraq were many, this program also had considerable problems. Specifically, the initiative came three years after the start of the war. Within this time the Sunni population had already become alienated from the political process and had formed an active insurgency against coalition forces and the fledgling Iraqi government. The Sons of Iraq were also established along ethnic lines, further driving a wedge between Sunnis and other ethnic groups, particularly the Shia. Furthermore, coalition powers had already spent three years constructing official Iraqi security forces; the Sons of Iraq created a problematic redundancy in Iraq's security sector. Last, neither coalition forces nor the Iraqi government had a viable plan for transitioning the Sons of Iraq to legitimate forces over the long haul, eventually leaving thousands of Sunni men unemployed once again, alienated from the government, and willing to passively or actively support the arrival of ISIL.

Ultimately, a population-centric approach to security could have helped foster the Iraqi nation by focusing on the community level first and drawing from an array of local leaders to help organize security at the local level. Occupying powers could have offered incentives—like training and advising, development grants, and other resources—for building security across ethnic lines. Furthermore, over the long haul, nonviolent means of security should also have been emphasized and taught in Iraq as a way to both improve security and strengthen national unity. Security should have been presented as a civic responsibility, not the sole requirement of the state. For example neighborhood watch programs could have been established throughout the country as a means of connecting citizens in towns and cities to the common concern of personal security and the protection of private property. Basic conflict-resolution skills and tolerance of others should also have been emphasized as a component of local security through school curricula, public service announcements, and other government-sponsored campaigns.

Coalition forces also could have helped establish and improve other security forces, including fire departments, emergency medical response, and disaster relief groups as a gesture of good will and to help Iraqis think of security as more than just the absence of violence. For example U.S. military reserve units, which typically have members of community-based fire and rescue units, could have formed partnerships with their fire departments in the United States, as an opportunity to share best practices and foster good will between the United States and Iraqi citizens. Coalition forces could have also helped facilitate partnerships with IOs and NGOs, like the Green Crescent, to help develop these services and create a broader definition of security that moves beyond just absence of violence.

Finally, coalition forces could have worked with national entrepreneurs to foster myths and rituals surrounding security forces and those who volunteer for them. All security forces should have taken an oath of office. For example, then-colonel Stephen Townsend, commander of 3-2 Stryker Brigade in Iraq during the 2007 Battle of Baqubah, proposed seven rules and one oath for the Iraqi military and turned insurgents fighting alongside U.S. forces. The rules were the following: "1) Protect your community from AQI, JAM and other terrorist militia. 2) Accept both peaceful Sunni, Shia and others. 3) Stay in your neighborhood /AO [area of operations] for your safety. 4) Take an oath of allegiance to the Constitution of Iraq. 5) Register with Iraqi Security Forces and Coalition Forces [biometrics for CF]. 6) For your safety, wear a standard uniform and markings. 7) Reserve hiring preference for Iraqi Police and Army."[5]

The proposed oath stated: "1) I will support and defend the Constitution of Iraq. 2) I will cooperate fully with the Iraqi government. 3) I will guard my neighborhood, community and city.

4) I will bear no arms outside my home without coordination of Iraqi Security Forces or Coalition Forces. 5) I will bear no arms against the Government of Iraq, Iraqi Security Forces or Coalition Forces. 6) I will not support sectarian agendas."[6] An oath like this should have been instituted across Iraq's security and emergency services, linking both local- and state-level requirements, as well as upholding the Iraqi military as an important historic institution. Alongside these oaths, national holidays, annual parades, statues, national cemeteries, and other commemorations for all of Iraq's security forces, should have been instituted to raise awareness of the personal obligation toward securing the community and the heroic efforts of all those who help in this endeavor.

LOCALLY LED GOVERNANCE

Closely connected to leveraging local ad hoc security forces, U.S. and coalition forces missed valuable opportunities to partner with local leaders and support impromptu governance in the wake of the invasion. In many cases these local leaders could have formed the earliest stages of population-based sovereignty and could have given U.S.-led efforts at regime change local legitimacy.

Instead, the United States government chose to work closely with Iraqi expatriates, who had spent considerable time lobbying various power brokers in Washington DC to run the country following the overthrow of Saddam Hussein. These leaders were accessible to decision makers in Washington and did not require "boots on the ground" or time to assess and understand the will of the Iraqi people. Alongside picking Iraqi expatriates to "put an Iraqi face" on governance during the early days of the occupation, the United States and its coalition made holding elections, particularly at the national level, a top priority and the means through which Iraqis would be able to choose their sovereign. As with creating security forces, establishing governance in Iraq was a top-down initiative.

U.S. efforts at establishing legitimate governance could have capitalized on the numerous instances of governance at the community level that sprang up in the days following the invasion.

As noted in chapter 5, some of these initiatives were supported by U.S. and coalition forces, and some were not. Of particular note, efforts in the ethnically divided city of Kirkuk, where three hundred leaders gathered and formed a council that included Sunnis, Shias, Kurds, and Turkomans, is a particularly good example of an instance where productive grassroots leadership could have been fostered for the early stages of local governance.[7]

At higher levels, U.S. and coalition powers could have worked with groups that had been self-organizing well before the 2003 invasion and planning for governing Iraqi after Saddam's removal, also noted in chapter 5. In particular the United States and its coalition could have worked with the council of Iraqi leaders that met in London in 2002 to draft the "Declaration of Shia in Iraq," in which they called for a continued unified Iraqi state and nation, the recognition of Kurdish autonomy under a federal system, and the end of ethnic discrimination and dictatorship.[8] The 2002 conference, in other words, took important steps to help govern in a post-Saddam Iraq. Decision makers in Washington should have engaged these leaders; however, they did not include them in the initial efforts at establishing the IGC in 2003. Instead they drew on leaders who were unknown to most Iraqis. The second governing body, the IIG, did engage some of these better-known leaders, but only after valuable time and first impressions for legitimate governance in Iraqi had been lost.

Moreover, the emphasis on holding elections within the first year of occupation in Iraq had lasting negative consequences for the country. As discussed in chapter 5, the overthrow of Saddam Hussein caused a power vacuum that, in turn, introduced new levels of political competition. In response to these rapid political changes, political parties had to mobilize votes quickly, and campaigning broke along ethnic lines. This development favored the Shias as the numerical majority ethnic group, and effectively gave no voice to Iraq's minority groups, including the Sunnis. Ethnic-based voting set the stage for the Shia-dominated government that ISIL toppled in 2014 with the tacit help of the disenfranchised Sunni minority.

Although doing so would have been controversial, the U.S. and coalition powers could have waited to hold national-level elections in Iraq and instead worked at the local level to build legitimate governance and help teach the principles of democracy to average Iraqis. A governing council of recognized leaders, such as the IIG, could have continued to manage the country from the top, along with guidance and oversight from the coalition powers. This approach most likely would have required working with religious leaders and leveraging their legitimacy for governance and stability, something that the United States seemed reluctant to do. However, as the religious leaders present at the 2002 "Declaration of Shia in Iraq" conference demonstrated, they are not de facto sectarian, antidemocratic, or antisecular; they could have work for pluralistic and representative forms of governance in Iraq.

The coalition powers could also have done more to help Iraqis develop initiatives aimed at educating their fellow citizens about the democratic process and the civic responsibilities of all citizens. Ultimately programs should have been rooted in the ideas of national entrepreneurs, but some examples of programs that the U.S. and coalition powers could have helped initiate include teaching democracy and holding elections in classes and schools, which would instill democratic values from an early age. Iraqi cities, districts, and the federal government also could have held annual essay competitions on democracy for children, or given grants and awards for civil-society building initiatives among children and youth. For adults greater public-service campaigns aimed at educating adults in their civic responsibilities beyond voting should have been more holistically initiated. Enlistees in the military and other security forces also should have been formally taught about their civic responsibilities as part of their indoctrination.

Finally, coalition forces and other international actors should have helped the Iraqi government devise a more comprehensive amnesty plan for insurgents, including bringing some into the political process, especially if insurgents had a popular base of support. Bringing willing insurgents into the political process could have held them accountable for their rhetoric and actions and given them a stake in the new Iraq.[9]

Alongside security perhaps the greatest positive impact the United States and its coalition could have had on a population-centric state- and nation-building program would have been economic programs for average Iraqis. After over a decade of crippling economic sanctions, the destruction of the marshes in Maysan Province and the farming it supported, and high unemployment, Iraqis most likely would have welcomed initiatives aimed at providing a consistent and meaningful livelihood. As with all other population-focused initiatives, economic programs at the local level would have required some degree of understanding of different areas in Iraq and the populations' needs and vulnerabilities. However, a simple baseline understanding most likely would have been possible based on pre-sanctions data on agriculture, industry, services, and oil production.

Instead, the United States and its allies focused heavily on Iraq's oil production, with the aim of harnessing its revenue for the country's reconstruction; as with other initiatives, this was a top-down effort. As noted in chapter 5, focusing on Iraq's oil had several problematic outcomes. First, it reinforced the idea that the United States invaded Iraq for its oil, and not to improve the lives of Iraqis or promote democracy, as it claimed. Second, focusing on oil exacerbated tensions over the rights of areas with untapped oil reserves—especially the Kurdish north and the Shia southeast—and the role of the Iraqi central government in partnering with international oil companies and distributing oil wealth throughout the country. Ultimately, the Iraqi government could not produce a hydrocarbon policy that resolved these questions, and it is unlikely that the Iraqi population as a whole benefited from the reemergence of Iraq's oil production.

Rather than focus on oil, the coalition powers could have initiated programs aimed at rapid employment and developing infrastructure and agriculture at the community level. These programs would have achieved several positive steps at once. First, they would have put people to work, offering income and means of providing for one's family. Second, these programs would have shown tangible results by building infrastructure at the local level and other initiatives from which average people could have benefited. Third, community-based infrastructure development would have given the local population ownership of these projects, as opposed to occupying powers or the Iraqi government. Fourth, if structured properly, community-based infrastructure development could have been used to foster civil society and to build committees that teach decision making, compromise, and leadership skills. Finally, community-based infrastructure development could have helped to drive a wedge between insurgents and the population—through employment, empowerment, organization, and ownership of projects. These projects also may have been "insurgent proof," meaning that if insurgents targeted these projects, they would be destroying the work of the communities whose support the insurgents needed to survive. It is also worth noting that these projects could have been implemented at a fraction of the cost of the massive development efforts initiated by the CPA or the U.S. government during the occupation.

Ultimately specific projects should have been based on the needs and wants of the local community; employment, organization, empowerment, civil-society building, and local ownership through manual labor should have been the goals, not the actual project per se. These programs did not need to be complex or elaborate to be effective. Examples of basic community-based infrastructure development programs include road improvements, cleaning irrigation systems, creating landfills, or developing parks and soccer fields.[10] More-complex programs could have been developed with the aid and mentorship of occupying troops, such as U.S. Civil Affairs, the Army Corps of Engineers, or U.S. Navy Seabees, or through civilian organizations like USAID. There is anecdotal evidence of individual units initiating programs like this in their areas of operation within the early stages of the war, including Civil Affairs Team-A 13, in West Baghdad, British teams in Maysan Province, and U.S. Special Forces teams in Ar Rutbah, to name a few.[11] However, this approach was not developed in earnest until years after the occupation had begun, squandering valuable time to involve the Iraqi people in rebuilding Iraq and taking ownership of their country.

Second, community-based economic development should have focused on agriculture over oil in the near term. Prior to the discovery of oil, agriculture was Iraq's biggest economic activity and is still the third largest industry after oil and government services. Focusing on agriculture would have had several positive benefits: it would have put farmers back to work and revived this industry; it would have produced food for Iraqis and possibly the region; and it would have potentially reduced conspiracy theories about U.S. intentions to take Iraq's oil. Beginning around 2007 several initiatives through USAID focused on Iraq's agriculture with promising results, as discussed in chapter 5. However, these initiatives began four years after the invasion and had barely taken hold when ISIL invaded the country.

Finally, since oil is Iraq's biggest economic sector, this industry should have been developed, but after basic programs that put Iraqis to work had first been initiated. Additionally, the United States and its allies should have pushed for an oil revenue distribution fund (ORDF), which gives a portion of oil revenue directly to individual Iraqis, as is done in the state of Alaska in the United States. This approach could have mitigated ethnic concerns over regional concentrations of Iraqi oil reserves, and it would have provided immediate tangible benefits to every Iraqi.

Longer-term programs for economic prosperity should have focused on developing Iraq's private sector and creating conditions that would have fostered direct foreign investment. The creation of the Iraq Economic Development Group in 2008, which aimed to encourage private investment in various sectors of Iraq's economy, is an example of an initiative that held promise for the long-term development and diversification of Iraq's economy. Unfortunately, partisan politics, lack of security, and the threat of ISIL have most likely stalled these efforts.

RULE OF LAW

Establishing a population-centric rule of law in Iraq was perhaps the most important aspect of setting the conditions to build civic nationalism following the overthrow of Saddam Hussein. However, of all the pillars of stabilization and reconstruction, it is the most difficult to build. As discussed in chapter 4, several scholars of state-building and stabilization name rule of law as the cornerstone of creating a viable state and popular buy-in to that state. Jens Meierhenrich, for example, argues that the creation of a consistent legal code and a healthy bureaucracy produce predictability and consistency that promote loyalty to the state, and "once legality and bureaucracy are established and relatively routine, secondary institutions can be introduced."[12] Furthermore, scholars of civic culture stress the importance of law and its consistent, even application as critical for establishing trust among citizens and between citizens and the state, particularly the creation of public policy.[13]

The United States focused on rule of law in the early stages of the occupation, but the emphasis was almost exclusively on drafting a constitution and punishing Saddam's inner circle. The logic behind this prioritization was to show swift justice for crimes perpetrated under Saddam's authority and to create the necessary rules and restrictions of the central government so that elections could be held in the near term. However, as noted in chapter 5, this process broke down almost immediately over who would be charged with drafting the constitution, the role of the central government vis-à-vis autonomous regions, and the role that Islam would play as a source of the law. The result was an interim law drafted primarily by the United States and the creation of a constitution in October 2005, almost two years after the invasion and overthrow of Saddam Hussein.

The focus on an Iraqi constitution, while important, was not done in a way that included key leaders or the population. The initial decision to draft a constitution without popularly recognized Iraqi leaders or any sort of ratification or debate that included the population was a mistake that the CPA had to correct, eventually requiring a process for selecting its drafters and a popular referendum on the constitution in 2005. Furthermore, the constitution did not impact the daily lives of average Iraqi citizens who faced both civil and criminal legal issues, such as property disputes or justice for sectarian-based murders. In some areas of Iraq, sharia criminal courts sprang up to fill the void and deliver justice.[14]

Creating rule of law that is evenly applied at the local level is perhaps the greatest challenge of building the state and the nation. As discussed above, it is important to create and implement law that resonates with the population and, at least in some respects, conforms to their sense of justice. However, at the same time, the law needs to be consistently applied across the whole population, not just among the majority or those in power. In the early stages of civic nation-building, populations may not have one common reference of justice, or they may have more than one system that operates simultaneously. Religion, culture, and other worldview-shaping systems all affect understandings of the law and justice. Therefore, although notions of law are rooted in cultural perceptions of justice, citizens still need to be taught their rights and responsibilities under the law. This process requires, first, creating a common framework and, second, instilling it in the population, both of which require time.

Furthermore, law and notions of justice are constantly evolving and changing to adapt to new developments and new understandings of what is right and wrong. Throughout this process the population needs to be consulted but also educated. One need only think about evolving issues of justice in the United States to understand this delicate process. Slavery was once legal, as were Jim Crow laws that perpetuated a separate legal system for African Americans. Women did not always have the right to vote. More recently, the rights of homosexuals to marry and receive benefits as married couples were hotly debated in both legislation and the courts. Legal rulings and the development of legislation, while rooted in the population, rarely rest on consensus. As with all aspects of civic life, law and justice must constantly be taught and reinforced to be evenly applied across the country. This process takes time and vigilance and requires resources.

More specific to Iraq, decades of dictatorial rule had left the population with a skewed sense of justice. Systems of patronage had favored specific ethnic groups and tribes over others. State-sponsored violence had targeted Kurds in the north and Shia marsh Arabs in the south, demanding some sort of restitution after the invasion. These actions most likely eroded popular confidence in Iraq's legal system and trust among its citizens. All these challenges required working with the people from the beginning to educate them on their rights and responsibilities as citizens and to begin restoring confidence in the legal system.

One means through which rule of law could have been taught in the early stages of the occupation was by pairing these norms and values with basic infrastructure development. The Afghan National Solidarity Program (NSP), which will be described in greater detail in chapter 7, gives incentives for people to work together to rebuild infrastructure and other development projects. The NSP requires individuals to form committees, develop project plans, and submit budgets for projects that are then funded by the central government. This approach teaches collaboration, team building, compromise, and basic skills like envisioning a project and developing a basic budget. Accountability rests not with the government but with the community, which has played an active role in selecting committee members and deciding on the project. This approach combines basic governance, economic development, and following rules to achieve a collective outcome.[15]

Ultimately, instilling in the population a common understanding of the rules, rights, and responsibilities of all citizens is a process that takes time and requires constant adjustment and education. Expecting Iraq to be transformed into a fully functioning state with citizens who embrace civic nationalism is an unreasonable expectation in the short run. However, the United States and its allies could have taken measures in the short run that would have helped build national unity and set the conditions for the values and norms of civic nationalism to take root.

SOCIAL WELL-BEING

Developing social well-being in Iraq following the overthrow of Saddam Hussein was another area in which the United States and its allies missed critical opportunities to engage and strengthen the Iraqi nation. As noted in chapter 5, occupying powers in Iraq focused heavily on the provision of electricity and other basic services, such as sewage management, water, and telecommunications, as a means of building social well-being. While these basic utilities were an important symbol of caring for the population under occupation, they did nothing to help build a sense of national cohesion among Iraqis. Furthermore, the occupying powers' inability to adequately provide these services, particularly in the early stages of the war, undermined their credibility and help fuel conspiracy theories about their true intentions for invading Iraq.

Rather than focus on utilities, coalition powers could have initiated programs that aimed to build national unity and provide Iraqis with a sense of normalcy. Although it may seem superfluous, sports could have been a means for helping Iraqis build their nation and improve morale. Soccer is perhaps the most popular sport in Iraq, and the Iraqi National Football team dates back to 1948. The team's nickname is Usood Al-Rafidain, or Lions of Mesopotamia. During the 1990s the football team endured threats to team players' lives and humiliating treatment under the leadership of Uday, one of Saddam's sons. However, following the overthrow of Saddam, the team won the West Asian Championship in 2002 and just missed qualifying for the World Cup. Iraq participated in the 2004 Summer Olympic Games in Athens and beat Portugal and Costa Rica before ultimately being defeated. One Iraqi fan claimed: "The Iraqi people have had so many problems, we need something good like this . . . Sunni, Shi'ite—everyone thinks he's the best. But tonight we are one together."[16] Following the Olympics the team went on to win a gold medal in the 2005 West Asian Games, and in 2007 it won its first Asian Football Confederation (AFC) Asian Cup.

As a means of strengthening national unity and improving social well-being, coalition forces could have capitalized on Iraq's love of soccer and built basic soccer fields and provided equipment, in addition to helping organize teams in their areas of operation.

These teams could have been matched along a variety of lines—police versus fire department, teachers versus students, by neighborhood and so on—and teams could have played one another in an intermural fashion. Furthermore, city teams could have played one another, fostering geographic rivalries that, if properly constructed, would have helped bring Iraqis from different ethnic groups and areas into contact with one another. Ultimately, this approach to well-being would have focused on something fun that built collaboration and collegial rivalries, as opposed to focusing just on the presence or absence of basic utilities.

Another source of well-being that could have encouraged national cohesion in Iraq was music, particularly pop music. Beginning in 2003, several shows based loosely on the *British Idol* and *American Idol* reality shows began airing in the Middle East, such as *Star Academy Arab World, Super Star,* and *Arab Idol.* These shows pit contestants from Arab countries against one another for the chance to be named the next big music sensation in the Middle East. In 2007 Shatha Hassoun, a singer of Iraqi and Moroccan descent, competed in *Star Academy.* Big screens were set up in several cities across the country to allow Iraqis to watch the competition. When Hassoun won, she waved an Iraqi flag and momentarily unified the country behind her success. She became known as the "daughter of the Mesopotamia," and continues to be one of the most popular Arab singers in the Middle East and North Africa.[17] This competition provided an opportunity not only for Iraqi recreation but also for national unity and pride behind an individual competing on behalf of her country. It was an opportunity for occupying powers to provide venues to hear Hassoun or possibly help organize a domestic tour.

Finally, education, while stressed as an important aspect of social well-being in Iraq, could have been emphasized more in the early days of the occupation and in a way that would have had a lasting impact on the population's well-being. Rory Stewart notes that during his year in Maysan Province following the invasion of Iraq, occupying forces refurbished schools in his area of responsibility, only to find that militants had taken over the buildings and were using the space to train new recruits.[18] Rather than focusing on rehabilitating schoolhouses, which was done in many regions throughout the country, coalition forces could have partnered with NGOs and agencies to organize and train teachers to jumpstart Iraq's education system. Training teachers would have developed a portable skill that could have been employed anywhere throughout the country.

Furthermore, building on the observations of Merriam outlined in chapter 2, over the long haul occupying powers should have encouraged Iraqi leaders to develop curricula that focused on ethnic collaboration, tolerance, and civic education. As Merriam argues, civic education and the role that it plays in creating responsible citizens who are respectful to one another and loyal to the state's rules and institutions is a never-ending process that requires constant attention in order to instill a sense of national unity within Iraq's youth and future generations.

A PILLAR OF NATIONAL UNITY

Finally, coalition forces should have worked with national entrepreneurs to institute programs that aimed to specifically work on fostering the Iraqi nation and leveraging the population's desire to keep Iraq unified. This pillar and its programs were almost wholly missing from plans to "nation build" in Iraq. As described in chapters 2 and 3, nations are not organic products of a group but rather are the result of conscious efforts to consolidate and meld members into an "imagined political community" that has a shared sense of past and destiny. This program of national-unity building, which would have helped pave the way for civic nationalism, should have not only capitalized on the functional aspects of the state to foster the nation but also developed programs aimed at creating in Iraqis an emotional sense of connection to one another and to the country.

First, occupying powers should have made the effort to find national entrepreneurs, to reach out to Iraqi intellectuals, and other local leaders and elites in order to help develop programs that would strengthen the Iraqi nation. Although undoubtedly intellectual freedom and the arts suffered under the rule of Saddam Hussein, academics, artists, and sports heroes have historically been some of the most defiant leaders in the face of oppression and occupation. Examples of individuals could have included sports figures, musicians, poets, TV personalities, even fashion designers. Moreover, occupying powers should have called on famous Iraqi exiles not to run the country but to help rally the people through art, music, and sports. Together, these intellectuals and high-profile figures could have helped foster a program of national-unity building that would have leveraged preexisting social and cultural icons and allowed Iraqis to lead the way.

Second, occupying powers should have worked with intellectuals to find points of pride shared by most, if not all, Iraqis. While often controversial, ancient history could have provided a common rallying point for Iraqis. Mesopotamia's rich history as the "cradle of civilization" alongside is millennia of empires and the art and other artifacts they created could have been one potential point of shared pride among Iraqis. As noted in chapter 5, the looting of Iraq's national museum in the days following the 2003 invasion destroyed not only artifacts but also a potential symbol of Iraqi pride.

Furthermore, a plan to return Baghdad to its rightful place as one of the great cosmopolitan cities of the world could possibly have been another rallying point for the Iraqi nation. Postinvasion Iraq presented a unique opportunity not just to rebuild crumbling infrastructure and a capital city but also to make these functional aspects of the state beautiful symbols of the nation. During the Great Depression, the United States government created the Public Works Administration (PWA) as part of the National Recovery Act of 1933, which aimed to put the country to work building infrastructure and public buildings. This initiative created not only bridges, dams, and buildings but also national landmarks that persist in the twenty-first century, such as the Triborough Bridge and the Lincoln Tunnel in New York.

The Hoover Dam was also part of a Great Depression jobs program initiative.

Similarly, the CPA and the fledgling Iraqi government could have sponsored architectural and city-planning initiatives that would not only have rebuilt Baghdad but made it a symbol of the Iraqi nation, a place that would have drawn Iraqis to visit its museums, parks, monuments, and federal buildings, similar to the initiatives undertaken by major European cities and the United States in the nineteenth century. Coalition powers could have supplied money, resources, and advisers but allowed Iraqi architects and urban planners to develop the city in a way that would resonate with the population.

Another program of national unity that occupying powers could have initiated was one to help preserve Iraq's diverse and beautiful landscape. As mentioned in chapters 3 and 4, European countries and the United States developed urban parks and national forests as places of recreation; however, these lands also became symbols of national pride. Iraq has several areas that could have served this purpose. For example, coalition powers could have taken steps to help the Iraqis clean up and preserve areas of the Tigris and Euphrates Rivers, make national parks in the mountains of the Kurdish north, and preserve the ancient cities of Babylon and Ur. These programs, if structured properly, could have employed Iraqis and helped to revitalize these symbols of national pride.

The United States government, together with NGOs, did take measures aimed at restoring Iraq's marshes, which Saddam Hussein's regime systematically drained during his rule; however this initiative was overshadowed by large-scale, top-down initiatives. In 2013 the founder of Nature Iraq, a U.S. citizen born in Iraq, won the Goldman Environmental Prize for efforts to reclaim Iraq's wetlands and restore many species they support.[19] These efforts, however, are most likely challenged by recent political dynamics in the country. Had the United States and its allies focused on such programs in the beginning of the occupation, it may have sent a very different and positive message to Iraqis about the intentions of intervening powers, along with helping Iraqis to forge their own destiny as a nation.

The United States and its allies also could have helped promote popular culture as a means of fostering Iraqi national unity. Pop music, as mentioned, became a rallying point for Iraqis, particularly when Shatha Hassoun won *Star Academy*; this is a medium that coalition powers could have leveraged to rally young Iraqis around the notion of the nation and built emotional pride and support for national pop art. Similarly, Iraq's cuisine could have been used as a means of highlighting both Iraq's regional diversity and its overall unity through the common denominator of food. Iraq's history of literature and its culture of poetry were another possible vehicle of uniting Iraqis. In particular coalition powers could have helped the Iraqi government organize national-level competitions in music, cooking, and literature, perhaps providing award money or other incentives to be named Iraq's artist of the year. They could have helped create national poetry contests or television shows similar to *Star Academy*, but on an Iraqi level, or *The Great British Bake Off*, which draws contestants from across the United Kingdom, as a means of both highlighting Iraq's diversity and showing its unique national attributes.

Coalition powers also could have done more to help foster symbols of the Iraqi nation. As discussed in chapter 5, the CPA's decision to disband Iraq's military shortly after the invasion not only had disastrous consequences for security in the country but also destroyed a symbol of Iraqi independence and national pride. Iraq's flag and national anthem were also missed opportunities for national unity. The CPA chose the national flag in 2004 along with its national anthem, based on the poem *Mawtini* (my homeland), which was written by a Palestinian poet in the 1930s. In 2008 the Iraqi government initiated a contest to find a new national anthem, soliciting input from national poets and artists. A new flag was chosen in 2008, but the government was unable to decide on a new anthem.[20] These proposals are summarized in table 5.

5. Hypothetical nation-building in Iraq

Pillar	What was done	What could have been done
Security	Established conventional security forces	Foster community-based security with local leadership
	soi after 2006	Encourage neighborhood watch
		Focus on all aspects of security forces including fire, emt, and disaster relief
		Partner with national entrepreneurs to foster oaths, myths, and rituals surrounding security
Governance	Worked with ex-pats	Engage 2002 Shia conference attendees
	Did not support local initiatives consistently	Support local governance issues in the wake of the invasion
	Held national elections	Delay elections
		Support Iraqi-led civic education and initiatives
		Bring willing insurgents into the political process
Economic development	Oil production	Establish jobs program to rebuild Iraqi infrastructure
		Focus on agriculture
		Develop oil revenue distribution fund
Rule of law	Drafted constitution	Include key leaders in drafting constitution
		Teach rule of law through locally led building and development programs
		Promote civic education at all levels to teach rule of law
Social well-being	Focused on providing basic utilities	Support national sports program
		Promote pop music
		Train teachers

National unity	Work through local celebrities and influencers
	Emphasize "cradle of civilization"
	Develop art, poetry, cooking competitions
	Rebuild capital city through locally led city planning and architecture
	Support national parks and wilderness
	Promote Iraqi competition for new flag and anthem

Ultimately, programs of national-unity building need to emanate from the population and national entrepreneurs. Programs like these will succeed only if the resonate with and inspire the population.

State-building and nation-building in Iraq should have included the Iraqi people throughout the process; in other words, the population's needs and dreams should have been an integral part of reconstructing Iraq from the earliest days of the occupation. This approach would have gone far to mitigate perceptions that the United States invaded Iraq solely for its oil and that it did actually care about the destiny of Iraq and its people. Furthermore, creating programs that consciously aimed to foster national unity within efforts to establish security, economic stability, governance, rule of law, and social well-being could have potentially reduced some of the country's ethnic tensions and worked toward establishing an overarching identity of civic nationalism.

7

STATE-BUILDING IN AFGHANISTAN, 2001-2016

In 2012 the conflict in Afghanistan became America's longest war, outpacing the six-year American Revolution, the eight-year war in Iraq, and the ten-year Vietnam conflict. The conditions that led to the invasion of Afghanistan were some of the most trying in U.S. history—an attack on the homeland by a shadowy force that left nearly three thousand dead. However, unlike the 1941 Japanese attack on Pearl Harbor, the United States faced a new type of enemy not confined to a state or bound by international rules and norms. Furthermore, securing the U.S. homeland against future attacks required a different strategy, one rooted not in defeating an adversary's military but in reducing the conditions that foster sympathy and support for a transnational movement that aims to destroy the international system.

To address these challenges, the United States declared a "global war on terror." As part of this initiative, the United States invaded Afghanistan in 2001 with specific goals: to capture key leaders including Osama bin Laden, to end Taliban rule, and to deny al-Qaeda and other transnational terrorists a safe haven in the country and the possibility of launching another attack on the U.S. homeland. However, following the invasion key Afghan and international leaders met in Bonn, Germany, to discuss the future of the country. In December 2001 they devised a plan to transform Afghanistan into a constitutional democracy with a functioning judiciary and rule of law. A month later, in January 2002, an international conference convened in Tokyo, Japan, in which sixty countries and dozens of NGOs pledged US$4.5 billion over the next five years to further develop its political, economic, and social institutions.[1]

The 2001 Bonn Agreement and the 2002 Tokyo conference effectively transformed the war in Afghanistan from a military operation with specific goals, to a massive international effort aimed at transforming the country from one of the poorest and least developed into a modern democratic state with the necessary social, political, legal, security, and economic institutions. Although intervening countries initiated several novel efforts aimed at realizing these goals and driving them down to the local level, development efforts still focused primarily on the construction of a central government and instruments of the state. By and large the population was left out of the state-building process. Furthermore, virtually no efforts were made to build national unity beyond creating power-sharing arrangements in the government and the military.

This chapter investigates what U.S. and international actors did to build the Afghan state. It begins with a brief overview of Afghan history, starting with the creation of the Afghan kingdom under Pashtun rulers and culminating with the circumstances that led to the rise of the Taliban and the U.S.-led invasion in 2001. It then looks at U.S., NATO, and UN efforts to develop Afghanistan in the wake of the 2001 invasion, including initiatives aimed at building the state along the pillars of stabilization and reconstruction: security, governance, rule of law, economics, and social well-being.

Brief History of the Afghan State and Nation

Anthropologist Thomas Barfield's account of Afghanistan's cultural and political history begins by challenging the common adage that Afghanistan is "the graveyard of empires" and that its ethnically diverse population and difficult terrain make it ungovernable. Barfield makes a few key assertions. First, Afghanistan's emirs, who ruled from 1747 until 1978, created a system of governance that provided security and basic resources for the population, and in return the population did not challenge these dynastic rulers. Within this system ethnicity was not politicized and therefore not a problem for governance. Second, this system of governance and ethnic cohabitation was interrupted by foreigners—the British, the Soviets, and most recently, the Americans—who empowered different leaders and created new systems of political power that, in turn, fostered competition for authority. Ultimately, this political competition was destabilizing and has contributed to the current challenges with governing the country.[2]

Barfield's argument suggests that, historically, Afghanistan's various ethnic groups were not a source of instability; rather, ethnic conflict is a recent development and tied to political competition. Afghanistan's main ethnic groups include a mixture of Pashtuns, Tajiks, Shia Hazaras, Uzbeks, Aimaq, Turkomans, Balochs, and others. Within these ethnic groups are different tribes and clans, further complicating the demographic landscape. Despite the fact that Afghanistan is over 99 percent Muslim, there is still considerable diversity within the faith; the majority (80–85 percent) adhere to Sunni Islam, but 15 to 19 percent (mostly Hazaras) practice Shia Islam, and there are also Sufis, particularly the Chishti, the Naqshbandi, and the Qadiri orders.[3]

Barfield is quick to note that some of these ethnic categories are not fixed but rather change according to time and circumstances. He argues that the most important defining factor of a group is its self-definition and recognition by others: "There is a practical rule of thumb for sorting out the large number of ethnic groups in Afghanistan: if people identify themselves as the 'such and such,' and their neighbors agree that they are such and such, then they *are* such and such."[4] Barfield also notes that, despite changing over time and in response to circumstances, Afghanistan's groups present their stories as immutable. "People do assert that ethnicity is both fixed and historically rooted. All ethnic groups give themselves elaborate histories that stress their unchanging character."[5] Finally, Barfield states that ethnic diversity has historically not been a problem for governing Afghanistan, and it is only within the last fifty or so years that groups have demanded political power based on their ethnicity.[6]

Within this complex landscape of different religious sects and ethnic groups, understanding Afghanistan's political history is essential for comprehending the governance and security challenges it faces today. Afghanistan's first period of political independence came in 1709, when the Pashtun Mir Wais Hotak rebelled against the Persian Safavids and created an independent state, led by the Hotaki Dynasty. In 1747 Ahmad Shah Durrani expanded the state's territory, effectively creating the Afghan Empire and a secession of leadership based on blood within this dynastic line. The right to govern, in other words, was inherited within key family lines, and not attained through broader competition. It was in this era that a particular social contract emerged between the rulers, who supplied security and stability, and the population, which did not challenge their authority in return.[7]

In 1838 Britain invaded Afghan territory, in what became known as the First Anglo-Afghan War (1838–42), with the goal of checking increasing Russian involvement and their possible invasion into Afghanistan. Despite initial successes the British suffered heavy casualties, including the 1842 massacre of 4,500 troops and 12,000 British civilians retreating from Kabul, where only a British doctor escaped. That same year the British counterattacked and installed Dost Mohammed as emir, beginning a period of prolonged British influence within the area.[8]

Barfield notes that British influence in Afghanistan introduced new sources of authority in the region. Specifically, the British worked with tribal warriors on Afghanistan's frontier, empowering them when it suited their needs and fighting them when they posed a threat. To this end the British engaged in another war with the Afghans (1878–80), which sought to pacify Afghan tribes on the border with India's western frontier and ultimately resulted in Britain gaining territory from the Afghans and increased influence.[9]

In the wake of the Second Anglo-Afghan War, the British helped bring Abdur Rahman to power in the hopes of creating a more stable region on the empire's border. Abdur Rahman, who became known as the "Iron Emir," began an era of aggressive state-building that included violent confrontations with relatives and tribes, especially Pashtun tribes that did not submit to his rule, effectively ending their autonomy. He also taxed the population and received funding from the British, which allowed the emir to strengthen his army. Abdur Rahman invoked jihad and considered defending Islam as a principal duty of Afghans. Ultimately, the Iron Emir's use of force created the Afghan state. Barfield notes, "These wars centralized political and economic power in Kabul, and made Abdur Rahman the undisputed ruler of Afghanistan." Despite this Barfield is quick to point out that the Iron Emir left rural Afghan society largely untouched.[10] Barfield further notes, "One might appeal to the common defense of Islam, but a national identity did not bubble up from below. It was the amir's standardized taxes, laws, currency, conscription and administrative structure that put all Afghans into a single system."[11] Ultimately, the Iron Emir's approach to governance created more enemies than supporters, and his successor was unable to maintain the necessary degree of coercion to keep tribes in line.

In 1893, during the reign of the Iron Emir, the British diplomat Mortimer Durand established a border between Afghanistan and what is today Pakistan, a demarcation that became known as the Durand Line. This border effectively divided Pashtun and Baloch tribes between the Afghan state and British-controlled India. The British fought one final war with the Afghans in 1919 to confirm this border.[12]

Following the Third Anglo-Afghan War, Britain largely withdrew from Afghanistan in 1919, leaving Amanullah Khan in control of the emirate. Amanullah introduced important changes to governance in Afghanistan and initiated a period of state-building. He oversaw the drafting of Afghanistan's first constitution in 1923, imposed new tax laws, created a more comprehensive legal system, developed universities and schools of higher learning, and imposed universal military conscription. The emir also initiated education for women and created laws against their abusive treatment, including child marriage.[13] These changes were not well received by tribal leaders who disagreed with the new policies and increased taxation they required. In January 1929 Shinwari Pashtuns revolted, and the emir fled to India. General Mohammed Nadir Khan seized power in October 1929 and was declared the king of Afghanistan.[14] In 1931 Afghanistan drafted another constitution, building on the 1923 version and adding elements of Persian, Turkish, and French law. Dupree contends that "the 1931 Constitution only partly suited the Afghan character and social system, which can be generally described as tribal, authoritarian, patrilineal, and patriarchal."[15]

Mohammed Nadir Khan was assassinated in November 1933, and Zahir Shah became the new king. The creation of the Soviet Union in 1922 and Afghanistan's proximity to the empire introduced new levels of foreign machinations in the country. Following a brief relationship with Nazi Germany during World War II, Afghanistan became party to Cold War competition between the United States and the Soviet Union, in which the Soviet Union ultimately prevailed with development and military aid.[16]

In 1953 General Muhammed Daud, a member of the ruling family, became prime minister. During his tenure he further opened relations with the Soviet Union. A decade later, in 1962, Daud was pushed out of office following a dispute with Pakistan that led to the closure of the border between the two countries, bringing trade to a halt and nearly bankrupting Afghanistan. Dr. Mohammed Yousuf, a Western-educated commoner, became Afghanistan's new political leader. Under Yousuf another constitution was drafted in 1964 and validated through the Loya Jirga, a general assembly of the country's tribal and religious leaders. The constitution limited the role of the royal family, defined "Afghan" as all citizens living within Afghanistan (not just Pashtuns), and included—but limited—the role of Islam and sharia law in the country. Of particular note the constitution states: "A law is a resolution passed by both Houses [of parliament], and signed by the King. In the area where no such law exists, the provisions of the Hanafi jurisprudence of the *Shari'a* shall be considered as law."[17] Dupree calls the 1964 constitution, for its time, "the finest in the Muslim world."[18]

In 1973 Daud staged a coup against the royal family and

declared Afghanistan a republic. King Zahir Shah fled to Italy. Daud drafted a constitution in 1976, which was legitimated by the Loya Jirga in 1977.[19] However, shortly after its ratification, Daud was assassinated in a Soviet-backed coup in 1978, sparking violent infighting in Kabul. In 1979 the Soviet Union invaded Afghanistan in an attempt to keep the Communist-sympathizing government in power. Afghanistan drafted two more constitutions, in 1987 and 1990, but these documents were largely ignored in the midst of the country's chaos.

The Soviet-Afghan War created lasting social and political problems for the country. Insurgent groups emerged almost immediately with the aim of resisting Soviet occupation and pushing back its forces. These groups, called mujahedeen (ones who engage in jihad), were predominately Sunni Muslim and mostly Pashtun, although Tajik and Hazara forces also appeared. In addition to small factions fighting independently throughout the country, seven main groups emerged: the Khalis faction, named after its leader; Hekmatyar's Hezbi Islami; Rabbani's Jamiat-e-Islami (which was primarily Tajik); Sayyaf's Islamic Union for the Liberation of Afghanistan; Gailani's National Islamic Front for Afghanistan; Mjoaddedi's Afghanistan National Liberation Front; and Mohammadi's Islamic and National Revolution Movement of Afghanistan. Ahmad Shah Massoud formed an eighth group in 1984, Shura-e Nazar, which was an offshoot of Jamiat-i-Islami. These seven groups, together with Massoud's group, formed the Islamic Unity of Afghanistan Mujahedeen in 1985. They received financial and military backing from the United States and Pakistan as part of Cold War politics and support from fellow Muslims and Saudi Arabia.[20]

In addition to the Afghan mujahedeen, foreign fighters traveled to Afghanistan to participate in what they believed to be a jihad aimed at defending a Muslim land and people against a secular force attacking Islam. Sheikh Abdullah Azzam, a Palestinian-born cleric trained at Al-Azhar University in Cairo, left Saudi Arabia, where he was teaching, and moved to Peshawar, Pakistan, to aid in the Afghan fight. Together with Osama bin Laden, the son of a wealthy Saudi businessman, and Egyptian

Dr. Ayman al-Zawahiri, they formed the Maktab al-Khidamat in 1984 with the aim of recruiting foreign fighters, mostly Arabs, and raising money for the jihad. This organization eventually became al-Qaeda.[21]

The Soviet-Afghan War also created massive social problems, and the Afghan people suffered ineffably during and after the conflict. The war produced a massive forced migration both within the country and into Pakistan and Iran, which had a reported 6.2 million refugees split between the two countries. By 1999 an estimated 4 million had returned to Afghanistan without international assistance; however, the number of Afghan refugees in neighboring countries still totaled more than 2.6 million.[22] In addition to forced migration, Afghanistan also had a record number of landmines laid during the conflict, an estimated 640 million, which continue to this day to injure people and hinder agriculture and other aspects of daily life.[23] Furthermore, Afghanistan's overall economy remained in shambles, and basic services following the war, such as access to potable water, education, and health care, were abysmal.

The Soviet-Afghan War ended in 1989 with the withdrawal of the Soviet Union's military and the installation of a government sympathetic to Moscow led by Dr. Mohammad Najibullah. The Najibullah regime attempted to create a power-sharing agreement among Afghanistan's ethnic groups and to maintain a multiethnic military as a means of stabilizing the country. Alongside these efforts the Soviet Union continued to provide military aid, financial assistance, advising, food, and other resources to Afghanistan. However, when the Soviet Union abruptly collapsed in December 1991, the fledgling government lost its paternal and financial support and quickly folded. Barnett R. Rubin summarizes this period by noting that "when the Soviet Union withdrew and then dissolved, and the United States disengaged, Afghanistan was left with no legitimate state, no national leadership, multiple armed groups in every locality, a devastated economy, and a people dispersed throughout the region, indeed the world."[24] The country quickly plunged into a civil war in which the major mujahedeen factions fought for control of cities and regions and their leaders became warlords. Barfield notes that through the creation of these mujahedeen forces and their efforts to drive out the Soviets, "the Afghans found that they had inadvertently made it ungovernable by anyone else."[25]

Afghanistan's civil war was quelled by the rise of the Taliban, a militant Pashtun group whose lineage can be traced back to the mass migration of Pashtun refugees from Afghanistan to Pakistan during the Soviet-Afghan War and Pakistani efforts to create a bulwark against potential Soviet advances into Balochistan and prevent a strong Afghan government from forming after the war.[26] The Taliban drew from the millions of Pashtun refugees in the Federally Administered Tribal Areas and, with financial and material aid from Arabian Gulf States, raised a fighting force of "students" that espoused a reductionist and literalist interpretation of Islam and sharia law. Legend has it that the Taliban first gained support in Afghanistan near Kandahar after freeing two teenage girls abducted by fighting forces and hanging the town's mayor from a tank barrel. This story perhaps explains the initial spread of the Taliban as a force that provided security and swift justice in the ongoing chaos of the civil war.[27]

Despite the initial tales of the Taliban's heroism, the movement quickly grew into a merciless and intolerant force. Under the leadership of Mullah Omar, the Taliban succeeded in gaining control of the majority of the country by 1996, declaring Afghanistan an Islamic emirate, and making Kandahar its capital. Around this time the Taliban and al-Qaeda formed an alliance; Mullah Omar gave Osama bin Laden sanctuary and allowed him to establish training camps in Afghanistan. In 1998 the United States targeted these same al-Qaeda camps in Afghanistan following the bombing of the U.S. embassies in Kenya and Tanzania.

Despite the Taliban's almost universal condemnation—only three countries recognized its authority: Pakistan, Saudi Arabia, and the UAE—its rule over Afghanistan persisted until the September 11 attacks against New York and Washington DC, after which Afghanistan became the central focus of the United States' retaliatory attacks.

Conditions and Goals for the U.S. Invasion of Afghanistan

The story of U.S. military involvement in Afghanistan, now the country's longest war, began with specific goals in mind: to capture bin Laden, Mullah Omar, and other key leaders; to overthrow the Taliban; and to prevent al-Qaeda from using the country as a safe haven to train operatives and plan attacks. However, these limited and specific goals quickly morphed into a full-blown agenda for transforming Afghanistan from a predominately rural society to a democracy with a stable economy and a modern military.

On October 7, after negotiations with the Taliban failed to produce bin Laden, the United States commenced its bombing campaign on targets in Afghanistan. This offensive complemented the incursion of U.S. Special Operations Forces and the CIA into the north of the country, where they worked with members of the Northern Alliance, the only organized opposition to the Taliban in the country. U.S. and Northern Alliance forces succeeded in toppling the Taliban government within a month. Despite considerable U.S. military and government efforts, Mullah Omar, bin Laden, and other key leaders ultimately escaped from Afghanistan, denying the United States one of its primary objectives.[28]

Following the demise of the Taliban, an international debate began over what to do with Afghanistan. In December 2001 the United Nations convened a meeting of twenty-five prominent Afghans and key international leaders in Bonn, Germany, to devise a plan for stabilizing Afghanistan. The Agreement on Provisional Arrangements in Afghanistan Pending the Re-Establishment of Permanent Government Institutions, more commonly known as the "Bonn Agreement," created a time line for transforming Afghanistan's government into a representative system. The Bonn Agreement established the thirty-person Afghan Interim Authority (AIA), which would govern for six months, followed by the two-year Transitional Authority (TA), followed by elections. The Bonn Agreement also set the conditions for drafting an Afghan constitution, calling for a

Loya Jirga—a nationwide assembly of elders and other people of authority—to debate and ratify its contents within eighteen months. Finally, the Bonn Agreement set the conditions for the judicial branch of government, including an Afghan supreme court.[29] This initial meeting was followed by a donors' meeting in Tokyo in 2002, which pledged money for humanitarian assistance, reconstruction, and stabilization of Afghanistan. At that meeting the newly formed Afghanistan Interim Authority named five key reconstruction priorities: "enhancement of administrative capacity; education, especially for girls; health and sanitation; infrastructure; reconstruction and agriculture."[30]

The Bonn Agreement together with the Tokyo conference effectively set the conditions for state-building in Afghanistan. As will be discussed, while some of these efforts worked at the local level and new initiatives were launched to more evenly develop Afghanistan politically and economically and to provide security, state-building was largely a top-down initiative and did not leverage Afghan understandings of security or leadership. Furthermore, few initiatives focused on creating a sense Afghan national unity.

Stabilization and Construction of Afghanistan

The process for stabilizing Afghanistan focused on top-down macro-level initiatives, including the creation of national security forces, the introduction of democratic processes, the drafting of a constitution, and the initiation of major infrastructure development. Ultimately, this approach, which followed the pillars of stabilization and reconstruction discussed in chapter 4—a safe and secure environment, democracy, rule of law, healthy economy, and social well-being—aimed to create a stable state that would inoculate the country against parasitic terrorist groups like al-Qaeda and to give its citizens a better life and more opportunity. Each of these lines of effort is described below.

SECURITY

Historically the ability of leaders to provide security was the key factor for legitimacy in Afghanistan. When discussing how foreign empires established authority in the premodern era, Barfield notes that "all foreign rulers and their successors needed to achieve was the restoration of public order, and perhaps put down a rebellion or two."[31] Fotini Christia and Michael Semple observe that even the Taliban's ability to provide security and order during Afghanistan's civil war in the 1990s is critical for understanding the spread of its authority across the country.[32] Security, therefore, was a natural place to begin building the Afghan state following the U.S.-led invasion in 2001 and the overthrow of the Taliban regime.

U.S. and NATO forces made establishing and training competent Afghan security forces the cornerstone to securing the country and, ultimately, one of the key conditions for allowing U.S. and NATO troops to withdraw.[33] Occupying forces began training the Afghan National Security Forces (ANSF) within a few months of the overthrow of the Taliban. A RAND report on Security Force Assistance (SFA) in Afghanistan states that in 2002 an initial plan for the creation of ANSF called for a seventy thousand end-strength force of ethnically balanced volunteers spread across the army, police, and air force, and for a twenty-nine-thousand-strong Afghan National Army (ANA) to be trained and operational by the summer. This plan was later revised to just nine thousand ANA by November 2003.[34] U.S. Army Special Forces soldiers conducted the initial training, which lasted ten weeks; these efforts also included a "train the trainer program" designed to eventually make Afghans capable of training their own forces. However, training suffered from lack of resources, shortened courses, and the absence of follow-up training and advising.[35]

Furthermore, responsibility and coordination for training Afghanistan's security forces changed over time, hindering progress. Initially, the United States trained the Afghan National Army, Germany trained the Afghan National Police, and Britain, Italy, and Japan oversaw specific tasks like counternarcotics training and demobilization of militias.[36] In 2003 U.S. Central Command implemented Joint Task Force Phoenix, which aimed to mentor newly trained Afghan Security Forces through embedded training teams. Coalition forces created the Afghan National Army

Training Command (ANATC) in 2005, which sought to provide mentoring and assistance to Afghans responsible for training new forces and to guide regional and special training centers throughout the country. In November 2009 the NATO Training Mission in Afghanistan (NTM-A) unified training efforts under a single command, and at the end of 2014, most training responsibilities were transferred to the Afghan government.

Given this evolution in efforts and responsibilities, the RAND report on SFA in Afghanistan notes that measuring progress in training was virtually impossible because no one method was used to create Afghan security forces: "Units in one part of the country have taken one approach; units in another part a different one—but no one has tracked the results as coalition units rotated in and out of Afghanistan."[37] This made analyzing what was done and measuring success virtually impossible. Furthermore, the RAND report notes that few efforts were initiated to coordinate these different security elements, particularly the army and police forces, or link them to the country's fledgling judiciary, thus hindering their effectiveness.[38]

In addition to the problem of tracking what coalition forces actually did, training efforts were also not without challenges. Lack of basic skills in Afghan recruits was a problem and impeded the training of security forces; a 2010 assessment, for example, placed literacy rates of recruits at 14 percent. In response ISAF initiated a literacy program within its military training effort aimed at providing basic literacy skills to all who enlisted.[39] However, a 2014 Asia Foundation report notes, "Despite large literacy training programs sponsored by the United States military, illiteracy rates within the ANSF remain very high (roughly two-thirds of ANSF are illiterate)."[40]

In addition to challenges posed by high illiteracy rates, which slowed training, Afghan security forces also had high attrition rates, particularly in the beginning. By one estimate, "Afghanistan's 1st Battalion had a desertion rate of approximately 50 percent. But the rate eventually dropped to 10 percent per month by the summer of 2003, between 2 percent and 3 percent per month by 2004, and 1.25 percent per month by 2006."[41]

Coalition forces' training efforts also suffered from what became known as "green-on-blue attacks," Afghan forces that attacked their ISAF trainers. The majority of green-on-blue attacks were the result of insurgent forces penetrating ISAF training centers and then using their access to kill coalition forces. In response ISAF attempted to employ more rigorous vetting standards and use biometric data gathering as means of reducing insider threats; however, this threat remained a persistent problem throughout ISAF efforts to train Afghan forces. As of June 2017 green-on-blue attacks accounted for 152 coalition deaths and 200 wounded.[42]

The actual performance of Afghan Security Forces was mixed at best. The RAND report on SFA in Afghanistan notes that the ambitious buildup of both Afghanistan's army and its police forces stressed quantity over quality and did not allow sufficient time to train these forces.[43] The ANP initially suffered disproportionally as it was deployed as the principal force for combating the Taliban, a mission for which it had not trained. Between 2007 and 2009, 2,329 ANP were killed, as opposed to 717 ANA.[44] These concerns were further echoed in a 2009 memo from the U.S. ambassador to Afghanistan, Karl Eikenberry, to Secretary of State Hillary Clinton. Eikenberry asserted: "The Army's high attrition and low recruitment rates for Pashtuns in the south are crippling. . . . Simply keeping the forces at current levels requires tens of thousands of new recruits every year to replace attrition losses and battlefield casualties."[45]

Alongside NATO efforts to create Afghan security forces, insurgent groups reemerged in the country, including the Taliban, the Haqqani network (which was headquartered in Pakistan), and other movements that fought both occupying powers and Afghan forces. Pakistan played a critical role in the resurgence of these groups, particularly by allowing these groups to base, organize, and train along its frontier with Afghanistan, as well as by possible funding and training from the Pakistani government.[46] Eikenberry's 2009 memo to Secretary Clinton clearly delineated the problem Pakistan posed to Afghan security and stabilization: "Pakistan will remain the single greatest source of

Afghan instability so long as the border sanctuaries remain. . . . Until this problem is fully addressed, the gains from sending additional [U.S.] forces may be fleeting."[47]

Insurgents became a serious security concern in several Afghan provinces. The Taliban became particularly active in Helmand Province, its original stronghold, while the Haqqani network was active in Patika, Khost, Ghazni, Wardak, and Logar Provinces in Afghanistan.[48] To address local security needs, U.S. Special Operations Forces initiated what eventually became known as Village Stability Operations (vso). vso aimed to create local security forces, called Afghan Local Police (alp), with the goal of leveraging these forces to push back insurgents and establish "white space," territory that is clear from insurgent activity. In addition to creating local security forces, vso also initiated development projects and helped establish local governance.[49]

Despite pushing security and development down to the local level and achieving short-term success in denying insurgents populations and territory, vso came with some important challenges and implications. First, vso was not systematically implemented until around 2010, nearly nine years after the beginning of the war. Second, the program created redundancies in security forces, establishing local security forces in addition to "official" Afghan security forces. Third, the program had vertical integration in theory, proposing long-term plans of integrating these forces into the official forces of the country, but in practice these plans were virtually never realized.[50] It is possible that this lack of vertical integration and control could lead to different alp forces fighting one another and government forces down the road. Finally, the program reinforced a martial culture, as opposed to teaching Afghan men new skills for earning a living. Thus, although this initiative was implemented at the local level and resonated with the population, all these limitations will most likely mean long-term instability for the areas in which vso was implemented.

Ultimately, U.S. and nato efforts at building Afghanistan's security forces relied heavily on a Western model of security and building forces at the state level that would be responsible for securing the country's borders and establishing order from within. This process went through several iterations of organization and training, as well as various challenges that impeded the forces' growth and progress. As of 2015 the Afghan government set the number of security forces at 195,000 for the Afghan National Army and 157,000 for the Afghan National Police, for a total of 352,000 personnel, and the United States had appropriated $60.7 billion to "equip, train, and sustain the ANSF," including at least $3.8 billion to pay salaries. A 2015 Center for New American Security report claims that the military was improving, quoting ISAF trainers who placed 33 to 40 percent of ANA forces as "capable or fully capable" and asserted that Afghans were now in the lead in the fight against the country's insurgents.[51]

However, an April 29, 2015, testimony to Congress by John F. Sopko, the special inspector general for the Afghan reconstruction, claimed that the number of Afghan security forces was difficult to verify because of lack of oversight and that millions of taxpayer dollars were potentially being squandered. Furthermore, Sopko asserted that this lack of oversight made measuring Afghan Security Forces' capabilities difficult, if not impossible.[52] In September 2015 the Taliban's successful advance and capture of the northern city of Kunduz and the two-week counteroffensive required to take the city back further threw into question the ability of Afghan Security Forces to stand on their own and secure the country's population and territory. Ultimately, the viability of Afghanistan's security forces may not be clear until after NATO forces have completely withdrawn from the country.

GOVERNANCE

The December 2001 Bonn Agreement set the conditions for transforming Afghanistan into a democracy, beginning with the Afghan Interim Authority (AIA), which would govern for six months, followed by the two-year Transitional Authority (TA), and culminating with elections. Initially, the conditions in Afghanistan looked promising for a political transition from the Taliban to a more democratic system. Afghanistan has a tradition of consensus building through *jirgas* and *shura* councils (Islamic

councils). A 2002 Loya Jirga, a grand assembly, was used to ratify the Afghan Transitional Authority, giving the body legitimacy
in the eyes of Afghan leaders and, presumably, the population.
A Loya Jirga was also used to ratify the constitution in 2003. In
2010 a Loya Jirga was called to discuss peace with the Taliban.
And a 2013 Loya Jirga helped reach a consensus on the Status
of Forces Agreement with the United States.

Afghanistan also had a charismatic leader who was appointed
in the 2001 Bonn Agreement, Hamid Karzai, who showed promise for keeping the country together during the transition from
Taliban rule to democracy. Karzai, a Pashtun, was the head of
the Popalzai tribe, which was a member of the Durrani confederation. In 1999 his father was assassinated, placing Hamid as
the head of the tribe. Karzai was well known for raising money
for the mujahedeen during the Soviet-Afghan War. He was an
important figure because he was Pashtun and therefore could
help bring Pashtuns into the new political process, but Karzai
was openly opposed to the Taliban, winning the support of non-
Pashtuns. He was also liked and trusted by the Americans and
other international actors involved in stabilizing Afghanistan.[53]

However, both the tradition of *jirgas* and the initial popularity of Karzai were insufficient for transitioning the country from
Taliban rule to democracy. The *jirgas* succeeded in sanctioning
the interim government and ratifying the constitution, but perhaps more importantly, they did not instill the concept of "one
person, one vote," which is a fundamental concept of democracy; rather, the *jirgas* reinforced the notion of elders and leaders deciding on behalf of the community.

Likewise, Karzai's initial promise as a leader who would transition the country to democracy bogged down over allegations
of growing corruption and the institutionalization of patronage
networks. A 2011 Asia Foundation Survey, for example, found
that the overwhelming majority of Afghans, around 75 percent,
believed the government to be corrupt, and this number did not
improve over time.[54] Furthermore, U.S. and allied forces lost
confidence in Karzai's ability to lead the country effectively and
promote democracy. The 2009 memo from Ambassador Eiken-

berry to Secretary Clinton underscored the particular problems of Karzai's leadership: "President Karzai is not an adequate strategic partner. The proposed counterinsurgency strategy assumes an Afghan political leadership that is both able to take responsibility and to exert sovereignty in the furtherance of our goal—a secure, peaceful, minimally self-sufficient Afghanistan hardened against transnational terrorist groups."[55]

In addition to the institutionalization of corruption and the shortcomings of Karzai's leadership, Afghanistan also faced considerable challenges in transitioning to a popularly elected leader. First, and perhaps most important, Afghanistan did not have a culture of democracy, at least not in the Western sense of the term. Barfield contends that political authority in the country derived from three prominent sources: it was passed through family line from father to son within a ruling family; it was determined by the consensus of elders in certain tribes; and, most recently, it was assumed through force and establishing order, as was the case with the mujahedeen and the warlords, and a mixture of coercion and the claim to uphold the true tenets of Islam, as was the case with the Taliban.[56] None of these sources of power was based on "one person, one vote" as a basis of legitimacy.

Another key challenge to popular sovereignty was Afghanistan's ethnic divisions. Although Barfield notes that, historically, Afghanistan's ethnic groups were not a political problem, particularly under the rule of dynastic families, ethnic divisions had become a political problem, particularly following the Soviet invasion, Afghanistan's civil war in the 1990s, and the rise of the Taliban. During the Soviet-Afghan War, mujahedeen fighting factions began to break along ethnic lines, particularly between Pashtuns and Tajiks, the two largest ethnic groups in the country. During the civil war, the Northern Alliance was primarily a non-Pashtun entity and formed in opposition to the Taliban, which was Pashtun. These conflicts helped mobilize and politicize ethnic divisions in the country. The creation of political parties and their competition in elections effectively created the conditions for these ethnic divides to be further politicized and threatened to alienate smaller ethnic groups that could not muster the votes to gain representation in the government. Eikenberry noted this dynamic in his 2009 memo to Secretary Clinton, in which he claimed, "There is no political ruling class that provides an overarching national identity that transcends local affiliations and provides reliable partnership."[57]

In addition to power struggles and ethnic representation in post-Taliban Afghanistan, transitioning the country to an electoral system also presented technical challenges. As previously mentioned Afghanistan has high rates of illiteracy. Prior to the overthrow of the Taliban, by some estimates only 28.1 percent of Afghans aged fifteen years or older were literate, and only 12.6 percent of women were able to read or write.[58] Illiteracy presented challenges for the entire electoral process, from informing voters to casting ballots. Alongside challenges posed by illiteracy, Afghanistan also needed to mount an extensive education program on democratic principles and rules. A 2013 survey of Afghans on the electoral process noted that "only 25 percent [of Afghans] said they had enough information to participate on election day," and nearly half reported that they were not informed about their local representatives or understood legislative activities in the National Assembly.[59] Afghanistan also presents considerable geographic obstacles to the election process. In some remote mountainous areas, ballot boxes had to be carried in and out by pack animals, illustrating the logistical challenges presented by Afghanistan's topography and lack of infrastructure.[60]

Afghanistan also faced challenges from parallel and competing political organizations, specifically warlords and the Taliban. Many of the country's warlords were key mujahedeen fighters during the Soviet-Afghan War. The 2001 Bonn Agreement specifically recognized the service of the mujahedeen in fighting both the Soviets and the Taliban and called for their inclusion in post-Taliban Afghanistan, although the agreement did not specify how to integrate these leaders into the new system. Mark Peceny and Yury Bosin argue that following the overthrow of the Taliban in 2001, the United States government and military used warlords when it suited their interests, to defeat the Taliban and search for al-Qaeda, but then tried to marginalize them in efforts to build a Western-style democracy and state institutions:

> The US achieved its initial victory over the Taliban by striking bargains with local warlords throughout Afghanistan and crafting a political settlement in which these warlords would support Hamid Karzai as the presiding officer of a constitutionally centralized, yet weak national government that generally would not disrupt warlords' control over their local districts. While this agreement brought short-term victories over the Taliban and the appearance of national reconciliation, it has fueled political fragmentation and corruption, making it essentially incompatible with the development model that policymakers have considered essential to long-term success in Afghanistan.[61]

This use of warlords helped ensure that the Afghan state would not have a monopoly over the use of force, as well as posing serious political and economic challenges. Peceny and Bosin further note that some warlords collect their own taxes, especially in the form of international "tariffs" in the border regions they dominate, and are major drug traffickers, which has undermined legitimate economic activity and institutionalized an illicit economy.[62]

The Taliban posed another important challenge to this new political system. Despite being unseated fairly quickly following the U.S.-led offensive in 2001, the Taliban was not defeated. Mullah Omar was not captured and escaped to Pakistan, where he became a member of the Quetta Shura, a confederation of tribal leaders and their militias. Beginning around 2003 these groups organized attacks on ISAF forces, including carrying out suicide bombings, laying IEDS, and launching small weapons attacks.[63] In addition to their guerilla operations, the Taliban also provided services for the population, including adjudication of civil and criminal disputes. Anecdotal evidence suggests that popular support for the Taliban grew, in part, because their courts could provide swift resolution to disputes ranging from contested property to criminal acts. Furthermore, polling evidence suggests that the Afghan people did not view the Taliban as a principal problem for Afghanistan's future, hinting at a popular base of support for the Taliban and its renewed presence in the country.[64]

The United States and NATO powers did make considerable efforts to negotiate with the Taliban, including the prospects of recognizing it as a political force in the country and holding talks in Qatar, but these meetings never succeeded in incorporating the Taliban into the political process. The Afghan government called a Loya Jirga in 2010 with the aim of forging peace with the Taliban; however, the Taliban rejected the initiative and actually launched an attack on the meeting. Reconciliation between the Taliban and the Afghan government reached its nadir when Taliban operatives assassinated President Burhanuddin Rabbani in 2011 under the guise of discussing a ceasefire with the government.[65]

Ultimately, elections in Afghanistan reflected the lack of necessary infrastructure and democratic culture in the country. In 2004 Afghanistan held its first national elections to determine its head of state, and Karzai was elected president. He was reelected in 2009 for a second and last term, following low voter turnout, claims of rampant fraud and corruption, and lack of security. Under these conditions the United States called for a runoff vote between Karzai and challenger Abdullah Abdullah, but Abdullah refused and conceded to Karzai. The 2014 elections for head of state faced many of the same problems as those in 2009: widespread corruption, accusations of ballot-box stuffing, and low voter turnout. In the face of close results and neither candidate receiving a majority of the votes, Ashraf Ghani and Abdullah Abdullah, the two main candidates, were forced into a runoff vote in June of the same year.[66] Ultimately, the two candidates announced a unity government in September 2014, in which Ghani became president and Abdullah was named chief executive officer.

Afghan parliamentary elections did not fare much better. Per the terms of the 2004 constitution, Afghanistan's parliament is divided into two bodies: the upper house, the Meshrano Jirga, of which 34 members are elected from provincial councils, 34 are elected from district councils, and 34 are appointed by the president; and the Wolesi Jirga, which consists of 249 members directly elected by the general population. The 2005 elections for the lower house experienced low voter turnout—49 percent of the eligible population, lower than the 2004 presidential elections—and had considerable voter irregularities. Over six thousand candidates ran, making the process overwhelming and confusing. In the end the elections favored warlords, who had a popular base of support or at least popular recognition. The constitution also stipulated a 25 percent gender quota for elected members of parliament; the 2005 elections resulted in women constituting 30 percent of representatives in the lower house.[67]

The 2010 parliamentary elections followed a similar trajectory. Political parties were required to reregister with the Department of Justice, a process that only five parties could complete on time. Due to security concerns and fear of fraud, several polls were closed at the last minute, preventing Afghans from voting. A post-voting audit called for the invalidation of 1.5 million votes due to fraud. Following the announced election results, the attorney general of Afghanistan contested the list, claiming rampant fraud. Despite allowing the parliament to open in January 2011, sixty-two candidates were ultimately disqualified, leaving 25 percent of the lower house unoccupied.[68] Thus like presidential elections, Afghanistan's parliamentary elections were marred by corruption, fraud, lack of infrastructure, and low voter turnout.

Finally, in addition to challenges with the process of creating a new government in Afghanistan based on democratic principles, the country also faced considerable obstacles with establishing a governmental presence in the hinterlands. Most areas outside cities had little to no concept of a central government or the relationship between governments and their citizens. To address this critical gap, the United States military initiated what became known as Provincial Reconstruction Teams (PRTS) in late 2002. USAID summarizes the mandate of PRTS as "key instruments through which the international community delivers assistance at the provincial and district level. As a result of their provincial focus and civilian and military resources, PRTS have a unique mandate to improve security, support good governance, and enhance provincial development."[69] By 2008 twenty-five PRTS existed in Afghanistan, with the United States managing twelve and a combination of participating nations, including Germany, Britain, Italy, Canada, Sweden, Norway, and the Netherlands, running the remaining thirteen.[70] In theory PRTS mixed military and civilian personnel who worked together to improve conditions at the provincial level. In practice, however, PRTS were often staffed with mostly military personnel, and considerable differences existed between different PRTS' priorities and execution of projects. In the end PRTS had mixed results with improving the reach of government in different provinces, and it is unclear if this concept will persist beyond the Afghan conflict.[71]

RULE OF LAW

In tandem with calling for a representative, electoral government, the 2001 Bonn Agreement also set the conditions for drafting an Afghan constitution, which would establish the rules for elections and the structure of the government, and for creating the judicial branch of government, including a supreme court.[72] The Bonn Agreement called for a Loya Jirga to debate and ratify the constitution within eighteen months of the creation of a transitional authority, which was established in June 2002.[73]

Despite setting clear guidelines for establishing an Afghan constitution, the process was much more difficult in practice. Afghanistan had two unique constitutions drafted in 1923 and 1964, along with several constitutions based on these two; however, decades of conflict followed by Taliban rule had rendered the concept of a common law moot within the country, and the processes for amending the 1964 constitution were not possible in the current political environment. Creating a new constitution began by establishing a constitutional drafting commission, consisting of nine members, in October 2002. This body was replaced by a constitutional commission on April 24, 2003, all of whose thirty-five members were appointed by Karzai.[74]

The task of drafting the constitution faced two main challenges: the role of Islam in the constitution and the role of the
central government vis-à-vis provinces and districts. A RAND
conference report on the Afghan constitution notes that while
naming Islam as a source of the law is in keeping with religious and cultural traditions in Afghanistan, even the Taliban
claimed to be upholding Islamic law, so clearly additional parameters were needed to keep Afghanistan on the path to democracy. The report concludes, "Thus, language in the constitution
should always recognize not only the basic principles of Islam,
but also the principles of democracy, pluralism, social justice,
rule of law, and Afghanistan's international obligations."[75]

In addition to the role of Islam in the constitution, the relationship of the central government to the rest of the country was
equally contentious. Afghanistan has a long history of regional
autonomy in certain areas. An International Crisis Group report
has warned that threatening this autonomy could result in
regional leaders dragging their constituents into war. Despite
this dynamic most Afghans have expressed a desire for Afghanistan to remain united and not to become highly federalized.[76]
The 2004 constitution sought to resolve this conflict with article 1: "Afghanistan shall be an Islamic Republic, independent,
unitary and indivisible state."[77]

Ultimately, the constitutional committee submitted a draft
for review on November 3, 2003, and ratified it on January 26,
2004. Despite successfully instituting a constitution within just
a few months of the original stated time frame, a 2003 International Crisis Group report criticizes the process of drafting a
constitution for its tight time line, which allowed roughly eighteen months for the process, start to finish. It also criticizes the
process for not including the public sufficiently and its overall opacity in debates that ensued in the process of drafting the
document. Finally, the 2003 International Crisis Group report
claims, "The Transitional Administration (TA) and the UN are
now heading down a well-trodden path in Afghan history whereby
a constitution is proclaimed but no one, let alone those in control of state power, has any incentive to respect it."[78]

In addition to the struggle with drafting a constitution, establishing rule of law in Afghanistan has remained a considerable challenge. The country has had to contend with multiple systems of justice, including sharia and *pashtunwali*, a tribal code of conduct. Furthermore, as important as establishing a rule of law is the ability to enforce it. Afghanistan has struggled with creating the necessary infrastructure to implement the law, including an adequate police force (discussed in the section on security), keeping trained lawyers and judges, and building courthouses, jails, and other necessary buildings. The U.S. government and the international community invested considerable money and effort aimed at building these necessary components of the law, including establishing training and mentoring programs for lawyers and judges, creating a better system of review between the central judiciary and courts at the provincial and district levels, and bringing female lawyers and judges into the judicial system.[79]

Despite these efforts, yearly reports to the U.S. Congress on the progress of security and stability in Afghanistan cite chronic obstacles to establishing an effective judiciary. With regard to Afghanistan's criminal courts, the 2008 report summarizes the challenges:

In many provinces, most Afghans are not aware of their rights under the constitution nor do they have a basic understanding of the justice system. Nationwide, fully functioning courts, police, and prisons are rare. Municipal and provincial authorities as well as judges have minimal training and little or no access to published law, often basing their judgments on their personal understanding of sharia law, tribal codes of honor, or local custom. Judges and prosecutors with jurisdiction over the districts often reside in the provincial capital. The lack of trained and qualified judicial personnel hinders the courts and results in very few cases being processed. Renovation of existing judicial infrastructure is needed and utilities, communication equipment, and basic office supplies are lacking. Prison conditions remain poor. Most Afghan prisons are decrepit, severely overcrowded, unsanitary, and fall well short of international standards. Many prisons hold more than twice their planned capacity.[80]

Afghanistan implemented a new criminal code in 2014. That same year a report to the U.S. Congress summarized developments in the application of law: "The Afghan population continues to struggle with embracing the often cumbersome formal justice process, compared to the familiarity and immediacy of informal systems of justice, although there are signs of progress. In the past, the populace relied on the Taliban's system of justice when formal courts were absent or perceived to be corrupt. Now there is some data that shows more Afghans were using the formal justice system than the informal justice system for the first time."[81]

However, despite the report's claim that citizens were choosing Afghan state courts, others have suggested that sharia courts continue to adjudicate cases and still may be the preferred method of conflict resolution. In particular Taliban forces have maintained sharia courts that provide quick resolutions, particularly in the hinterlands, where government courts are either nonexistent or where the population views them as corrupt and ineffective. A 2012 Integrity Watch Afghanistan report on Taliban courts states that, despite being targeted by ISAF and Afghan forces, the Taliban had managed to maintain civil and criminal courts throughout the occupation, resulting in mobile courts that had become less just but were still more effective than the government's legal system.[82] Similarly, a 2015 New York Times article describes how two men claiming ownership of the same land tried to go through the state courts but did not receive a resolution, despite paying an estimated $1,000 in fees; the Taliban resolved the case in a matter of days and free of charge.[83]

Ultimately, despite adhering to the time line established by the Bonn Agreement for creating a constitution and laying the ground work for developing civil and criminal law following the overthrow of the Taliban, Afghanistan continues to struggle with realizing rule of law in the country. The challenges facing international efforts to establish rule of law—a necessary ingredient for a healthy, functioning democracy and civic nationalism—demonstrate how difficult this process is and the amount of resources required not only to draft the law but also to implement it. Furthermore, the law is only as effective as the population's awareness of it and adherence to its rules and norms; neither of these conditions was met in the first decade of the post-Taliban era.

ECONOMICS

Despite being landlocked, which several economists note is a challenge for economic development, Afghanistan has the potential for economic growth and viability.[84] First, Afghanistan's agriculture holds important prospects for improving food security in the country and as a major sector in the economy. For example, USAID notes, "Prior to decades of conflict, Afghanistan's agricultural products earned a global reputation for excellence, particularly almonds, pomegranates, pistachios, raisins, and apricots."[85] Historically, Afghanistan was also known for its timber, particularly in Kunar Province. In addition to agriculture, Afghanistan has considerable mineral deposits. One report suggests that "Afghanistan may hold 60 million tons of copper, 2.2 billion tons of iron ore, 1.4 million tons of rare earth elements such as lanthanum, cerium and neodymium, and loads of aluminum, gold, silver, zinc, mercury and lithium."[86] Other potential areas of economic growth include Afghanistan's textile industry, clothing manufacturing, and tourism.[87]

However, Afghanistan also has considerable challenges obstructing its economic growth. The country has limited infrastructure, including roads, electricity, and rail lines, which are all important resources for developing an agricultural industry and extracting Afghanistan's mineral wealth. Afghanistan also has a highly illiterate and uneducated workforce, which hinders the management of these and other potential industries. Of greater challenge to Afghanistan's economic development is the presence of illicit economies, particularly its opium poppy production, the Taliban's illegal mineral extraction, and black market timber sales. Furthermore, the Afghan government's weak capacity and limited reach beyond the capital has allowed these illegal economies to flourish and prosper warlords, the Taliban, and other opportunists. This lack of political reach and ability to offer alternatives to black market economies has arguably been the greatest hindrance to economic development in the country.

Despite plotting a course for Afghanistan's political and legal development in the 2001 Bonn Agreement, the fledgling Afghan government and international community were relatively slow to come up with an economic plan for the country. A January 2002 conference of more than sixty countries and dozens of NGOS met in Tokyo and raised more than US$4.5 billion over five years.[88] While heralded at the time as a healthy amount, this sum paled in comparison to past postconflict development efforts. For example, according to a RAND study, Bosnia received roughly US$1,400 per person in the first two years after the war, whereas Afghanistan received less than US$100.[89] With regard to humanitarian aid specifically, a 2011 report on aid to Afghanistan noted, "Afghanistan is one of the world's leading recipients of humanitarian aid, and yet on a per capita basis, it receives far less than OPT/Palestine and significantly less than Somalia. In its peak year (2002), Afghanistan received US$39.60 per person compared with Iraq (2003) US$44.30, Somalia (2008) US$63.20, and OPT/Palestine (2009) US$284.90."[90]

Furthermore, a comprehensive plan for economic development did not initially accompany these pledges. The World Bank, together with thirty-three donor states and the Afghan government, created the Afghanistan Reconstruction Trust Fund in 2002 with the aim of coordinating development efforts in five sectors: agriculture, rural development, infrastructure, human development, and public-sector capacity and governance.[91] Alongside these efforts, the Afghan government itself drafted "Securing Afghanistan's Future" in 2004, with the aim of better coordinating economic development through building social and human capital; developing physical infrastructure; initiating public administration reform and economic management; enabling trade, investment, and the private sector; improving security; implementing plans; and creating a budget.[92] In 2008 the Afghan government released another strategy, the Afghan National Development Strategy (ANDS), which aimed to plot a course for viable security, economics, governance, and social development by 2020. With regard to Afghanistan's economic development, the ANDS aims to create "a society of hope and prosperity based on a strong, private-sector led market economy, social equity, and environmental sustainability." The ANDS names establishing security, strong fiscal policies, and the development of the private sector as major goals for not only improving Afghanistan's economy but also reducing the country's rampant poverty. However, the ANDS also notes the numerous obstacles to implementing economic development and poverty reduction through the private sector, including lack of infrastructure, unreliable electrical grids, lack of security and rule of law, limited access to finances, and corruption.[93]

Not only did the development of a comprehensive economic development plan lag, but very little international aid money went to the Afghan government, which hindered implementing a plan and more basic functions, such as paying the salaries of civil servants. A report from Global Humanitarian Assistance that covered aid to Afghanistan from 2002 to 2010, for example, notes that 77 percent of aid to Afghanistan had "little or no Afghan government support."[94] These observations are echoed in *Fixing Failed States*, which, among other things, considers the problems with the way aid is distributed to fragile states. The authors note: "The aid system as currently configured tends to undermine rather than support state institutions. The thousands of small projects designed to aid a particular school, village, or district end up recruiting the very teachers, administrators, and doctors they are designed to support to work instead as secretaries and drivers for international staff."[95] The authors go on to assert: "In Afghanistan, for instance, approximately 280,000 civil servants work in the government bureaucracy and receive an average salary of $50 per month. Meanwhile, approximately 50,000 work for NGOS, the United Nations, and bilateral and multilateral agencies, where support staff can earn up to $1,000 per month. Unsurprisingly, there has been a brain drain. "[96]

Following the overthrow of the Taliban, both small and large projects relied heavily on foreign NGOs and contractors, bypassing the Afghan government. For example the U.S. government launched a major initiative aimed at refurbishing Highway 1, the "Ring Road," which connects Afghanistan's major cities: Mazar, Kabul, Ghazni, Kandahar, Farah, and Herat. This project was awarded to a U.S. contracting firm, the Louis Berger Group (which a U.S. court later found guilty of fraud for its work in Iraq and Afghanistan), along with Japanese, Indian, and Iranian firms, as opposed to allowing the Afghan government to implement the project or even hiring an Afghan company for its design and construction.[97] In places where the Ring Road was constructed, it had a positive effect on the citizens. Between Kabul and Kandahar, for example, the road cut travel time down from roughly eighteen to six hours. A 2014 USAID factsheet on Afghanistan noted that 80 percent of the population lived within fifty kilometers of the Ring Road, thus promoting better physical connectivity throughout the country.[98] However, that same year a *Washington Post* article noted that lack of maintenance by the Afghan government had caused the road to decay, squandering billions of U.S. taxpayers' dollars and one of the great symbols of progress in the post-Taliban era.[99]

In addition to big initiatives, both the U.S. military and NGOs created micro-development programs aimed at building influence with populations and improving the lives of Afghans; however, these efforts were made independent of the Afghan government. The U.S. Department of Defense initiated the Commander's Emergency Response Program (CERP) in Iraq in 2004, which gave military units the ability to rapidly fund programs with the aim of "winning hearts and minds" in their area of responsibility. In Afghanistan units used CERP for a variety of initiatives ranging from basic infrastructure development to sewing classes for Afghan widows. A 2014 Center for Financial Inclusion blog entry put the amount of U.S. micro-lending in Afghanistan at "$136 million across 251,846 borrowers."[100] NGOs also engaged in local-level development projects aimed at improving the lives of Afghans. These initiatives, while useful for helping some Afghans meet their most immediate needs and improve their lives, did not help the Afghan government develop the capacity to deliver these services to the population directly.

In an attempt to better connect the government to the population through development initiatives, the Afghan government, together with international advisement, created the National Solidarity Program (NSP) in 2004 as a means of fostering development projects at the local level, empowering communities, and connecting villages and districts to the central government. Together with a suite of initiatives—including the National Emergency Employment Program, the National Transportation Program, the National Health Program, and the National Accountability and Transparency Program—the NSP issued grants of up to $60,000 per village that locally elected Community Development Councils (CDC) decided how to spend through the creation of a budget and a time line. Alongside the federal funds it received, the village was required to provide 10 percent of the overall budget either through monetary contributions, materials, or in labor. The CDC was also mandated to provide frequent updates and post expenditures to promote transparency.

Equally important as the projects initiated under the program, the NSP aimed to teach decision making, consensus building, leadership, accountability, and community ownership of development projects. The NSP also attempted to create development projects that were "insurgent-proof"—attacking these initiatives would be destroying projects that the population had created through its own efforts, thus alienating the very support the insurgents could not live without. The NSP has been credited with the creation of schools, bridges, roads, irrigation systems, and water pumps, to name a few projects.[101]

The Afghan government also sought direct foreign investment to build the country's economy, particularly through its rich mineral reserves. In 2007 two Chinese companies bid $4.4 billion to extract copper from Logar Province; the deal included building a rail line to the Chinese border and a power plant.[102] In 2011 a Chinese oil company formed a partnership with Watan

Oil and Gas, an Afghan company, to begin tapping the country's petroleum reserves.[103] These contracts were controversial for the United States, which had contributed billions to developing Afghanistan's security sector, governance, rule of law, and infrastructure, essentially creating the conditions for foreign investors to profit. However, these investments promised infrastructure development, revenue, and the potential for jobs creation, all of which were sorely needed in Afghanistan. By 2013, however, the slow pace of developing the necessary infrastructure for mining and persisting insecurity in Afghanistan threw these contracts into renegotiation.[104] Throughout the reconstruction warlords and the Taliban continued to illegally mine marble and minerals and use the profits to help fund their influence with the population and fight against the Afghan government.[105]

Alongside major and minor efforts to rebuild Afghanistan's economy and infrastructure, countering Afghanistan's illicit opium poppy cultivation became another major initiative. The 2001 Bonn Agreement, in addition to setting the agenda for political transition in the country, also named countering Afghanistan's opium poppy cultivation as a major priority. The United Kingdom was initially put in charge of counternarcotic efforts, including training the Afghan military in counternarcotic operations. In May 2003 the Afghan Interim Government released its National Drug Control Strategy (NDCS), which aimed to eradicate opium poppy production. It set as its goal securing "a sustainable decrease in cultivation, production, trafficking and consumption of illicit drugs with a view to complete and sustainable elimination." The NDCS created a four-stage process for opium poppy reduction: disrupting the drug trade; "strengthen[ing] and diversify[ing] legal rural livelihood"; reducing the demand for drugs by rehabilitating drug users; and strengthening state institutions.[106] This strategy, in other words, sits at the intersection between economics, governance, and security.

Efforts to counter Afghanistan's opium poppy cultivation have been disastrous on a number of fronts. First, targeting opium poppy cultivation hurt the livelihood of average farmers, who had few viable alternatives for earning a living. Rubin's assessment of this counternarcotics approach claims that "the Afghan people believe that poppy cultivation is undesirable. But it is inevitable in situations of dire poverty and insecurity where there are no secure economic alternatives."[107] Vanda Felbab-Brown notes that this approach not only hurt farmers but also turned them against the fledgling government and the International Security Assistance Force (ISAF).[108] Second, this strategy required targeting warlords in the country; however, the United States and ISAF needed warlords to hunt for al-Qaeda and to suppress the Taliban. Ultimately ISAF's counterterrorism and counterinsurgency pursuits outweighed its counternarcotic ambitions, and ISAF forces continued to empower warlords to address these security concerns. Third, the Taliban reemerged, in part, by harnessing profits from the opium trade, reflecting the overall failure of ISAF's and the Afghan government's approach to countering narcotics. Rubin contends, "Poppy eradication does not reduce the amount of drug money available to fund insurgency, terrorism, and corruption. On the contrary, eradication raises the price of opium, thereby making more money available for insurgency, and causes cultivation to migrate to more remote areas."[109] The 2014 special inspector general for Afghan reconstruction (SIGAR) found that, after over a decade of development efforts and $7 billion in counternarcotics operations, Afghanistan's opium production was at an all-time high.[110]

Ultimately, despite all these efforts to develop Afghanistan's economy, and its potential for agriculture and mineral extraction, prior to 2015 the overwhelming majority of Afghanistan's GDP was aid, and the illicit opium market accounted for an estimated four hundred thousand jobs and 6 percent of the country's GDP.[111] A 2012 International Crisis Group report notes that, despite an outpouring of money from the international community, a decade of efforts aimed at rebuilding Afghanistan, including its economy, has very little to show for the effort. "Poor planning and oversight have affected projects' effectiveness and sustainability, with local authorities lacking the means to keep projects running, layers of subcontractors reducing the amounts that reach the ground and aid delivery further undermined by corruption in Kabul and bribes paid to insurgent groups to ensure security for development projects."[112]

SOCIAL WELL-BEING

Following the overthrow of the Taliban in 2001, the United States and its allies faced considerable challenges with improving the basic social well-being of Afghans. Decades of war, minimal infrastructure and public services, virtually no access to health care and vaccines, high illiteracy rates, and the absence of basic education all rendered Afghanistan one of the least developed countries on the planet. In 2004 the UN Development Program, in coordination with an independent team of Afghans, prepared its first National Human Development Report on Afghanistan using the Human Development Index, the Human Poverty Index, and the Human Gender Index. The report ranked Afghanistan at 173 of 177 countries, virtually at the bottom of the list in terms of infant mortality rates, literacy, life expectancy, and school enrollment.[113] The Human Gender Index was also one of the lowest in the world, and the lack of reliable data made measuring the Human Poverty Index impossible.

Access to basic health care became a particularly important social well-being benchmark. In 2002 a combination of foreign countries and NGOs, together with the fledgling Afghan government, initiated the Basic Package of Health Care (BPHC) for Afghanistan, a program designed to improve "maternal and newborn health, child health and immunizations, nutrition, communicable diseases, mental health, disability, and pharmaceutical supply" with the overall goal of providing these basic services to 90 percent of the population by 2010.[114] By 2006 the Afghan government estimated that 82 percent of the population had access to the BPHC, and by 2010 the life expectancy of Afghans had soared from forty-two for men and women in 2004 to sixty-two for men and sixty-four for women.[115]

Another area of international focus was the improvement of gender equality. At the time of the invasion in 2001, Afghanistan had one of the lowest gender-equality ratios in the world. Women had been confined to their homes, prevented from attending school and working, and denied access to basic health care. The United States and its allies aimed to improve this discrepancy by increasing access to education and health care for all, with a special emphasis on girls and women, and by including gender quotas in the central government. The 2005 Brookings Institution *Afghanistan Index Report* noted that school enrollment had climbed from roughly 1 million during Taliban rule to an estimated 4.8 million boys and girls by December 2004.[116] By 2011 an estimated 2.4 million girls were enrolled in school, up from virtually none under the Taliban, although a 2012 Care International report put the numbers of actual attendees at a much lower rate and noted that girls' education was virtually nonexistent beyond primary school in rural areas.[117] By 2009 women made up 28 percent of the Afghan parliament, and women had joined the country's security forces and civil service.[118] In 2010 the Afghan parliament passed the Law on Elimination of Violence against Women (EVAW). However, a 2013 UN report investigating the enforcement of the EVAW found that, while reporting of violence against women had increased by 28 percent, prosecution had risen only 2 percent, suggesting that the law's application was progressing too slowly.[119]

Perhaps one of Afghanistan's greatest challenges for social well-being has been basic poverty reduction. As Muhammad Yunus, Amartya Sen, and other economists observe, poverty reduction is primarily about sustainable access to the most basic necessities, especially food.[120] In 2007 the Afghan government conducted the Afghanistan Living Condition Survey as part of the wider National Risk and Vulnerability Assessment (NRVA) of the Afghan population. The report found that poverty was greatest in rural areas, which is 80 percent of the population, followed by among nomadic Kuchi, and then in urban areas. More telling, the report also notes that "the latest NRVA survey (Spring 2007) indicates that 42 percent of the population lives below the . . . poverty line. . . . That is, almost half of the Afghan population is unable to purchase a basic food basket to provide 2,100 calories per day."[121]

As part of its plan to reduce poverty and improve development, the Afghan government released the Afghan National Development Strategy in 2008. As described the ANDS provided a five-year integrated "strategy for security, governance, economic growth and poverty reduction." The report named "a weak asset base," insufficient government and economic institutions, lack of health care, vulnerability to conflict and natural disasters, a "non-diverse livelihood," low literacy rates, indebtedness, and remoteness as key drivers of poverty. The ANDS proposed a strategy of poverty reduction by "promoting broad based private sector led growth," and "fiscally affordable social protection safety nets," along with allocating funds to develop better "security, education, health, and social protection," providing resources to rural areas, fostering jobs creation, establishing metrics of success and gathering data, and building partnerships with NGOs.[122] In other words the ANDS proposed developing all aspects of the Afghan government, creating robust institutions, improving security, and fostering economic growth as a means of poverty reduction in five years' time, an ambitious, if not unreasonable, goal.

Improving basic services, particularly electricity and potable water, became another goal of bettering social well-being. In 2002 Afghanistan's total megawatt capacity was 243; by 2012 that number was at 1100.[123] However, a 2014 USAID estimate cited only 28 percent of Afghans with access to reliable electricity. The 2014 report also notes that only 39.4 percent of rural Afghans, in contrast to 70.9 percent of urbanites, had clean drinking water.[124] Despite these improvements congressionally mandated SIGAR reports on Afghanistan chronicle incidents of contractor fraud, misuse of funds, and shoddy work on development efforts, including schools, hospitals, and trash incinerators—projects all designed to improve Afghanistan's well-being.[125] Furthermore, the country's HDI score has remained abysmally low. The 2007 "Afghan Human Development Report" put the HDI unchanged from 2004 at 174 out of 178 states.[126] In 2011 Afghanistan was ranked 172 out of 187 states and in 2012 175 out of 187. Data from 2012 put Afghanistan at 147 out of 148 states for gender inequality, and lack of reliable data prevented the UN Development Project from calculating a Multidimensional Poverty Index.[127]

6. Coalition forces' state-building efforts in Afghanistan

Pillar	Coalition action	Effect
Safe and secure environment	Created state-level security forces	Difficult to build, did not positively affect population
	Pursued counterterrorism	Empowered warlords, undercut state monopoly on force
	Developed village stability operations	Engaged population but was implemented late in the war, created redundancies, lack of vertical integration
Governance and democracy	Created interim government, ratified by Loya Jirga	Appeared to legitimate interim government
	Held elections for president and parliament	Low voter turnout, allegations of corruption and fraud
	Negotiated with the Taliban	Failed to resolve insurgency
Rule of law	Oversaw drafting of constitution	Ratified in 2004, does not appear to have taken hold with population
	Created criminal legal code	Taliban-run sharia courts still widely used
Sustainable economy	Pursued counternarcotics efforts	Put farmers out of work, opium poppy production increased
	Promoted infrastructure development	U.S. contractors completed the Ring Road, now in decay
	Chinese initiated mine development	Stalled due to lack of security
	Promoted local-level development	Believed to be effective but difficult to validate
Social well-being	Developed basic services	Improvement in infrastructure but still minimal electricity, limited rural potable water
	Pursued health care efforts	Improvement in life expectancy and BPHC
	Promoted gender equality	Increased school enrollment, access to health care, women's presence in government and security forces
	Promoted education	Increased school enrollment

Ultimately, despite successes providing basic services to the population, improving access to health care, and increasing life expectancy, it is uncertain if these basic improvements in social services, opportunities for girls, and hints at poverty reduction will result in a population that participates in the social contract and supports the Afghan government, or if these advancements will be understood as the result of outside efforts, including ISAF countries and NGOs. Findings regarding these issues are summarized in table 6.

The international community faced considerable challenges in developing Afghanistan following the demise of the Taliban's government in 2001, including over thirty years of atrophied governance and lack of a democratic culture, virtually no physical infrastructure, the inability to secure the country's borders, and rampant poverty. Despite employing measures aimed at driving development down to the local level, including programs like Provincial Reconstruction Teams, Village Stability Operations, and the National Solidarity Program, the main effort of stabilizing Afghanistan focused on building the structure of the state, including a constitutional democracy, national security forces, rule of law, and physical infrastructure, including roads, delivery of potable water, and electricity. Despite these efforts poverty remains a perennial challenge, particularly in rural areas. Furthermore, the withdrawal of ISAF forces and persistence of insurgent threats have placed Afghanistan on a precarious road to the future.

The next chapter will take an ex post facto, hypothetical look at how the United States and its coalition could have better engaged the population in its state-building exercise with the aim of developing national unity and a more stable Afghanistan.

8

COUNTERFACTUAL STATE-BUILDING AND NATION-BUILDING IN AFGHANISTAN

Following the U.S.-led invasion of Afghanistan in 2001 and the overthrow of the Taliban, international actors focused heavily on rebuilding (or building) the structure of the state, including creating a constitutional democracy, a conventional military, and rule of law. However, despite some innovative initiatives, the population was largely left out of the state-building process; intervening powers missed valuable opportunities to use state-building as a means of creating local empowerment and fostering national unity. Furthermore, programs aimed specifically at building national unity were almost wholly missing, overlooking opportunities to create this necessary ingredient of the state.

This chapter offers an ex post facto, hypothetical look at how the United States and coalition powers could have helped foster programs aimed at national-unity building as part of their efforts to develop a viable state. It begins by discussing the conditions for nation-building, noting evidence that Afghans had a sense of national unity, even in the post-Taliban era. It then looks at how the U.S. and coalition powers could have helped foster national unity within their state-building programs, focusing specifically on the five pillars of stabilization and state reconstruction—security, governance, economic development, rule of law, and social well-being—in addition to what a sixth pillar of national-unity building would have looked like.

Ultimately U.S. and coalition powers' efforts at building the state and the nation should have understood and focused more on the population, pushing authority and resources out from

Kabul, and less on the macro-level structures of the state. Moreover, given the predominantly rural nature of Afghanistan, about 78 percent of the population as opposed to 34 percent in Iraq, building the Afghan state and nation should have prioritized two broad goals: better connecting people physically and virtually, and addressing the everyday issues of poverty within the rural population. State-building and nation-building should have focused on addressing these very real needs, and building hope and a sense of common destiny by empowering Afghans to improve their own lives.

Conditions for Fostering National Unity in Afghanistan

As discussed in chapter 7, Barfield notes in his analysis of the culture and politics of Afghanistan that ethnic divisions, historically, were neither a social nor a political problem for the country because power was concentrated in a ruling family, and thus the region's various tribes and ethnic groups did not vie for political power because it was not up for grabs. Barfield further notes that foreign invaders set the conditions for political competition by empowering tribes for their specific security and geopolitical needs, and it was this foreign-led process that created ethnic antagonisms in Afghanistan. The 2001 invasion and state-building of Afghanistan could be seen as a continuation of that process, particularly the creation of large conventional security forces and the insistence on making Afghanistan a full-fledged democracy. These programs changed sources of power and legitimacy within the country.

Nonetheless, Barfield strongly asserts that post-Taliban Afghanistan was not the ethnically fractured society that the world seemed to think it was. He goes so far as to claim that Afghanistan was "a failed state but not a failed nation" and that Afghans did not have a desire to see their country partitioned along ethnic or regional lines.[1] Barfield further notes that the Afghan sense of national unity "was not rooted in an ideology of nationalism, but rather in the will of its people to persist together, united by a common experience that transcended ethnic or regional differences."[2] He concludes that capitalizing on this sense of unity was one of the biggest missed opportunities of state-building in Afghanistan.

Barfield is also quick to note that the U.S.-led intervention of Afghanistan and the state-building efforts that followed were not met with immediate cries of resistance and jihad as when the Soviets invaded in 1979. Barfield suggests that this initial silence was due to several factors: first, the population was reluctant to return to war, and second, this round of invaders, unlike the British and the Soviets, had no intentions of seizing and holding land. But he surmises that the most important reason why an insurgency or jihad did not immediately form was because the population was optimistic that the coalition of interveners would improve their lives. "The large sums of money pledged for reconstruction first raised the expectations of ordinary Afghans to unreasonable levels, but as the years passed people had a right to be disappointed by how little was being accomplished at such great expense." Barfield further asserts, "Unfortunately this unexpected measure of good will from the Afghan people in 2002 was heedlessly squandered in the coming years by inept policies that failed to bring security to many regions and did little to improve the people's dire economic condition."[3]

Building on Barfield's observations, the following discussion offers a hypothetical, ex post facto consideration of how the pillars of state-building could have been pursued by the United States and its allies, with an emphasis on empowering the population and instilling a sense of national unity among Afghan citizens.

SECURITY

The international community rightly understood that security was a priority for post-Taliban Afghanistan. Historically, whichever power provided security and stability to the region won the support of the people; therefore starting with security made sense. Furthermore, establishing security was an increased priority given the fact that the country had endured more than thirty years of violence and instability, beginning with the Soviet invasion in 1979, followed by the civil war after the collapse of the

Soviet Union, and continuing with the rise of the Taliban. Given these factors, security was a logical place to start.

The United States and its coalition partners' principal means of creating security and stability in the country rested on the construction of hundreds of thousands of trained, competent, and professional Afghan security forces. In 2015 the Afghan government reported its security forces' numbers at 195,000 Afghan National Army soldiers and 157,000 Afghan police, for a total of 352,000 security personnel.[4] However, as noted in chapter 7, this aggressive plan for building security forces foundered on a number of problems, including the limited length of time required to train forces and make them competent, the quality of instruction being provided, high desertion rates, low performance rates, and "green-on-blue" attacks that killed hundreds of ISAF forces. Afghan security forces also suffered from more basic challenges, such as high illiteracy rates, which further slowed training.

Ultimately, building large numbers of conventional security forces took too long and did not create order outside major cities. Taliban and other insurgent strongholds in the south and east of the country remained particularly unstable and insecure. Poll after poll of Afghans showed that poor security remained one of the main concerns of average citizens, and that this concern did not improve over time. For example in 2014, the year of U.S. troop withdrawal, an Asia Foundation poll found that 64.5 percent of Afghans reported that they "always, often, or sometimes fear[ed] for their personal safety."[5] This was an increase from the 2013 survey, in which "a majority of Afghans (59%) report[ed] always, often, or sometimes fearing for their own safety or security or that of their family."[6] The 2017 Asia Foundation Poll put the number at 70.7 percent, the highest it has been since polling began in 2004.[7]

Following the resurgence of the Taliban and a shift in strategy in 2009, U.S. forces aimed to improve security at the local level by creating ad hoc, local security forces—what became known as the Afghan Local Police (ALP)—through Village Stability Operations (VSO). Ultimately, this initiative created an estimated twenty-seven thousand ALP distributed throughout 137 districts.[8] However, while VSO might have had some initial success in creating "white space" in rural villages and valleys, it came late in the game and after years of instability and violence in the wake of Taliban rule. The 2014 Asia Foundation survey notes that "the ALP, which was established in 2010 to help smaller communities protect themselves from AOGS [armed opposition groups], has had uneven success."[9] The 2013 Asia Survey report asserts, "In some areas, the establishment of the ALP and arbakai [tribal security] may be undermining local government and may have even led to an increase in criminal activities."[10] The 2017 survey showed similar, at best uneven results.[11]

In addition to VSO's mixed performance, the creation of ALP under VSO also created problematic redundancies in security forces, as well as long-term problems with vertical integration. Interviews with U.S. Special Forces soldiers who conducted VSO missions in Afghanistan revealed that, despite producing security in the near term, there were concerns over the role of these forces in producing long-term stability. One soldier even went so far as to say that he thought ALP members might turn and fight one another after the withdrawal of U.S. forces, essentially producing a localized civil war.[12]

Ultimately, intervening powers did not have many good options for creating both immediate and lasting security in Afghanistan following the overthrow of the Taliban. The construction of conventional security forces along Western lines took too long, did not reach the local level, and required extensive training and mentoring, producing a near-term vacuum in security. Conversely, the formation of local ad hoc security forces improved security at the local level in the near term but presented considerable challenges for integration and oversight in the long run. Furthermore, these forces needed to resonate with the local population but at the same time possess some degree of vertical integration with the government in order to have accountability and prevent regional fights. Creating ad hoc security forces at the village level may have met the first requirement of local security, but it did not address the second issue of statewide accountability.

One missed opportunity that ISAF forces could have used was leveraging regional leaders such as the mujahedeen or even tribal elders in the aftermath of the Taliban and placing them in charge of security in their areas of influence in the near term, while developing plans for national forces over time. U.S. Special Operations forces and other coalition SOF units could have offered training and oversight, similar to VSO, but at a higher level than villages. Regional leaders who showed signs of good governance could have been rewarded with National Solidarity Program grants for development projects and other incentives, along with a seat in district governments. Ultimately, these forces could have been transitioned to a national guard–like service for the districts in which they lived and operated.

Alongside issues of establishing security at the local and district levels, the United States and coalition powers should have done more to create viable programs aimed at demobilizing illegally armed individuals and integrating them back into society, what is often called demobilization, disarmament, and reintegration (DDR). DDR is essential for successful long-term statebuilding and nation-building because it gives the country's youth an alternative to fighting. Furthermore, not only do comprehensive DDR programs work with integrating fighters back into society, but they also prepare society for receiving past fighters, including amnesty programs and community-based development aimed at addressing grievances and concerns.

Several DDR programs were started and stopped during the tenure of the war. Following the overthrow of the Taliban, Japanese forces were tasked with funding and managing a demobilization program that became known as the Afghan New Beginnings Programme, which aimed to demobilize one hundred thousand fighters. This program was ended in 2005, despite having demobilized only around fifty thousand fighters.[13] Simultaneously, the Afghan government started another initiative, Takhim e-Sohl, with the aim of offering amnesty to Taliban fighters and drawing low-level fighters away through jobs programs. This program also failed to demobilize large numbers of fighters.[14]

In 2010 the Afghan government began a new initiative, the

Afghan Peace and Reintegration Policy, which was accompanied by an amnesty law for illegally armed fighters.[15] The 2014 Asia Foundation survey noted that "the Afghan Peace and Reintegration Program (APRP) reintegrated 1,600 combatants back into their communities in 2013, out of a total 7,800 since the High Peace Council established the program in 2010. While an increasing number of the reintegrated combatants come from Afghanistan's more insecure southern and eastern provinces, most combatants in the program are from the less troubled northern and western provinces." The 2014 survey of Afghan people further noted: "The reconciliation and reintegration process is expected to slow down during Afghanistan's political transition. However, 72.6% of Afghans remain optimistic that reconciliation efforts can help stabilize their country. Among intercept interviewees living in insecure areas, 76.7% in 2014 think the government's reconciliation efforts and negotiations will be successful, up from 68.4% in 2013."[16] These assessments suggest that establishing a safe and secure environment in Afghanistan requires not merely creating security forces but also addressing the underlying causes of security in the country, including reintegrating members of the Taliban and other illegally armed fighters back into society.

Ultimately Afghanistan requires national forces, but beginning security efforts with their construction was ill advised because of the extensive time involved, and these efforts did not provide adequate security at the local level. Had international actors acknowledged these issues in a systematic and effective way up front, they could have helped address some of the country's security concerns. Furthermore, leveraging local leaders could have provided a critical conduit for creating near-term security, allowing time for the construction of national-level forces.

POPULATION-CENTRIC GOVERNANCE

Within weeks of overthrowing the Taliban, the 2001 Bonn conference created the conditions for democratic transition in Afghanistan. The goal of democracy promotion was to place the population in charge of the political destiny of the country.

The Bonn Agreement specifically states that it is "the right of the people of Afghanistan to freely determine their own political future in accordance with the principles of Islam, democracy, pluralism and social justice."[17] The Bonn Agreement called for the creation of the thirty-person Afghan Interim Authority (AIA) that would govern for six months, followed by the two-year Transitional Authority (TA), ratified by a Loya Jirga, ending with elections. However, as discussed in chapter 7, elections quickly became mired in allegations of fraud and corruption. Simultaneously, voter turnout continued to decline through the iterations of national elections. The 2014 presidential elections had a reported turnout of 32 percent of eligible voters.[18]

The rush to democratic elections clearly has not produced the desired results of increased popular sovereignty, legitimacy of the government, or state stability in Afghanistan. It appears that international state builders see democratic elections as the only legitimate form of popular sovereignty. However, if true, this maxim places considerable burdens on transforming a society that has been under the yoke of a nondemocratic entity, the Taliban, to one that understands the rights and responsibilities of democratic culture in the astoundingly short period of three years.

For Afghanistan the transformation to democracy included practical considerations, such as conducting a census, registering voters, making a determination on the eligibility of refugees to vote, establishing voting polls, ensuring security during the election season, and creating a system of campaigning and elections that do not require literacy—a staggering requirement for a country that is predominately rural, has just emerged from Taliban rule, and lacks the most basic infrastructure. More important than logistics, instilling a sense of democratic culture is also essential, including introducing the idea of political platforms, campaigning, and the construction of political parties based on ideas over identity. Liberal democracy requires safeguards for minorities and preservation of key values such as freedom of speech, assembly, the press, and religion. Democracy also requires the norm that the losing party does not overthrow the system but rather waits until the next elections to change power *through* the electoral process. This understanding also assumes that the process itself is robust enough to endure nonviolent challenges to the system and changes in leadership. Finally, democracy requires believing that all citizens have the right to choose their sovereign; while obvious to those raised in a democratic republic, this idea may be novel in places where democracy is newly introduced.[19] Clearly three years was not enough time to establish all these cultural and structural requirements for a democratic system in Afghanistan.

Rather than make democratic elections an immediate goal, Afghan leaders, with the help of the international community, could have leveraged the culturally acceptable means of decision making in Afghanistan, the Loya Jirga, to select the country's leadership while the necessary democratic values and infrastructure were developed.[20] The 2001 Bonn Agreement was quick to understand that *jirgas* needed to play a critical role in legitimating both the interim government in Afghanistan and its constitution. The Loya Jirga and other *jirgas* could have continued to play this role of managing and legitimating Afghanistan's government in the near term, allowing for a process of consensus building but also of continuity while the country worked to build, rebuild, and educate its population about the democratic process.

In a 2009 testimony before the U.S. Senate Committee on Foreign Relations, Clare Lockhart, director of the Institute for State Effectiveness, delineated the concept of "good enough governance" as a pathway to restoring sovereignty in Afghanistan. Good enough governance focuses on working through existing local systems to provide security, initiate accountability in public finance, establish basic services, and instill fair and equitable decision making in accordance with a framework of rule of law. It is a results-based approach to governance, as opposed to process based, and allows room for means of determining leadership other than democratic elections. Lockhart further notes, "To recognize that governance is central also means understanding that the most critical factor is not what we, as outsiders, do but how the Afghans are organized to govern themselves."[21]

Another critical issue for governance was the creation of a central government vis-à-vis a more federal system that would push power out to the provincial and district levels. As noted in chapter 7, this issue became one of the major points of debate in the drafting of a constitution. The 2001 Bonn Agreement and subsequent international efforts at stabilizing Afghanistan focused heavily on the creation of a central government. This was most likely because it was easier for international actors to work with a more centralized government concentrated in Kabul than with dozens of regional and local leaders.

However, pushing power out to the regions would have created the conditions for several aspects of good governance in Afghanistan. First, it would have capitalized on already-existing leadership at the local level. Several experts on Afghanistan have noted that in the early stages of the invasion, regional and local leaders, including tribal elders and civil servants, already existed throughout the country and had legitimacy that could have been used to stabilize the country. Lockhart, for example, states in her 2009 testimony to U.S. Congress: "When I travelled across Afghanistan in January 2002, in most provinces there were functioning provincial offices, with trained civil servants successfully carrying out their work."[22] Second, Barfield argues that a decentralized political system was more culturally and historically acceptable to Afghans, who were used to highly localized leadership, particularly in the last twenty years. Barfield goes so far as to point out that the efforts of Abdul Rahman, the Iron Emir, and Amanullah to create a strong centralized government ultimately produced insurgencies and civil war.[23] Third, Barfield further notes that a decentralized system "would have proven more effective and given people more of a stake in the local administration."[24] In other words a decentralized system would have driven power down to the local level and empowered the people better.

Alongside the debate over how to distribute political power in the country, the way in which Afghanistan's warlords were managed following the overthrow of the Taliban was detrimental to the political stability of the country. The 2001 Bonn Agreement recognized the importance of giving Soviet-Afghan War–era mujahedeen a place in the new Afghan government; however, this goal was never fully realized. Several scholars note that the United States' empowerment of warlords to help track down al-Qaeda and fight the Taliban, while simultaneously promoting and recognizing only the legitimacy of a central government, ultimately served to destabilize the country.[25]

In retrospect warlords and other regional power brokers should have been included in the political process. By not giving these elites a stake in the new government, they ultimately became a liability, undermining the system instead of supporting it. Steven Biddle and his colleagues argue for what they call a "mixed sovereignty" approach to stabilizing Afghanistan politically, one in which warlords and other local leaders could maintain a degree of power and authority while a central government managed international affairs and border security.[26]

The same could be said for bringing the Taliban into the political process. It appears that no concerted effort was made to negotiate with leaders in the Taliban or bring them into the new political system until relatively late in the reconstruction process. Visible signs of negotiation included the 2010 "Peace" Loya Jirga, which unsuccessfully aimed to create reconciliation with the Taliban, and the 2013 creation of a Taliban office in Doha, Qatar, with the goal of improving opportunities to negotiate with the Taliban. The fact that the Taliban has not gone away, despite being militarily deposed in 2001 and one of the targets of counterterrorism operations, suggests that it may have a popular base of support that is allowing it to persist. If the Taliban does have a degree of legitimacy, it is unlikely to be eradicated militarily, at least not without significant cost.

Finally, international efforts aimed at creating political stability in Afghanistan were not without some important innovations. As described in chapter 7, the creation of Provincial Reconstruction Teams (PRT), the National Solidarity Programs (NSP), and even Village Stability Operations (VSO) were initiatives aimed at pushing power and the positive effects of governance out to the districts and local levels. However, these concepts either came too late, as in the case of VSO; were unevenly created, as with

PRTS; or appear to have been overshadowed by the corruption and ineffectiveness of the central government, which effectively obscured their progress, as with the NSP. Ultimately, the overemphasis on creating a central government and a political system to support it took precedence, and its shortcomings affected political stability as a whole.

RULE OF LAW

In addition to setting a time line for establishing a democratic political system in Afghanistan, the 2001 Bonn Agreement also called for the creation of a constitution. As noted in chapter 7, despite some rough patches and significant debates over the role of Islam in the law and the strength of the central government relative to regions, provinces, and districts, the Afghans were able to draft a constitution in a timely fashion and legitimate it through a Loya Jirga. The constitution, in turn, set the conditions for holding national, provincial, and district-level elections.

But drafting a constitution is truly only the first step, and quite possibly the easiest, in creating rule of law in any country. In addition to drafting a constitution and a template for rule of law, the state requires human capital and critical physical infrastructure to implement and uphold the law, as well as trained police and other security forces that understand their limits under the law. Similarly, upholding the law requires trained lawyers and judges who are capable of presenting and adjudicating cases. In most internal conflicts, these are some of the first professionals either to be killed or to flee the country, effectively ruining the state's ability to uphold the law. Practicing the rule of law also requires physical infrastructure, especially jails and courthouses. Afghanistan has struggled with all these aspects of implementing the law in the post-Taliban era, as discussed in chapter 7, which has resulted in the delay in hearing cases and delivering justice.

Perhaps even more important than creating the necessary infrastructure is instilling the law in the population and truly making it an institution, or the informal and formal rules that structure human interaction without the need for enforcement.[27]

Afghanistan faces several challenges in this regard. First, the country's rugged terrain and lack of roads, electricity, phones, and other critical infrastructure present certain barriers for informing the population about the law. As noted in chapter 7, polling data show that many Afghans had no idea of the constitution or its purpose years after its creation. Second, for a country that is widely illiterate, teaching the population about the law requires approaches other than print media. Given Afghanistan's remoteness and lack of physical infrastructure, radio would most likely have been the best medium, as will be discussed further below. Third, children can learn about the constitution and rule of law in schools, as Americans and others do, but this approach does not address how to teach the law to adults, the ones that will be upholding it in the near term. Therefore, while the rule of law should be instilled through schools, this approach is not sufficient for informing the entire population about the law and institutionalizing it.

As of 2017, it appears that the Taliban has the upper hand with upholding justice in rural Afghanistan. As described in chapter 7, the Taliban continues to adjudicate civil and criminal cases in areas where the state has failed to create the necessary infrastructure and human capital to uphold the law. Furthermore, the population most likely has some familiarity with Taliban law because it is rooted in Islamic and *pashtunwali* principles. The Taliban's ability to settle disputes quickly, free of charge, and legitimately in the eyes of the population will most likely mean that it will continue to be the law of choice in rural Afghanistan in the near future.

As with Iraq creating, upholding, and instilling the rule of law in society is perhaps the most difficult pillar to construct in a state-building initiative because it requires so many different types of resources and takes time to develop. Similar to the situation in Iraq, building national unity in Afghanistan on the foundation of civic nationalism—which is rooted in common belief and adherence in the law—is unreasonable, and another form of national unity is required in the near term.

The international community could have helped instill the

rule of law in Afghanistan by, first, providing resources that would have helped spread knowledge of the constitution, rule of law, and its purpose for average citizens. For example, the international community could have helped develop public-service announcements for television and especially radio that could have circumvented literacy issues in the country. The international community could have also helped Afghans develop curricula for teaching rule of law to children in school and the rights and responsibilities of all citizens. Other means of spreading information about rule of law and instilling it in the population could have included the creation of comic books that teach justice and social responsibility. Television or radio dramas about the rule of law could also have been both entertaining and informative, as law shows are in the United States. The Afghan government could have held yearly poetry contests or quizzes on the subject, like a spelling bee, with scholarship money for the winners.

Alongside these initiatives, the government would still need to develop the necessary resources to apply the law, which would take time. Perhaps one of the most important places to begin is to realize that establishing rule of law requires much more than just drafting a constitution.

ECONOMICS

Despite pledging billions of dollars in aid at the 2002 Tokyo conference, the international community was slow to develop a systematic plan aimed at economically developing Afghanistan. It was as if the international community did not believe that Afghanistan had economic potential, which is clearly not the case. As discussed in chapter 7, Afghanistan has a history of agriculture that held potential for revitalization in the post-Taliban era. Afghanistan also holds considerable mineral deposits that, if properly managed, could be a significant source of jobs and economic development.

Afghanistan, of course, faces considerable challenges in economic development. It is a landlocked country, placing it at a disadvantage for trade and the cheap import of fossil fuels for industry. Perhaps more crucially, Afghanistan's illicit economy has not only gone unchecked in the post-Taliban era; rather, it has flourished. This is especially true of opium poppy production and the opium trade but also of illegal mining, smuggling, and other illicit activities. Allowing these black and gray market economies to prosper has slowed the growth of legitimate industries, especially in the agricultural realm. These illicit markets have also denied the Afghan government important revenue in the form of taxes and other payments that help fund services to the population that generate the social contract.

Given the predominantly rural nature of Afghanistan and its high levels of poverty, a population-centric approach to economic development should have focused on creating jobs programs, reinvigorating the country's agriculture sector, and developing mining down the road. Polling data suggest that, next to security, lack of jobs is one of the biggest, chronic grievances of the population. The 2014 Asia Foundation survey on Afghanistan, for example, queried Afghans about reasons for migrating and found that "among those who left the country, 27.0% say they did so due to the economy or lack of jobs, and among those who moved from one province to another, an even higher proportion (38.8%) moved for economic or employment reasons."[28] At the local level, the 2014 survey reported that unemployment was the single biggest concern of respondents at 33.1 percent.[29] In the 2017 survey, 54.5 percent of Afghans cited unemployment as the reason for wanting to leave; security concerns were the second largest reason for wanting to emigrate.[30]

One of the earliest projects initiated after the overthrow of the Taliban was the country's Ring Road, which aimed to connect Afghanistan's five major cities and place 80 percent of the population within a reasonable distance from this major thoroughfare. However, as noted in chapter 7, the contract to build this road was awarded primarily to non-Afghan companies. Big and small infrastructure projects like this should have focused on hiring Afghans throughout the process, including Afghan firms, engineers, suppliers, and laborers. Hiring a U.S. firm to oversee the project was expedient: the United States government was capable of cutting contracts to these firms more

quickly and easily because the firms knew the government contracting process—they literally and figuratively spoke the same
language. However, expedience should not have been the goal;
rather employing the population and jump-starting the economy, taxation, services, and the social contract should have been
the objectives.

There were endless projects that the United States and its allies
could have initiated at the onset of the occupation that would
have helped employ Afghans, ranging from building roads, to
stringing electrical lines, to improving irrigation in agricultural
zones, to developing landfills. For the purposes of strengthening national unity, as will be discussed further below, helping
Afghans to develop their basic communications infrastructure,
such as roads, cell phone capabilities, and radio towers, would
have been a particularly good investment for the international
community. This infrastructure could have allowed for a better
flow of information, and people and goods in the case of roads,
thus helping to create a sense of connectivity among Afghans,
particularly in rural areas and remote villages.

Some initiatives had these goals in mind. The Afghan-initiated
National Solidarity Program (NSP), for example, was an important effort that sought to empower and employ Afghans while
developing critical infrastructure and other projects. As described
in chapter 7, this initiative allowed villages and communities
to generate proposals and apply for development grants from
the government to construct infrastructure that they deemed
critical, all while teaching decision making, accountability, and
transparency. The NSP should have been supported more by
international donors, as well as implemented on a number of
different levels, not just in villages.

The U.S. military's use of Commander's Emergency Relief
Project (CERP) money, including micro-grants, was also a good
initiative because it brought "seed" money to the local level, especially villages that were vulnerable to insurgents; this money went
for projects ranging from income-generating initiatives for widows to basic infrastructure development. In some cases VSO also
tied the creation of ad hoc security forces in vulnerable villages

to payment through infrastructure development and other projects. However, these development projects suffered from lack of oversight and consistency, given the short rotation schedules of troops and the need to move U.S. security forces to different villages and areas based on the location of insurgent forces.[31]

A larger, longer-lasting initiative to jump-start Afghanistan's economy should have begun with agriculture. In various forms developing the country's agriculture sector would have touched more rural Afghans, who are the majority of the population. International assistance to the agricultural sector could have focused on a number of programs, including providing the resources for Afghans to clean and improve irrigation canals in their villages, courses on basic soil and seed maintenance, and training Afghans in basic veterinarian skills. In 2012 U.S. Civil Affairs reservists initiated a pre-deployment training program aimed at equipping soldiers with these basic agriculture skills, which they could then pass on to Afghans.[32] Such initiatives should have been executed on a much larger scale and earlier.

U.S. forces and the Afghan government also could have helped to facilitate markets at the local level with the aim of providing a place for Afghans to sell their produce and livestock, but also as an opportunity for Afghans to mingle and learn their common interests and vulnerabilities. In a country where over 40 percent of the population is still struggling to get basic nutrition, improving sustainable agricultural production at the local level may not have made a sizable impact on the country's GDP, but it would have affected average Afghans positively.

Bigger initiatives, like developing Afghanistan's mining industry, should have also been pursued, but not in the near term. Ghani and Lockhart contend that management of natural resources is one of the ten critical functions of a sovereign state, and mismanagement of these resources can lead to disastrous consequences for state stability, the environment, and sovereignty.[33] The Afghan government's haste to sign contracts with Chinese mining companies in 2007 resulted in a failed start in developing this sector of the economy, due to a combination of weak governance and lack of security.

Ultimately economic development at the local level should have attempted to do several things at once: create jobs, initiate sustainable projects, foster leadership and decision making, develop community and civil society, teach planning and budgeting, and instill norms and the value of institutions. Given that roughly 90 percent of Afghanistan's GDP was foreign aid in 2015, it is critical that the country begin to develop a sustainable economy, one that will allow for the virtuous cycle of the social contract to be put in motion. However in the near term, these programs should produce visible results for average rural Afghans and foster positive externalities.

SOCIAL WELL-BEING

Of the five pillars of state-building and reconstruction, social well-being arguably has been the most successful endeavor in Afghanistan. As noted in chapter 7, the average life expectancy of an Afghan has climbed from forty-two to sixty-two for men and sixty-four for women since the fall of the Taliban at the end of 2001. Access to basic health care—including maternal, newborn, and child health care; immunizations; and basic medicines—has grown from almost nothing to reaching an estimated 80 percent of the population. Basic infrastructure has improved, allowing better connectivity between villages, cities, and their people. Public utilities, including electricity and potable water, made sizable gains between 2002 and 2014, although rural areas are still at a considerable disadvantage for access to both. Reducing the gender gap, an international priority, has also experienced considerable gains; women now hold seats in provincial and federal government. And a reported 10 million children are enrolled in school, including an estimated 2.4 million girls.

However, despite these gains Afghanistan still has considerable progress to make in basic well-being, and social well-being more broadly. As discussed in chapter 7, Afghanistan still hovers at the very bottom of the Human Development Index and basic poverty reduction has stalled, with around 40 percent of the population still unable to secure adequate nutrition on a consistent basis. Furthermore, Afghans still name personal security and jobs, which should be included in social well-being, as principal concerns in polling data. It is also unclear if the agenda that the international community set for the social well-being of Afghans is the same as the agenda that Afghans would have set for themselves.

Given the severe underdevelopment of Afghanistan, it is perhaps best to distinguish between physical well-being and social well-being. Physical well-being would include access to basic health care, nutrition, and security. Despite the considerable gains that have been made, more could be done to develop sustainable access to health care and empower Afghans. A good example of an initiative that aims to be sustainable and empower Afghans is the Community Midwifery Education (CME) Programme, a collaborative effort between the Afghan government, NGOs, and UNICEF. Afghanistan's infant and mother mortality rates are some of the highest in the world, and to combat this the CME instituted an eighteen-month program that trains Afghan women to be midwives in their local communities. A 2008 report notes that the number of Afghan midwives had risen from 467 in 2002 to 2,167 in 2008, with a goal of 4,546 to cover 90 percent of deliveries in the country.[34]

Another example of a sustainable initiative for physical well-being comes from Rwanda, where post-genocide reconciliation efforts have focused on a range of issues, including improved health care. Under the new system, communities elect local health workers who are then given basic medical training and tasked with providing immediate heath care for rudimentary problems. Dr. Fidele Ngabo, the civil servant in charge of the program explains the process: "They are elected by the community. The only criteria we give is [that] they can read and write. We give them basic training like how to screen for malaria, how to take temperatures, how to check respiration. For complicated treatment, they are obliged to transfer patients to the health facility." Community workers are paid by the number of patients they treat and vaccinate. Ngabo states, "The most important thing is to bring service closer to the community, that's what people can really learn from our country."[35]

In addition to basic health care, poverty reduction and consistent access to basic nutrition should have been one of the primary goals of the Afghan government. Afghans should have been empowered at the local level to reduce this problem, particularly the challenges associated with rural poverty. As noted in the previous section, one means by which poverty could be reduced and access to basic nutrition improved in rural areas is through training in improved agricultural techniques, including irrigation, soil care, selection of ideal crops, food storage, and herd maintenance. Basic knowledge in these techniques could have improved consistent access to adequate food.

Social well-being concerns not only addressing access to services and basic needs but also the way in which access to these services shapes social dynamics within a country. One of the international community's priorities for social well-being was improving access to education. As noted in chapter 7, Afghanistan has one of the highest illiteracy rates in the world. Illiteracy has, in turn, become a concern for training security forces, raising a competent civil service and government, and economically developing the country. Education is also a social well-being concern because it has been shown to improve gender and social equality, lower fertility rates, and even increase health and wellness.[36]

The international community's focus on education was certainly not a bad thing, but its near obsession with primary school education left postsecondary education and vocational training underattended. Ghani and Lockhart note that virtually no money was allocated for higher education or vocational training at the 2002 Tokyo meeting, and it is rarely mentioned in fact sheets regarding education improvements in the post-Taliban era.[37] This gap in education has inhibited the country's ability to train civil servants, lawyers, doctors, engineers, and other professionals in-house, forcing college students to go abroad and risking brain drain of this critical resource. Ghani and Lockhart further note that, by not investing in education for adults, the development of a middle class will be greatly slowed in Afghanistan, which in turn will likely affect civic participation in governance and the growth of an important tax base.[38] As it is, Afghanistan will have to wait virtually a generation to see educated children grow into a responsible middle class.

From the standpoint of building national unity in Afghanistan, the emphasis on education was not misplaced, but it should have also included resources for young adults and adults. Significant portions of the male population have been fighting in some capacity for most of their lives, and not studying or learning vocational skills, resulting in a form of internal brain drain.[39] The prospects for lasting peace will be greatly inhibited if these men do not find some alternative form of existence. Vocational training in basic agricultural skills, metal smithing, construction, mechanics, and so on would have offered something for these generations of fighters and a pathway out of combat.

Another area of social well-being that was strongly pushed by the international community was girls' and women's education. Girls' education became a priority for donor countries and the increase in girls' enrollment is a statistic that is cited as a significant improvement toward gender equality in Afghanistan. Moreover, quotas for women's participation were included in the Afghan constitution, setting the minimum requirement of women in parliament at 25 percent. It may be worth considering, however, that this concentrated focus on gender equality and women's rights may have been too much too fast. Barfield, for example, notes that in particularly conservative Pashtun areas, this agenda was understood as an effort to destroy the country's culture and faith, beliefs that helped generate support for the resurgence of the Taliban.[40]

Introducing social change, especially gender and ethnic equality, is a difficult undertaking and requires pushing at the parameters of accepted norms. However, it is worth considering that this pressure for change needs to, on some level, come from within the society, as the civil rights movement and the women's rights movement did in the United States. Without some degree of legitimacy from within, the effects of externally driven campaigns for equality are not likely to work.

Finally, promoting sports was another underutilized aspect of social well-being that could have helped foster national unity. Soccer is perhaps the most popular sport in Afghanistan, although cricket and basketball are also popular. The Afghan National Football team dates back to 1922; it joined FIFA in 1948 and the AFC in 1954. In 2013 the Afghan team won against India in the South Asian Football Federation, earning the team's first title in the post-Taliban era. The Afghans also formed a women's football team in 2011. And in 2012, the country's first professional football league, the Afghan Premier League, had its inaugural season, with eight regional teams competing within the country.[41] U.S. and coalition forces could have helped support this national pastime by providing necessary resources, facilitating partnerships between soccer teams in Afghanistan and those around the world, and in doing so, helping to build national unity.

Of the pillars of state-building and reconstruction initiated by the United States and its allies after the 2001 invasion, physical well-being has been the most successful endeavor in Afghanistan. Undoubtedly Afghans' physical well-being has improved, as the dramatic increase in life expectancy, reduction in infant mortality rates, and improved access to potable water demonstrate. However, the international community could have done more to create sustainable initiatives that empower Afghans and build national unity over the long haul. Moreover, well-being should have included educational and training initiatives for adults, not just children, and recreational activities that capitalize on preexisting institutions, such as national soccer leagues.

NATIONAL UNITY

The United States and the myriad of international support that aimed to stabilize and develop Afghanistan ultimately did very little to foster national unity as part of their overall state-building exercise. Following the overthrow of the Taliban, Afghanistan had both unique challenges and opportunities for building national unity. Roughly 78 percent of the Afghan population was rural, and prior to 2001 the country had exceptionally poor infrastructure, creating challenges for physically and virtually connecting people. Furthermore, Afghanistan's high illiteracy rate and low levels of education presented unique challenges for creating programs aimed at fostering and spreading a sense of national unity. The country also struggled with providing the most basic resources to the population, including sufficient nutrition, basic sanitation, and potable water. These were all important challenges that needed to be addressed in their own right and to facilitate executing programs aimed specifically at building national unity.

However, Afghanistan also had some unique opportunities for building national unity. In many ways the challenges were also the opportunities; infrastructure development, poverty reduction, literacy programs, and fostering education all offered the possibility of buildings these resources in a way that empowered Afghans and instilled a sense of hope and common destiny. Nation-building should have focused on addressing these very real needs while also acting as the vehicle through which to show the utility of a government and the common destiny of the people.

Three major state-building initiatives in particular could have been used to foster national unity in Afghanistan: basic infrastructure development, education, and improved access to nutrition. As noted above, basic infrastructure—particularly roads—not only plays an important role in improving security and commerce, but it also provides the conduits that connect people physically and informationally. Rome understood this; the adage that "all roads lead to Rome" was as much about physically connecting the empire's territory and holding it as it was about connecting its people through this vital piece of infrastructure. The international community also understood the importance of roads for Afghanistan and made reconstructing the Ring Road one of its priorities. However, as described above, the work largely fell to U.S.-based contractors, took considerable time to complete, and then became a target of the Taliban once it was finished. Although probably taking more time in the near term, the international community could have used constructing roads as a means of employing Afghans, creating better connectivity between cities and villages, and making the road a symbol of destiny for the country.

Another critical piece of infrastructure that the international community could have focused on improving was making the country 100 percent accessible to radio frequencies in the near term, with eventual expansion into television, internet, and other forms of information technologies over time. Radios, unlike televisions and computers, are inexpensive and can run on batteries or be manually operated, thus making them the most accessible form of information technology for a predominately rural, illiterate, and impoverished society.

Historically, radio broadcasts have been a critical form of information sharing within and across countries, in addition to providing entertainment to listeners. In the United States, for example, radio broadcasts became a critical part of nation-building following the creation of commercial broadcasting companies in the 1920s, which would later become the country's major television stations. During the Great Depression, impoverished Americans gathered around radios to hear "fireside chats" from President Roosevelt, dramas, comedies, sports broadcasts, and music. Similarly, radio remains the best means of informing and connecting Afghans, at least in the near term.

Second, the international community should have focused on an array of training and education, not just at the primary school level, as a means of building national unity in Afghanistan. Adult education and training, as noted above, could have focused on teaching improved farming techniques, vocational skills, and other traits that would have offered fighting-age men an alternative livelihood. Although considerable efforts were made on these fronts, as noted above, adult education should have also trained more teachers, basic health-care providers, and individuals with rudimentary veterinary skills. To be sure, international actors engaged in such training, as with the NGOs committed to training midwives and U.S. Civil Affairs personnel learning basic farming techniques to teach Afghans, but this form of assistance could have been undertaken sooner and on a larger scale. Within all these initiatives, Afghans could have used these opportunities for training and education to instruct fellow citizens about the rule of law and civic responsibility.

Within primary and secondary education, there should also have been an effort to educate students on the rule of law, civic responsibility, and their fellow citizens throughout the country.[42] Afghans should have learned about other regions, groups, and cultures in their country as a means instilling a diverse sense of what it means to be Afghan and, potentially, to foster a sense of connectedness with Afghans in other regions whom they are unlikely to ever meet.

Third, poverty reduction in Afghanistan could have been a vehicle for building national unity. As described earlier nearly half the population suffers from malnutrition and access to basic resources, such as potable water and sanitation. Nation-building should have focused on addressing these very real needs and building hope and a sense of common destiny by empowering Afghans to improve these areas. Focusing more on agriculture—including providing resources for farming and training in improved techniques—could have helped with better securing consistent access to food. Agriculture also could have better connected Afghans by strengthening local markets and the need to swap or sell produce between villages.

Finally, the United States and its allies could have worked with national entrepreneurs to foster programs that focused on Afghans' common destiny as a nation. Sports, as mentioned above, could have been a common connection among Afghans, and the intervening powers could have provided resources and helped organize teams at the local, district, provincial, and even national levels. Music and poetry recitations could have also been a vehicle for building national unity, including competitions at the national level. The creation of the Afghanistan National Institute of Music in 2010 through the collaborative efforts of the Afghan Ministry of Education and Australian and other international donors is an excellent example of initiatives that should have been pursued earlier.[43]

The preservation of Afghanistan's ancient history could have also been a vehicle for national-unity building and could have created the potential for tourism in the country. Initiatives like Turquoise Mountain, a nonprofit cooperative between the British royal family and the Afghan government, aims to preserve the many aspects of Afghanistan's historic culture, including its ancient architecture, art, and craftsman-ship. The cooperative helped Afghans restore the old city of Kabul and offers vocational training in woodwork and other artisan crafts. In 2008 Turquoise Mountain established the Afghan Contemporary Art Prize, which seeks "to find the best young artists in Afghanistan, and spur interest in both traditional and contemporary Afghan art."[44] Initiatives like these not only offer training and micro-employment, but they restore aspects of Afghan culture that could become points of pride for all Afghans. The aspects of national-unity build-ing are summarized in table 7.

Ultimately, rallying points for national-unity building could be any number of things, so long as they resonate with Afghans, offer hope, and provide the opportunity for Afghans to recog-nize their common destiny. Working with Afghanistan's many national entrepreneurs could have helped identify points of unity and destiny that the U.S. and coalition forces could have fos-tered earlier.

It is unclear at this point if Afghanistan will suffer the same fate as Iraq has in the wake of internationally driven efforts to state build. However, intervening powers could have done more to foster national unity in Afghanistan, and these missed opportu-nities, along with an overemphasis on building the central pow-ers of the state and not addressing the basic needs of most rural Afghans, may pose significant problems for making Afghani-stan stable down the road. Despite all these challenges, the 2017 Asia Foundation Survey on Afghanistan found that average cit-izens are slightly more optimistic about their country's future than the previous year, "from 29.3% in 2016 to 32.8% in 2017," with rebuilding the country cited as the most significant rea-son. Respondents were also more positive about the govern-ment and its services.[45]

Chapter 9 will build on these ideas to offer summary thoughts and propose a strategy for building imagined communities in the twenty-first century.

7. Hypothetical nation-building in Afghanistan

Pillar	What was done	What could have been done
Security	Establishing conventional security forces	Promote community-based security with local leadership (similar to vso)
	Instituting vso after 2008	Vertically integrate local forces
		Transition vso to national guard
		Establish comprehensive DDR program
Governance	Used *jirgas* to validate interim government	Include willing warlords and Taliban in political process
	Held national elections	Use *jirgas* to validate longer interim government
	Sidelined warlords and other leaders	Delay elections
		Support "good enough governance" in the near term
		Push power out to province and district level, limit central government, and create "mixed sovereignty"
Rule of law	Drafted constitution	Include key leaders in drafting constitution
	Created criminal legal code	Teach rule of law through locally led building and development
		Provide civic education at all levels to teach rule of law
		Educate adults, train lawyers and judges
		Bring effective and timely courts to the local level
Economic development	Launched counternarcotics efforts	Set up massive jobs program to rebuild infrastructure
	Provided micro-grants	Focus on agriculture and vocational skills
	Partnered with Chinese firms for mining	Foster local markets
		Delay mining until government is strengthened

Social well-being	Provided basic utilities	Focus on more-aggressive poverty-reduction programs
	Promoted women's rights	Train teachers and health-care providers
	Furthered children's education	Support national sports programs
	Provided basic health care	
National unity		Build roads and radio towers to connect people
		Focus on poverty reduction as national unity goal
		Provide basic education at all levels, not just for children
		Promote sports
		Establish music, poetry, and art scholarships and competitions

9

A PROGRAM FOR POPULATION-CENTRIC
STATE-BUILDING AND NATION-BUILDING

Given the lackluster track record of state-building efforts in the post–September 11 world, it would seem logical that the United States would be done with both large- and small-scale missions aimed at fixing dysfunctional and failing states. However, the United States is likely to engage in future state- and nation-building efforts for several important reasons. First, weak and failing states offer undergoverned spaces in which violent non-state actors can reside, recruit fighters, plan operations, and gain momentum. Some but not all of these violent nonstate actors are committed to targeting the U.S. homeland, its people, and its key interests. Therefore, trying to fix undergoverned spaces with the aim of denying nonstate actors a safe haven will most likely remain a U.S. priority. Second, weak and failing states pose a considerable security challenge for the regions in which they are located. Internal governance and security problems rarely remain within the borders of a state and often become regional problems in the form of transborder refugees, weapons and drug trafficking, and the proliferation of nonstate and trans-state actors. Third, the United States appears unable to stay out of these conflicts due to international pressure. In the conflicts where the United States has not intervened, such as the Syrian civil war, it has received international criticism for its delayed and limited response.

Therefore, understanding what went wrong in the U.S.-led efforts to state build in Iraq and Afghanistan and recognizing the missed opportunities for national-unity building in these countries are both a worthwhile and a necessary endeavor. Moreover, the United States has invested trillions of dollars in Iraq and Afghanistan, over four thousand U.S. service members' lives, and an estimated one million U.S. service members' injured with a suspected one in five suffering from post-traumatic stress disorder; these costs are significant and demand consideration for how to do better in the future.[1] The Iraqi and Afghan people also have paid dearly with countless numbers killed and displaced as a result of state-building efforts and the violent conflict these initiatives helped fuel. Furthermore, with the collapse of the Iraqi military and government in 2014, the United States finds itself being pulled back into the region. The demise of the Islamic State in 2017–18 still leaves unanswered how Syria and Iraq will create viable governments that can provide for their people, create order, and defend their borders. Moreover, ISIL as a counter-state force will most likely remain in the region for the near future, or its next incarnation will appear to threaten states' stability in the Middle East and beyond. In other words the battle against the Islamic State may have been won, but the war against ISIL is not over. The stakes for understanding how to aid failing states and put them on the path to long-term stability could not be higher.

This concluding chapter offers summary thoughts on U.S.-led efforts to state build, missed opportunities to build national unity, and lessons learned that, hopefully, could be considered in the inevitable efforts to stabilize weak and failing states in the future. In particular it offers six principles for state-building and national-unity building: start with the population; identify and incorporate local leaders into state-building and nation-building; allow the necessary time for change; stabilize the top, focus on change occurring at the local level; emphasize national unity in all efforts; and remember that building the state and the nation never end. The ultimate hope is that these observations and suggestions will spark a debate within the U.S. government, the military, and other key state and non-governmental actors for how to better engage in building the state and national unity.

Sovereignty, Nations, and States

The book began by asserting that sovereignty has undergone a significant shift since the creation of early states in Europe and especially since the time of the Westphalia accords of the seventeenth century. The birth of modern-day democracies, the creation of security through the *levee en masse*, the transformation of monarchies, the rise of private property, increased levels of education, the birth of the public sphere, the Industrial Revolution, the ideas of the Enlightenment, and the revolution in information technologies have all shifted sovereignty from governments and territories to the population.

Perhaps at no other time in modern history has sovereignty more truly rested in the people than today, aided by technology, education, and a sense of rights and empowerment. Within this drastic shift in sovereignty, the state still matters and, for the foreseeable future, is the best form of political organization to provide domestic, regional, and global stability and to secure rights and resources for the population. However, any effort at state-building and national-unity building needs to recognize this dramatic shift in sovereignty and begin with the people.

Furthermore, states need to be more than brokers of resources to succeed as states. The social contract—the idea that citizens give up some of their rights and resources for state services in return for provisions like security, public utilities, education, and health care—is an important and necessary function of a healthy state. However, the "usable state," as Meierhenrich calls it, is necessary but not sufficient for creating a viable state. As important—and often overlooked by state builders—is the emotional attachments that citizens need to have to one another and to their state. These attachments provide the glue that holds the population together and builds loyalty to the state. Nations can exist without states, as the Palestinians, the Kurds, and the Hmong have shown, but states need nations in order to cohere, to traverse difficult times, and to imagine a common purpose and future. Fostering this form of emotional unity is truly nation-building; it is creating and reinforcing imagined communities.

As with state-building, national-unity building requires specific programs aimed at fostering attachments among the people. However, unlike state-building, the process of developing national unity requires a subtler approach. When successfully done, national-unity building almost appears to have no conscious construction; the nation merely was, is, and always shall be. As described in chapter 3, nation-building in Europe and the United States was the process of subtle and ever-changing efforts to create and reinforce national unity. These efforts included a wide array of programs, ranging from language construction and mass education, to the development of national myths of origin and founding fathers, to the creation of capital cities, monuments, national parks, and forests. These programs, which were developed in tandem with state-building, created and then reinforced what it means to be a member of the nation.

Furthermore, national-unity building programs were not solely the product of governments, although governments certainly contributed to the process; rather, they were largely the efforts of nation-building entrepreneurs: academics, artists, socialites, businesspeople, activists, and other private citizens who created programs aimed at fostering or preserving symbols, artifacts, and monuments of national unity. As such the very process of imagining the common threads of unity and destiny was a group effort. The inclusive and successful imagining of the nation therefore is greatly reliant on identifying national entrepreneurs with an inclusive vision for the nation.

Within these national-unity building programs, history played an important role, but more as myth than fact. History was not just about the past; it served an important role of telling citizens where they came from, who they are, where they are going, and how they should behave. Thriving nations, therefore, are not only backward looking; they use the past to create a sense of common purpose and destiny. The United States, in particular, developed a narrative of the nation that was optimistic, forward looking, and stressed a common sense of destiny. European nations were perhaps more reliant on the past and myths of common ancestry as a source of national unity. This approach to nation-building appears to be under considerable duress in the twenty-first century.

Finally, nationalism, the fusion of the sense of nation with a political program, is another important component of nation-building and state-building. Chapter 2 highlighted three types of nationalism: ethnic, which is based on the perception of common ancestry and usually a common language; civic, which is rooted in common norms and rules that produce trust among citizens and between citizens and the state; and religious, which seeks to make religious beliefs and practices the governing principles of the state. Ethnic and religious nationalisms may be easier to create because they draw on preexisting perceptions of common ties, either through myths of ancestry or religious norms and values. However, these forms of nationalism are also exclusive and restrict who can join the nation based on these limiting criteria. Civic nationalism, which creates a sense of unity and common destiny through the rule of law, is inclusive, but it takes a longer time to develop and is especially difficult to build after violent conflict and state collapse, which reflect a breakdown of social capital, rule of law, and other state services. Although perhaps not a full-blown form of nationalism, creating a sense of common destiny among citizens and between citizens and the state—a program of national unity—is a productive starting point. National unity emphasizes the common destiny of a state's people, and their need to work together to build a healthy prosperous state. Fostering a sense of the common destiny of all citizens paves the way for civic nationalism to eventually take hold.

These observations about state-building and nation-building offer clues for missed opportunities that the United States and its allies could have used to help stabilize Iraq and Afghanistan following the overthrow of Saddam Hussein and the Taliban.

Missed Opportunities for State-Building and National-Unity Building in Iraq and Afghanistan

Ultimately, two key variables were missing from U.S. and coalition efforts to "nation build" in Iraq and Afghanistan. First, nation-building did not include efforts to truly build the nation—the people's sense of common destiny, interdependence, and emotional connection to one another and to the state. Rather, "nation-building" efforts focused specifically on building the structure of the state: security forces, government, key infrastructure and services, and a robust and viable economy. The assumption with this approach appears to be that, by providing key resources, the population in return would feel a sense of national unity and be loyal to the state; in other words, the creation of the social contract between the government and the population would create both a viable nation and a viable state. Second, within this approach the population was not sufficiently included in state-building efforts; instead the focus rested more on quickly creating the structure of the state from the top down by establishing central governments, constitutions, and conventional security forces.

In Iraq U.S. and coalition forces focused heavily on building key functions of the state, which included establishing a democracy in Iraq that would be both domestically and internationally responsible, securing a functioning economy based largely on restarting the country's oil production, creating responsible security forces that would not be a menace to Iraq's neighbors, and providing key social services to the population. This approach sought to mitigate Iraq's ethnic grievances by building multiethnic security forces and a democratic government. The focus was almost exclusively on creating macro-level instruments of the state, overlooking programs and initiatives aimed at working with and through the population to stabilize and rebuild the country.

The results of this state-building program in Iraq were disastrous. The political and social upheaval caused by the overthrow of Saddam Hussein helped fuel multiple insurgencies against coalition forces and the fledgling government. Disenfranchised Sunnis staged a boycott of the country's first elections, further alienating this segment of the population and creating a Shia-dominated political system. The Iraqi government could never agree on a hydrocarbon law that would equitably distribute oil wealth to the population; and public services, such as electricity, garbage removal, and sewage management, were slow to be delivered. On top of these problems, the country experienced high numbers of civilian casualties during the occupation; and security remained a challenge both during and after U.S.-led efforts to state build. These shortcomings culminated with U.S. and coalition–trained Iraqi security forces imploding in 2014 as ISIL rolled over Iraq's border; officers abandoned their troops, and thousands of enlisted personnel were slaughtered in addition to untold numbers of Iraqi citizens. ISIL maintained its foothold in Iraq, in part, through the tacit and active support of the Sunni population, which had been thoroughly disenfranchised by the Shia-dominated government.

Despite the demise of the Islamic State in 2018, the future of the Iraqi state remains in question. Kurds voted to secede from Iraq in 2017 and attempted to take Kirkuk by force, requiring Iraqi forces to push them back and declare the referendum on independence vote. The future of the Sunnis in Iraq remains bleak, with limited options for meaningful representation in government, as the 2018 elections showed, and likely reprisals for average citizens' tacit and active support of ISIL.

State-building in Afghanistan began under different circumstances than in Iraq, a deadly attack on the U.S. homeland that demanded some sort of response. The 2001 U.S.-led invasion of Afghanistan aimed to end Taliban rule and to deny al-Qaeda and other transnational terrorists a sanctuary for launching another attack on the U.S. homeland. The December 2001 Bonn Agreement, which brought together Afghan leaders and a host of international actors, aimed to transform Afghanistan from one of the least developed countries in the world into a constitutional democracy with a functioning judiciary and rule of law. And an international meeting of over sixty countries and dozens of NGOs in Tokyo the following month set the conditions for a massive state-building program. Within Afghanistan state-building efforts faced considerable challenges, including over thirty years of atrophied governance and lack of a democratic culture, high illiteracy rates, a predominantly rural population, virtually no physical infrastructure, an illicit opium poppy industry, the inability to secure the country's borders, and rampant poverty.

Despite these important differences, the process of state-building in Afghanistan still remained largely the same as it was in Iraq. Development efforts focused primarily on the construction of a central government and instruments of the state, including a constitution, a liberal democracy, multiethnic conventional security forces, and infrastructure development. As with Iraq virtually no efforts were made to build national unity beyond creating power-sharing arrangements in the government and the military, and the population was left out of the process.

The results of this massive state-building exercise in Afghanistan show significant signs of instability. The country has experienced rampant fraud and corruption in its elections coupled with low voter turnout, suggesting that the population either does not understand the democratic process or does not recognize it as legitimate. On top of political challenges, illicit opium production is at an all-time high. Furthermore, the Taliban remains vibrant, and insurgent threats persist, as do the influence and power of warlords. And statistics suggest that the lives of average Afghans have improved only marginally, and poverty remains a perennial challenge, particularly in rural areas. These indicators suggest that Afghanistan is on a precarious road to the future.

In addition to these state-building efforts, the United States and coalition forces missed valuable opportunities to truly nation build in both Iraq and Afghanistan. In Iraq intervening powers could have leveraged locally led initiatives to establish order in towns and cities following the invasion in 2003. Similarly, U.S. and coalition forces could have worked with local initiatives aimed at building a population-centric approach to security. Economics could have focused less on oil production, which divided the country over rights to this resource, and more on agriculture, which could have created local jobs and improved food security throughout the country. U.S. and coalition forces also missed valuable opportunities to foster a sense of Iraqiness through a host of initiatives, ranging from protecting museums and artifacts that display Iraq's ancient history as "the cradle of civilization," to creating modern symbols of Iraqi pride, such as its national soccer team, or competitors in *Star Academy*, a popular singing competition in the Middle East. Ultimately, programs of national-unity building need to emanate from the population and their national entrepreneurs; but programs like these were almost entirely overlooked.

Afghanistan presented considerably different challenges and opportunities for national-unity building. Unlike Iraq Afghanistan is predominantly rural and faces basic challenges of virtual and physical connectivity between the people in villages, cities, districts, and provinces. National-unity building should have focused on empowering Afghans to build physical infrastructure that serves to connect people, specifically roads and radio infrastructure. Furthermore, although considerable strides were made in the improvement of life expectancy and access to basic human needs, coalition powers should have focused more on addressing the everyday issues of poverty, malnutrition, and lack of potable water, which still persist after over a decade of international development. Nation-building should have focused on addressing these very real needs and building hope and a sense of common destiny by empowering Afghans to improve these issues themselves. Finally, national-unity building in Afghanistan should have developed an array of education and training resources for Afghan adults—not just children—that provided tools for employment, gave youth alternatives to fighting, and taught basic rights and responsibilities in the new Afghanistan.

Ultimately, the U.S. and its coalition partners missed key opportunities to empower the people to rebuild their states in Iraq and Afghanistan, in addition to providing resources to help the Iraqi and Afghan people recognize their common destiny and national unity. The preference for quick, top-down state-building has had disastrous consequences in Iraq and made Afghanistan vulnerable to political and social collapse.

Key Considerations for State-Building and National-Unity Building in the Twenty-First Century

Building on the lessons learned from U.S.-led efforts in Iraq and Afghanistan, one can say that state-building may be less about what is actually done and more about *how* it is done. In other words successful state-building and national-unity building are more an orientation than a checklist of tasks that need to be completed and measured for their success. This new orientation requires a different approach for thinking about the problem. Below are six suggestions for reorienting state- and nation-building efforts in the twenty-first century.

Start with the Population

If the sovereignty and stability of a state rests in the people—who legitimate the government and its security forces and institutionalize rule of law—then any state- and nation-building initiative needs to begin with the population. This is where the ultimate success of state-building and national-unity building lies. Starting with the population includes understanding its perceptions of security, its concerns and vulnerabilities, what its expectations are of the government, points of commonality and divergence with other members of the state, economic expectations, and its hopes for the future. In other words any initiative aimed at building the state and national unity needs to begin by assessing the hopes and desires of the population.

Based on this assessment of the population, programs should be encouraged that empower the people—that give them ownership—and that foster a sense of destiny and national unity. Wherever possible intervening powers should act as facilitators, not as instigators. Intervening powers should provide some of the resources, help with organizing efforts, and provide technical advice on best practices, where appropriate.[2] The focus should be on projects that resonate with the people, improve their daily lives, empower them, and give the them a sense of hope.

Projects like these are often "low tech" in their approach and manpower intensive. For example, rather than hire a foreign and more experienced firm to rapidly build a road, the population could be put to work building the road manually. This approach would employ thousands of people and create opportunities to foster local-level management and leadership skills, and the road could be a symbol of national pride, built by national hands. Intervening powers could provide the salaries (in part or whole), help with organizing laborers, mentor managers, and offer technical advice on road construction. This approach would also teach those within the country how to build and therefore maintain a road, making the project sustainable over time. Finally, this approach would help "insurgent proof" the project; attacking the road would destroy the fruits of local labor—not a foreignmade project—and thus run the risk of alienating the very population the insurgents need to survive.

Furthermore, projects should not only focus on the basic physical needs of employment, agriculture, industry, and infrastructure but should also include art, music, sports, entertainment, and other forms of recreation. All people crave and deserve beauty and moments of laughter and fun in their lives. Sports, art, and entertainment can also be powerful tools of unity building, helping people to see their commonalities and providing hope and inspiration.[3] Moreover, recreational activities, especially sports, can teach teamwork, sportsmanship, and leadership skills, which are useful for building the state and the nation. Ultimately, projects should seek to build the state and the nation through addressing both the physical and the emotional needs of the population.

In addition to meeting immediate physical and emotional needs, population-based stabilization and development projects should aim to build trust among the people and between the people and the government. Every project should address, on some level, building national unity, the state, or both. Some projects will more obviously satisfy these goals than others. The construction of a road, for example, provides a critical piece of infrastructure that physically links cities and villages to one another, improving the opportunities for commerce, security, and connectivity of citizens. A national sports league may not build the structure of a state, but it could improve national unity. A local school, by itself, may not build the state and the nation, but if it includes classes on civic responsibility and improves the quality of human capital, it works toward these goals.

Creating programs that start with understanding the population's needs, vulnerabilities, and hopes comes with several significant challenges. First, this approach demands gaining some sort of understanding of the population, which requires "boots on the ground" beyond the capital city. This approach is labor intensive and also takes time. Local populations are unlikely to host a contingent of strangers and answer endless questions without expecting something in return. Therefore, assessors need to be quick in gaining an understanding of the dynamics on the ground and finding local leaders to leverage in programs to build state and national unity.

Second, the populations of postconflict countries are likely to be fractured from years of violence and unrest, and they may not know or agree on their top needs, vulnerabilities, and desires. A population-centric approach to state-building and nation-building will, therefore, require a process of consensus building within the population. Within this process there will certainly be losers— those that do not get what they want. Local communities need to be taught how to deal with dissenters and possible spoilers in the process of prioritizing and developing projects to build the state and national unity.

Identify and Incorporate Local Leaders into Building the State and the Nation

A population-centric approach to state-building and nation-building requires not only understanding the vulnerabilities and desires of the people but also identifying and leveraging local leaders. Local leaders are an integral aspect of state-building and national-unity building for several reasons. First, local leaders are recognized by their communities and therefore carry a degree of legitimacy that can lend credence to whatever program is initiated. Second, local leaders have knowledge of the local community that will be of use in the assessment stage. Third, when properly utilized, local leaders can act as a "force multiplier" and greatly increase the level of coordination and productivity in an area. Conversely, excluding local leaders threatens these individuals' status and could create enemies who will undermine outside intervention in any form.

Not all local leaders are good, however, which presents some interesting challenges for leveraging their authority in initiatives to build the state and national unity. Leaders who rely solely on coercion are unlikely to be both truly legitimate and useful in any efforts to build lasting popular-based stability. Those who are highly corrupt (by the local standards) should also be managed with care. However, aside from purely coercive and corrupt authority, the default position of intervening powers should be to work with all forms of local leadership and include them in some capacity in state- and nation-building initiatives. Even insurgents should be considered in a strategy of leveraging local leadership. Successful insurgencies require good leadership, and if insurgents have a substantial base of support among the population, they most likely will need to be included in the postconflict society in some capacity.[4]

Perhaps more than any other policy decision the United States and its allies made in Iraq and Afghanistan, its treatment of local leaders had lasting, negative consequences for state-building and national-unity building. In Iraq the decision to implement de-Baathification not only greatly affected Sunnis in the country also excluded and alienated leaders who were well trained and equipped to help run the country. It is widely believed that this decision fueled the country's Sunni-led insurgency. In Afghanistan the United States leveraged warlords in tracking down al-Qaeda and key Taliban members after September 11 but then focused on building a central government, largely leaving them aside. Warlords have become a perennial challenge for Kabul and state stability overall. The United States, its allies, and the fledgling Afghan government also failed to successfully bring willing members of the Taliban into the political process, which could have been a path to managing parts of this group and its support from the population.

In addition to their value in state-building initiatives, local leaders are also vital for national-unity building. National entrepreneurs—local academics, artists, socialites, pop stars, athletes, and other prominent figures—play a critical role in developing symbols, myths, and programs that help promote and reinforce the nation. Intervening powers, therefore, should identify and incorporate national entrepreneurs to help create and champion programs of national-unity building. Intervening powers can aid in this process by supplying resources, including financing, publicity, and other necessary tools, to help foster programs that these local entrepreneurs create. Without national entrepreneurs who reflect the culture on some level and have credibility, nation-building is unlikely to resonate with the population and therefore unlikely to succeed.

Allow the Necessary Time for Change

Perhaps no challenge is greater for state- and nation-building programs than time. For the United States, time was an enormous obstacle for building productive and viable states in Iraq and Afghanistan. It is unclear exactly how much time the United States and the international community thought it would take to build modern states with functioning democracies, competent conventional security forces, public services, and happy citizens who support the state; whatever the time frame, it was certainly not enough in Iraq or in Afghanistan.

Time presents an exceptional challenge to state-building and national-unity building for several reasons. First, it is unlikely that intervening powers, particularly democracies, can create an open-ended engagement when state-building, especially if the initiatives are large and require significant sums of money and manpower; their own populations are unlikely to support these initiatives indefinitely, especially if troops are dying. Ultimately, intervening powers should not embark on efforts to build the state and national unity without being honest about the time required and the support their own populations are willing underwrite. This level of support will most likely be tied to a combination of costs and understanding of how these efforts secure their own country's vital interests.

Second, although short- and long-term goals are paramount for state-building, the *process* is equally important in making a state sustainable and creating local ownership. Trying to build the structure of a state as expediently as possible misses important opportunities to better understand the population, identify and work with local leaders, and create state- and nation-building programs that are sustainable long after intervening powers have left. Shortcuts such as bringing in U.S. contractors to build infrastructure, or allowing three weeks to retrain the country's security forces are unlikely to succeed because they do not allow the critical time necessary to bring local leaders and the population along and give them ownership.

Third, managing local expectations over time is also critically important to successful state-building and national-unity building. Expectations were not well maintained in either Iraq or Afghanistan, and the U.S. and coalition powers overpromised both what they could do and how quickly they could do it. For example, Barfield argues that the vast array of international money and attention paid to Afghanistan after the fall of the Taliban raised Afghans' expectations that their lives would be vastly improved; when little visible change occurred, they became disillusioned.[5] Somewhat similarly, when Iraq fell into a state of insecurity and chaos after the U.S.-led invasion, some Iraqis believed that the United States intentionally created the chaos to justify staying in the country and profiting from its oil. Following the 2014 invasion of ISIL in Iraq, many Iraqis believed that ISIL was actually a U.S. creation aimed at further weakening and dividing the state.[6] Managing local expectations, therefore, is paramount.

Perhaps the best way to manage expectations and time in efforts to build the state and national unity is to divide tasks between near-term stabilization efforts and long-term development. In the near term, efforts should be made to leverage cultural practices and local leaders and bring the population on board in all initiatives. However, within these initial steps, it is important not to foster programs that could undermine long-term stability. Leveraging culture is key in the short term, but the creation of a healthy, functioning democracy, rule of law, responsible and competent security forces, enhanced social well-being, and a social contract between the government and the people most likely cannot be accomplished without changing some aspects of the people's culture. Changing culture is a delicate process that is best done slowly and through national entrepreneurs, allowing ample time for leaders and the population to adjust.

Emphasize Symbols of National Unity in All Efforts

The historical cases of Europe and the United States demonstrate that state-building and nation-building are best conducted simultaneously, and not only by a state's government but also by private citizens and civil society. The fledgling government in the United States made efforts to knit the population together and bind it to the state, including drafting a constitution and framework for common law that limited the government and delineated the rights and responsibilities of citizens, and through the adoption of a flag that symbolized both the independence of the states and their unity. Simultaneously, citizens created the first American newspapers, such as the *New England Courant*, founded by James Franklin (Benjamin's brother); and Benjamin Franklin's *Pennsylvania Gazette*; the *Virginia Gazette*; and the *Massachusetts Spy*, which bound people together not only through information but also with satire and humor. Following independence from Britain, key thinkers penned *The Federalist Papers*, which defended the creation of a central government. U.S. history is replete with this interplay between the construction of the state and popular efforts to reinforce these initiatives by building national unity.

States will only thrive, particularly in the modern world, with the buy-in and support of the population. But this support is not purely instrumental and requires conscious efforts to bind the people to one another and build attachment and loyalty to the state; this is true nation-building. National-unity building requires a delicate handling of drawing on the past as a tool for building myths of unity and destiny; the past can never be completely written out of the nation. However, *how* the past is understood becomes critical for its use in building national unity.

In U.S.-led efforts to reconstruct (or construct) Iraq and Afghanistan, national-unity building was all but left out of the process, particularly programs that fostered an emotional sense of unity and destiny. U.S.-led state-building efforts did attempt to create ethnic power sharing through elections and multiethnic security forces, but these initiatives actually reinforced ethnic differences among Afghans and Iraqis, instead of developing a narrative of national unity and destiny.

U.S. and coalition forces missed key opportunities to fold nation-building into the development of the state. First, in both states the United States and its partners should have looked for national entrepreneurs—artists, academics, athletes, businesspeople, and other individuals with whom they could have partnered in building national unity. In Iraq coalition forces could have better understood the role of Iraq's military, one of the first in the Middle East, as a symbol of national pride. Iraq's ancient history as the cradle of civilization could have been upheld as something that all Iraqis share, regardless of religion or ethnicity. In Afghanistan the country's rich and ancient cultural traditions, particularly in textiles and woodworking, could have been highlighted as a unifying symbol of the past, and rugged persistence in the face of an austere environment could have been themes to uphold as part of the Afghan nation. The unique landscapes and vegetation in both countries offer opportunities to remind Iraqis and Afghans of the beauty of their countries and to potentially attract tourism.

Pop culture could also have been a tool of national-unity building in both countries. As described in chapters 6 and 8, soccer is a national obsession in Iraq and Afghanistan. The creation of national teams and their competition in regional and international events could have been better fostered as a modern symbol of national unity. Music, art, movies, and cuisine are also present-day symbols that could have been used to show both the diversity and the unity of the Afghan and Iraqi nations. Finally, national competitions in poetry readings, music, recitations, and other forms of art could have been financially sponsored by U.S. and coalition powers with the goal of bringing young people together from different parts of the country to compete and earn national-level recognition.

If state-building and national-unity building require working through and empowering the local population, beginning with creating a central government is likely to miss this critical approach. However, beginning at the grassroots level presents equally problematic challenges. Specifically, who controls and coordinates statewide initiatives in the absence of a central government? Who interacts with neighboring states and the international community more broadly?

Clearly provisions need to be made to create some sort of central authority to provide stability and continuity throughout the country, but at the same time the population needs to be empowered and integrated into state- and nation-building initiatives from the earliest stages. An approach is needed that allows for the people to be brought on board to the political process while educating them about their rights and responsibilities as citizens, but it must also create some sort of interim authority at the center that can manage the development of the state and the nation.[7]

Although controversial, one approach would be to keep an interim government in place longer than was done in Iraq and Afghanistan and to delay elections until the people are acculturated to their rights and responsibilities as citizens. This approach would create time for education and national-unity building at the local level while holding the central government constant, which, if done properly, would help foster continuity across the country and normalize relations with neighbors and the international community. This approach could also allow time for vertical integration between the local level, the district, the province, and the central government, which is necessary to create unity of effort within a country. Naturally this approach comes with some serious challenges, namely, finding the right leadership that would have the people's best interest at heart, that would earn their trust and respect, and that would not take advantage of the situation to seize the state or turn it into a kleptocracy or a tool of oppression.

This challenge in political development is further complicated if the population is demanding that elections be held in
the near term. Without the proper understanding of the democratic process and the norms that undergird liberal democracy,
including minority rights and freedom of speech, press, assembly, and religion, elections are likely to turn into census taking
(as it did in Iraq, ultimately allowing Shias as the numerical
majority to seize control of the state) or to be seen as ineffective and illegitimate (as the weak voter turnout in Afghanistan
suggests). Clearly, the necessary level of democratic education
and nation-building was not in place in either country prior to
holding elections. Under these conditions elections were less
the reflection of the will of the people and more a procedure to
install illegitimate regimes. Thus it is no surprise that these governments have become targets of insurgents and other competitors for state power.

Ultimately, intervening powers need to work through the population to find the mechanisms that will allow for an interim
authority to be identified and put in place while the population
is educated about the political process. Afghanistan had the
concept of the Loya Jirga, the national assembly of tribal elders
and other leaders, to approve and legitimate the interim government in Afghanistan. Iraq's initial interim government, the IGC,
was heavily composed of expatriates and formed by the United
States; it lacked the legitimacy of the population, and most people had never heard of the members or even knew that there was
an interim government. However, the second attempt, forged by
Iraqis, the UN, and the United States, included more local leaders and received better support from the population as well as
endorsements from other key leaders such as Ayatollah Sistani.
However, this body, the IIG, was only in power for about eighteen months before national elections were held. Perhaps if the
IIG had been allowed to stay longer, it would have allowed more
time and space to work with the population at the local level.
The same is true for Afghanistan, which also kept its interim
government for eighteen months.

Finally, it is important to manage popular expectations with regard to voting and to allow time for the necessary values that undergird voting to take root. Intervening powers should also be patient and not see voting as the sine qua non of state-building and not use elections as the benchmark for creating a government that is of the people, as the United States and its allies did in both Iraq and Afghanistan. Building popular legitimacy is more involved than casting a vote.

State-Building and Nation-Building Never End

Building the state and the nation is not a finite exercise; it is not a program that is initiated at a certain point and then completed in five, ten, or fifty years. Rather, building the state and the nation is an ever-continuing process that requires constant adjustments to meet the demands of the people, their sense of national unity, and the role of the state. Furthermore, state- and nation-building efforts are not linear; these initiatives have impressive leaps forward at some points and slide back to previous stages of development at others. State-building and nation-building, therefore, should be thought of not as unidirectional progress over time but more as a dialogue within the population and between the population and the government. As such, state-building and particularly nation-building are ever evolving and occasionally devolving.

One need only look at modern-day Europe to see this process in action. Changes within individual states and between governments and the European Union are ongoing. Scotland put to vote the possibility of declaring independence from Great Britain in 2014. Greece threatened to withdraw from the Eurozone in 2015. The United Kingdom voted to leave the EU in 2016. Catalonia voted to secede from Spain in 2017. Even the birthplace of states is in flux over what it means to be a state. Similarly debates over what it means to be French, Dutch, British, Spanish, or German are contentious and in transition, particularly with the influx of non-European migrants to these countries.

Similar adjustments are visible in the United States. The United States continuously struggles with what equality means, arguably one of the most important tenets of its constitution.

The United States fought a civil war over the issue of slavery and equal rights, had a civil rights movement a century later over equal rights among races, followed by women's rights, immigration rights, and gay rights, all around this foundational issue of the Constitution. Similarly, the United States has struggled with the rights of its central government vis-à-vis states' rights, the right of women to vote, what the legal voting age should be, and whether health care is a right or a privilege. States or nations are never fully made for all time. Expectations should be set with both developing states and those aiding these states that state-building and nation-building require constant vigilance.

State- and Nation-Building Forces for the Twenty-First Century

In theory most of the tasks of state-building and nation-building should fall to civilian agencies. U.S. agencies such as USAID and the U.S. Department of State, and NGOs and IOs more broadly, have access to an infinite repository of knowledge, specialization and expertise on population engagement, education, civil-society building, democracy promotion, and so on. These should be the forces that develop states and nations.

In practice, however, militaries will most likely be the entity to which these tasks fall, particularly in the near term, for several key reasons. First, not all civilian entities are equipped or prepared to work amid violence and significant unrest, what the U.S. military calls a "semi-permissive" environment. Militaries, by definition, are capable of providing their own security and, if tasked, of protecting the population in semi-permissive environments. This capability makes them the natural choice in the early stages of state-building and national-unity building, particularly in a state fraught with security problems.

Second, resources, funding, and manpower present a major challenge for civilian agencies engaged in building the state and the nation, particularly on a large scale. For example, in the United States, the U.S. Department of State (DOS) receives a fraction of the annual budget relative to the Department of Defense (DOD). For fiscal year 2015, the DOD was allocated $495.6 billion for its total operating budget, while the DOS and USAID were given just $50.3 billion and over $46 billion for overseas operations.[8] Alongside significantly greater financial resources, the DOD outmans the DOS exponentially, with nearly 1.4 million active-duty troops and another 850,000 reservists compared to the State Department's 13,000 foreign service officers and foreign service specialists. Moreover, the U.S. military is unparalleled in its ability to move large numbers of troops and matériel around the world, by both air and sea, giving it an operational edge over its civilian counterparts.

Furthermore, leadership and chain of command differ between the military and civilian agencies, giving militaries better unity of effort and accountability than their civilian counterparts. While some civilian organizations, such as the Department of State, have a clear chain of command, other civilian agencies, such as NGOS, are structured differently; most do not have an operational chain of command as in the military, making coordination within agencies across space and between agencies exponentially difficult and most likely hindering unity of effort.

Given these observations, militaries—including the U.S. military—need training and education to prepare for these missions, particularly the officers' corps, which will be responsible for much of the operational planning. Population-centric warfare, state stabilization, state-building, combatting non-state actor safe havens, and natural disaster interdiction are all examples of complex operations that require working with and through the population to achieve mission success. To prepare for these missions, the U.S. military should be educated beyond conventional state-on-state warfare, for which it has historically been trained, because population-centric warfare will undoubtedly continue to be more prevalent in the foreseeable future.

To be sure, there are those who claim that training the military in anything other than the management of "kinetic operations," the use of force, is a mistake. Within the military are voices that proclaim "war is about killing and destruction; it is not armed social science." Within the civilian and NGO world, there are those who assert that using the military in these complex operations militarizes humanitarian space.[9] However, the cost of being unprepared for managing these complex forms of warfare is too great to continue with just a state-on-state mentality of warfare.

Militaries, however, should plan to hand off operations to civilian agencies and groups as quickly as possible. To prepare for this, the United States specifically should think of state-building and national-unity building as a "whole of nation" approach, as opposed to a U.S. military and Department of State effort, or even a "whole of government approach." The U.S. government has considerable resources that should be mobilized for state- and nation-building efforts, including experts in agricultural management in the U.S. Department of Agriculture, forest and park management in the U.S. Department of Forestry and Bureau of Land Management, regulations in finance in the Department of Treasury, and legal issues in the Department of Justice, to name but a few. Individuals from these departments and agencies were deployed to Iraq and Afghanistan on an ad hoc basis. But moving forward the U.S. government should create a culture of deployment within these departments, particularly with incoming junior civil servants, and reward assignments in state-building initiatives with promotions and other career advancement. The vast array of U.S. government resources are too useful to go unutilized.

Beyond the U.S. government, efforts at state-building and fostering national unity should include mobilizing the whole nation. This could include encouraging private enterprise to form partnerships with fledgling industries in stabilizing states. It could also foster collaborations between universities, including faculty and student exchange programs. U.S. sports, art, music, and museum curation should be leveraged as a resource that could help recovering states construct and maintain these important tools of national-unity building. Sister cities relationships should be fostered between American cities and cities in stabilizing countries, and their local fire departments and emergency services could create partnerships with the aim of sharing best practices.

Just as state-building needs to start with the people in countries that are weakened and fractured, so too should the United States start with its own people to foster state-building and national-unity building. In fact the strongest asset for building the state and national unity in the United States is its people, and together with its government, the people can do much to erode negative perceptions of the United States and its intentions while working toward the stability and prosperity of the countries it aims to help.

NOTES

1. Bringing the Nation Back into Nation-Building

1. Scott Atran, "The Role of Youth in Countering Violent Extremism and Promoting Peace," brief to UN Security Council, April 23, 2015, http://blogs.plos .org/neuroanthropology/2015/04/25/scott-atran-on-youth-violent-extremism -and-promoting-peace/, emphasis in original.

2. Atran, "Role of Youth," emphasis in original.

3. Perito, *Guide for Participants*, xxxiv.

4. Anderson, *Imagined Communities*, 6, italics in original.

5. Fukuyama, *State-Building*, 99.

6. Livingston and O'Hanlon, *Iraq Index: 2007*; and Barfield, *Afghanistan*, 277–78.

7. These interviews were conducted on the basis of anonymity to protect participants' identities and in accordance with the Naval Postgraduate School's Institutional Review Board for Protection of Human Subjects.

2. States, Nations, Nationalism, and National Unity

1. Eller, *From Culture to Ethnicity*, 16.

2. See, for example, "Treaty of Westphalia: Article CXVII," The Avalon Project, http://avalon.law.yale.edu/17th_century/westphal.asp.

3. Weber, "Politics as Vocation." See also Weber, *Economy and Society*, 2:956.

4. Strayer, *Medieval Origins of the Modern State*; Tilly, "Reflections on the History," 6 and 70, respectively.

5. Eller, *From Culture to Ethnicity*, 16–17.

6. Ghani, Lockhart, and Carnahan, "Closing the Sovereignty Gap." See also Ghani and Lockhart, *Fixing Failed States*.

7. Rotberg, "Failure and Collapse of Nation-States," 2.

8. Buzan, *People, States and Fear*, 65–67.

9. Posner, "Civil Society."

10. Tocqueville, *Democracy in America*, 1:106.

11. Tilly, "Reflections on the History," 6 and 7, respectively.

12. Connor, *Ethnonationalism*.

13. Greenfeld, *Nationalism*, 3–9.

14. Connor, "Timelessness of Nations," 36.

15. Connor, "Timelessness of Nations," 37. See also Connor, "Nation-Building or Nation-Destroying?," 320.

16. A. Smith, *National Identity*, 40.

17. Mill, *Considerations on Representative Government*.

18. Eller and Coughlan, "Poverty of Primordialism." See also Bayar, "Reconsidering Primordialism."

19. Brubaker, *Nationalism Reframed*; Gellner, *Nations and Nationalism*; Hobsbawm, *Nations and Nationalism since 1780*.

20. Renan, "What Is a Nation?," 6, 5.

21. Renan, "What Is a Nation?," 8.

22. Renan, "What Is a Nation?," 9, 10.

23. Renan, "What Is a Nation?," 10.

24. Renan, "What Is a Nation?," 10.

25. Renan, "What Is a Nation?," 11.

26. Connor, "Timelessness of Nations," 35.

27. Anderson, *Imagined Communities*, 6, italics in original.

28. Brubaker, *Nationalism Reframed*, 16. Brubaker, "In the Name of the Nation."

29. Weber, *Economy and Society*, 2:922–23.

30. Gellner, *Nations and Nationalism*, 1. Also cited in Hobsbawm, *Nations and Nationalism since 1780*, 9.

31. Greenfeld, *Nationalism*, 8–11.

32. For economies, see Gellner, *Nations and Nationalism*, 89–109.

33. Anderson, *Imagined Communities*, 4. For communications as a key driver of nationalism, see Deutsch, *Nationalism and Social Communication*.

34. Breuilly, *Nationalism and the State*.

35. Breuilly, for example, names the following forms of nationalism: religious, unification, separatist, anticolonial, subnational, reform, and pan-nationalism; see *Nationalism and the State*.

36. A. Smith, "Ethnic Sources of Nationalism," 28–29.

37. A. Smith, "Dating the Nation," 65, quoted in Connor, "Timelessness of Nations," 37.

38. Connor, "Nation-Building or Nation-Destroying?," 331.

39. See, for example, Van Evera, "Hypotheses on Nationalism and War."

40. See, for example, Eliade, *Myth of Eternal Return*; Campbell, *Power of Myth*; Levi-Strauss, *Myth and Meaning*; K. Armstrong, *Short History of Myth*; Segal, *Myth*.

41. Eliade, *Myth and Reality*, 5, 18–19.

42. K. Armstrong, *Short History of Myth*, 2, 4, and 7.

43. Levi-Strauss, *Myth and Meaning*, viii.

44. Segal, *Myth*, 4.

45. Armstrong, *Short History of Myth*, 10.

46. Segal, *Myth*, 61, 63, italics in original.

47. Greenfeld, *Nationalism*, 10.

48. See, for example United Nations General Assembly Resolution 1514 (XV), "Declaration on the Granting of Independence to Colonial Countries and People," December 14, 1960, http://www.un.org/en/decolonization/declaration.shtml.

49. See, for example, Horowitz, *Ethnic Groups in Conflict*; Ramet, *Balkan Babble*; Brown, *Nationalism and Ethnic Conflict*; Brown, *Ethnic Conflict and International Security*; Brubaker, *Nationalism Reframed*.

50. Juergensmeyer, *New Cold War?*, 30–35.

51. Juergensmeyer, *New Cold War*; and Juergensmeyer, *Terror in the Mind of God*. See also Gregg, *Path to Salvation*.

52. Verba, "Introduction."

53. Verba, "Introduction," 4.

54. See, for example, Zakaria, *Future of Freedom*.

55. Tocqueville, *Democracy in America*, vol. 1.

56. Tocqueville, *Democracy in America*, 1:107.

57. Tocqueville, *Democracy in America*, 1:106, 110.

58. Lipset, *Political Man*.

59. See, for example, Lubragge, "Manifest Destiny."

60. Verba, "Introduction," 5, quoting Jean-Jacques Rousseau, *Social Contract*, 41.

61. Eller, *From Culture to Ethnicity*, 29.

62. Kaufmann, "Possible and Impossible Solutions."

63. Snyder, *From Voting to Violence*, 322–38.

64. "The Supreme Court of the United States: Mission," U.S. Supreme Court, http://www.supremecourt.gov/about/about_us.aspx.

65. Fukuyama, "Social Capital."

3. State- and Nation-Building in Europe and the U.S.

1. Epstein, "Rise and Fall of Italian City States."

2. See, for example, P. Jones, *Italian City-State*; Stark, *Victory of Reason*.

3. Van Zanden and Prak, "Towards an Economic Interpretation," 112.

4. Machiavelli, *Discourses on Livy*.

5. Van Geldern and Skinner, *Republicanism*, vol. 2.

6. Parker, *Thirty Years' War*. There is considerable debate about the actual numbers killed.

7. Habermas, Lennox, and Lennox, "Public Sphere," 49. See also Habermas, *Structural Transformation of the Public Sphere*.

8. Gellner, *Nations and Nationalism*, 19–38

9. Hobbes, *Elements of Law*; Hobbes, *Leviathan*.

10. Locke, *Political Writings*.

11. Rousseau, *Social Contract*.

12. "1689 English Bill of Rights," The Avalon Project, http://avalon.law.yale.edu/17th_century/england.asp.

13. Locke, *Second Treatise of Government*; and Locke, *An Essay concerning Human Understanding*.

14. Montesquieu, *Spirit of Laws*.

15. "Declaration of Independence," July 4, 1776, http://www.archives.gov/exhibits/charters/declaration_transcript.html.

16. For the common defense, see *Federalist Papers* nos. 2–5, and *Federalist Papers* no. 24; for the right to tax, see *Federalist Papers* nos. 31–36; for the structure of government and checks and balances, see *Federalist Papers* nos. 51–84, all at http://thomas.loc.gov/home/histdox/fedpapers.html.

17. Hobsbawm, *Nations and Nationalism*, 51.

18. Hobsbawm, *Nations and Nationalism*, 54.

19. Hobsbawm, *Nations and Nationalism*, 54–58.

20. Boli, Ramirez, and Meyer, "Explaining the Origins."

21. Gellner, "Nationalism," 757.

22. Tocqueville, *Democracy in America*, 111.

23. Anderson, *Imagined Communities*.

24. Copeland, *Colonial American Newspapers*.

25. Beard, "Written History," 219.

26. Gellner, *Nations and Nationalism*, 37; and Blanning, *Culture of Power*.

27. Finer, "State- and Nation-Building," 88.

28. Lytle, "Robespierre, Dalton and Levee en Masse."

29. "The Levee en Masse, August 23, 1793," Modern History Sourcebook, http://www.fordham.edu/halsall/mod/1793levee.asp.

30. "Levee en Masse."

31. Finer, "State- and Nation-Building," 144–45.

32. Finer, "State- and Nation-Building," 144–51.

33. Vagts, *History of Militarism*, 13.

34. Finer, "State- and Nation-Building," 163.

35. Weber, *Economy and Society*, 956.

36. Weber, *Economy and Society*, 957.

37. Braun, "Taxation in Britain and Prussia," 244.

38. Braun, "Taxation in Britain and Prussia," 233; Kiser and Linton, "Determinants."

39. Tilly, "War Making and State Making."

40. Braun, "Taxation in Britain and Prussia," 244, citing Mann, "Sociology of Taxation," 225.

41. Gellner, "Nationalism," 757.

42. Hobsbawm, *Nations and Nationalism*, 56–57.

43. Kyridis et al., "Nationalism through State Constructed Symbols."

44. Cerulo, "Symbols and the World System," 245.

45. Cerulo, "Symbols and the World System," 244.

46. See, for example, Whitney, *Flags throughout the Ages*.

47. After the Republic of Ireland's independence in 1921, it adopted its own flag. The Union Jack has continued to represent Northern Ireland. "The Union Jack," Official Website of the British Monarchy, https://www.royal.gov.uk/MonarchUK/Symbols/UnionJack.aspx.

48. Cerulo, "Symbols and the World System," 245.

49. Madden, "Flags," 125.

50. For the Dutch national anthem, see "Wilhelmus," Het Koninklijk Hus, http://www.koninklijkhuis.nl/encyclopedie/monarchie/volkslied-(wilhelmus). For the British national anthem, see "The British National Anthem," Official Website of the British Monarchy, https://www.royal.gov.uk/MonarchUK/Symbols /NationalAnthem.aspx. For "The Star-Spangled Banner," see "The Star-Spangled Banner," Smithsonian Institution, http://amhistory.si.edu/starspangledbanner /national-anthem.aspx.

51. Trachtenberg, *Statue of Liberty*, 15.

52. Pohlsander, *National Monuments*, 20.

53. Pohlsander, *National Monuments*, 13, 14, 18.

54. Trachtenberg, *Statue of Liberty*, 15–40.

55. Cannidine, "Context, Performance, and Meaning of Ritual," 126.

56. "Trafalgar Square: A Brief History," https://www.london.gov.uk/priorities /arts-culture/trafalgar-square/history.

57. "Royal Residences; Buckingham Palace," The Royal Family, https://www .royal.uk/royal-residences-buckingham-palace.

58. Saalman, *Haussmann*. See also Blanning, *Culture of Power*.

59. Cannidine, "Context, Performance, and Meaning of Ritual," 126–27.

60. Oliver, *From Royal to National*.

61. Smithson quoted in Meringolo, *Museums, Monuments, and National Parks*, 7.

62. Meringolo, *Museums, Monuments, and National Parks*, 31–32. Anderson also notes the importance of the creation of museums for building imagined communities. See Anderson, *Imagined Communities*, 167–90.

63. See Saalman, *Haussmann*.

64. Meringolo, *Museums, Monuments, and National Parks*, 11–12.

65. Fox, *John Muir and His Legacy*.

66. Meringolo, *Museums, Monuments, and National Parks*, 48–55.

67. Pohlsander, *National Monuments*, 27. See also Blanning, *Culture of Power*.

68. Pohlsander, *National Monuments*, 29.

69. "Mark Twain," The Official Website of Mark Twain, http://www.cmgww .com/historic/twain/about/quotes.htm.

70. Hobsbawm, "Introduction," 1.

71. Cannidine, "Context, Performance, and Meaning of Ritual," 121–22. See also Blanning, *Culture of Power*.

72. Cannidine, "Context, Performance, and Meaning of Ritual, 122.

73. Loewen, *Lies My Teacher Told Me*.

4. State-Building Programs Post 9/11

1. Dobbins, et al., *America's Role in Nation-Building*; Dobbins et al., *UN's Role in Nation-Building*; Dobbins et al., *Europe's Role in Nation-Building*; Dobbins et al, *Beginner's Guide to Nation-Building*.

2. For example, see Dobbins et al., *un's Role in Nation-Building*; Dobbins et al., *Europe's Role in Nation-Building*; Perito, *Guide for Participants*.

3. Perito, *Guide for Participants in Peace*, xxxiv.

4. U.S. Institute of Peace and U.S. Army Peacekeeping and Stability Operations Institute, *Guiding Principles*, 8–98.

5. Perito, *Guide for Participants*, xxxvii.

6. U.S. Department of the Army, "FM 3-07: Stability Operations," 2008; and U.S. Department of the Army, "FM 3-07: Stability Operations," 2014.

7. U.S. Department of the Army, "FM 3-07," 2014, 1–1.

8. U.S. Department of the Army, "FM 3-07," 2014, 1–2.

9. Dobbins et al., *Beginner's Guide to Nation-Building*, xvii.

10. Dobbins et al., *America's Role in Nation-Building*, 149.

11. See, for example Dobbins et al., *un's Role in Nation-Building*; and Dobbins et al., *Europe's Role in Nation-Building*.

12. Dobbins et al., *Beginner's Guide to Nation-Building*, 95–102, here 95.

13. Dobbins et al., *Beginner's Guide to Nation-Building*, 191.

14. Fukuyama, *State-Building*, ix.

15. Fukuyama, *State-Building*, 7.

16. Fukuyama, *State-Building*, 99.

17. Fukuyama, *State-Building*, 100–101. Fukuyama also edited a volume on nation-building, with a focus on U.S. efforts. See Fukuyama, *Nation-Building*.

18. Meierhenrich, "Forming States after Failure," 155.

19. Meierhenrich, "Forming States after Failure," 155, emphasis mine.

20. Meierhenrich, "Forming States after Failure," 156.

21. Meierhenrich, "Forming States after Failure," 159.

22. Ghani and Lockhart, *Fixing Failed States*, 124–63.

23. Ghani and Lockhart, *Fixing Failed States*, 144.

24. Kilcullen, *Accidental Guerilla*, 265–69.

25. Etzioni, "Self-Restrained Approach."

26. Dodge, *Inventing Iraq*, xxiv.

27. Dodge, *Inventing Iraq*, xxvi.

28. Lemay-Hébert, "Statebuilding without Nation-Building?"

29. Fukuyama, *State-Building*, 99.

30. As described by George Z. F. Bereday, "An Introduction," 18. See also Merriam, *Making of Citizens*.

31. Merriam, *Making of Citizens*, 34, 297–301.

32. Merriam, *Making of Citizens*, 309.

33. Merriam, *Making of Citizens*, 309–38.

34. Kilcullen, *Accidental Guerilla*, 263–90.

35. Rothstein, "Lessons from Reconstructing Security Forces."

36. Fukuyama, *Great Disruption*, 3–26; Fukuyama, "Social Capital."

37. Merriam, *Making of Citizens*, 18.

38. Perito, *Guide for Participants in Peace*, xxxvi.

39. Mansfield and Snyder, "Democratization and War."

40. Weber, *Theory of Social and Economic Organization*, 328.

41. Weber, *Theory of Social and Economic Organization*, 324–432.

42. Ghani and Lockhart, *Fixing Failed States*, 202–11.

43. Perito, *Guide for Participants in Peace*, xxxvi; Ghani and Lockhart, *Fixing Failed States*, 124–66.

44. Dobbins et al., *America's Role in Nation-Building*, 149–66.

45. Perito, *Guide for Participants in Peace*, xxxvi.

46. Fukuyama, "Social Capital."

47. Widner, "Building Effective Trust."

5. State-Building in Iraq, 2003–2011

1. "Remarks by the President and First Lady on the End of the War in Iraq," The White House, December 14, 2011, http://www.whitehouse.gov/the-press-office/2011/12/14/remarks-president-and-first-lady-end-war-iraq.

2. Trotta, "Iraq War Costs More Than $2 Trillion: Study," *Reuters*, March 14, 2013, http://www.reuters.com/article/2013/03/14/us-iraq-war-anniversary-idUSBRE92D0PG20130314.

3. Dodge, *Inventing Iraq*, 4–30. See also Marr, *Modern History of Iraq*, 5–8.

4. Dodge, *Inventing Iraq*, 1–41. See also Dodge, "Iraq"; Tripp, *History of Iraq*, 44–50.

5. Tripp, *History of Iraq*, 48.

6. Tripp, *History of Iraq*, 64.

7. Al-Rawi, *Media Practice in Iraq*, 8–10.

8. Al-Rawi, *Media Practice in Iraq*, 10.

9. Al-Rawi, *Media Practice in Iraq*, 11–13.

10. Baram, "Neo-Tribalism in Iraq."

11. Tripp, *History of Iraq*, 215.

12. International Crisis Group, "Shiite Politics in Iraq," i.

13. International Crisis Group, "Shiite Politics in Iraq," 3.

14. Tripp, *History of Iraq*, 234–37.

15. Dave Johns, "The Crimes of Saddam Hussein: Suppression of the 1991 Uprisings," *Frontline*, January 24, 2006, http://www.pbs.org/frontlineworld/stories/iraq501/events_uprising.html.

16. Robinson, "Notes on Iraqi Identity," 11.

17. Tripp, *History of Iraq*, 244–65.

18. "Iraq Economic Data (1989–2003)," Central Intelligence Agency, https://www.cia.gov/library/reports/general-reports-1/iraq_wmd_2004/chap2_annxD.html.

19. "Iraq Economic Data (1989–2003)."

20. Ricks, *Fiasco*, 3.

21. Ricks, *Fiasco*, 22.

22. Ricks, *Fiasco*, 48, emphasis in original.

23. Ricks, *Fiasco*, 43.

24. Ricks, *Fiasco*, 32.

25. "Iraq's Continuing Program for WMD," National Intelligence Estimate, September 2002, http://www2.gwu.edu/~nsarchiv/NSAEBB/NSAEBB129/nie.pdf.

26. Ricks, *Fiasco*, 35, 56–57.

27. Ricks, *Fiasco*, 37.

28. Ricks, *Fiasco*, 70–73.

29. Ricks, *Fiasco*, 67.

30. Eric Schmitt, "Army Chief Raises Estimates of G.I.'s Needed in Post War Iraq," *New York Times*, February 25, 2003, http://www.nytimes.com/2003/02/25 /international/middleeast/25CND-MILI.html.

31. Schmitt, "Army Chief Raises Estimates."

32. Clawson, *How to Build a New Iraq*.

33. See Karadaghi, "Managing Ethnic Tensions."

34. "The Future of Iraq Project: Overview," U.S. Department of State, May 12, 2003, http://www2.gwu.edu/~nsarchiv/NSAEBB/NSAEBB198/.

35. Bensahel et al., *After Saddam*, 41–72.

36. Aaron and Meyers, "Cost of Exile."

37. Dobbins et al., *America's Role in Nation-Building*, 149–66.

38. Recognizing this, the Brookings Institution began to measure civilian casualties, among other things, in Iraq beginning in 2003. See Livingston and O'Hanlon, *Iraq Index: July 26, 2013*.

39. Ricks, *Fiasco*, 135–38.

40. Bogdanos, "Thieves of Baghdad," 725. See also Bogdanos, "Casualties of War"; "The Looting of Iraq's National Museum," Stanford University Cultural Heritage Resource, https://web.stanford.edu/group/chr/drupal/ref/the-2003 -looting-of-the-iraq-national-museum.

41. Bensahel et al., *After Saddam*, 36, 121.

42. Edmund L. Andrews, "Envoy's Letter Counters Bush on Dismantling of Iraqi Army," *New York Times*, September 4, 2007, http://www.nytimes.com /2007/09/04/washington/04bremer.html?r=0. See also Dobbins et al., *Occupying Iraq*.

43. Bensahel et al., *After Saddam*, 121–22.

44. Bensahel et al., *After Saddam*, 125, 139–42.

45. International Crisis Group, "*Iraq*," 139–45.

46. "Disbanded Army Draws Praise, Condemnation," *Washington Post*, January 5, 2004, http://www.washingtontimes.com/news/2004/jan/5/20040105 -114522–6340r/?page=all.

47. Bensahel et al., *After Saddam*, 124–28.

48. "Iraq 'Death Squad Caught in the Act,'" BBC *News*, February 16, 2006, http://news.bbc.co.uk/2/hi/middle_east/4719252.stm.

49. Bensahel et al., *After Saddam*, 142–44.

50. Bensahel et al., *After Saddam*, 147.

51. Deady, "MiTT Advisor."

52. Class conversation with U.S. and international officers as part of "Culture and Influence," Fall quarter 2009.

53. See, for example, Rose, "Heads in the Sand." See also Wilbanks and Karsh, "'Sons of Iraq' Stabilized Iraq."

54. Tom Peter, "The Sons of Iraq Made Iraq Safer, What Is Their Mission Now?," *Christian Science Monitor*, July 30, 2008, http://www.csmonitor.com/2008/0730/p10s01-wome.html. See also Scott Peterson, "An Uncertain Future for the Sons of Iraq," *Christian Science Monitor*, October 3, 2008, http://www.csmonitor.com/2008/1003/p07s02-wome.html.

55. Thomas and Barry, "New Way of War."

56. Greg Bruno, "Finding a Place for the Sons of Iraq," *Council on Foreign Relations Backgrounder*, April 23, 2008, http://www.cfr.org/iraq/finding-place-sons-iraq/p16088.

57. Alexandra Zavis, "Daughters of Iraq: Women Take on a Security Role," *Los Angeles Times*, June 4, 2008, http://www.latimes.com/news/nationworld/world/la-fg-daughters4-2008jun04,0,7497772.story.

58. Porter, "Iraqi Prime Minister Al-Maliki."

59. "President Bush Discusses Freedom in Iraq and the Middle East," The White House, November 6, 2003, http://georgewbush-whitehouse.archives.gov/news/releases/2003/11/20031106-2.html.

60. Douglas Jehl with Eric Schmitt, "U.S. Reported to Push for Iraqi Government, with Pentagon Prevailing," *New York Times*, April 30, 2003, http://www.nytimes.com/2003/04/30/international/worldspecial/30POLI.html. See also Bensahel et al., *After Saddam*, 160–64.

61. Emphasis theirs. "The Future of Iraq Project: The Iraqi Component," U.S. Department of State, March 10, 2006, https://nsarchive2.gwu.edu/NSAEBB/NSAEBB198/20020005.pdf.

62. Regarding Chalabi, see Rajiv Chandrasekaran, "Exile Finds Ties to U.S. a Boon and a Barrier," *Washington Post*, April 27, 2003, http://www.washingtonpost.com/archive/politics/2003/04/27/exile-finds-ties-to-us-a-boon-and-a-barrier/0b87f222-6ccb-49e3-a521-fa3e1dd41b01/.

63. Bensahel et al., *After Saddam*, 166.

64. Bensahel et al., *After Saddam*, 175–76. See also Rajiv Chandrasekaran, "Interim Leaders Named in Iraq," *Washington Post*, June 2, 2004, http://www.washingtonpost.com/wp-dyn/articles/A7879-2004Jun1.html; Robin Wright, "Iraqis Back New Leaders, Poll Says," *Washington Post*, June 25, 2004, http://www.washingtonpost.com/wp-dyn/articles/a3433-2004jun24.html.

65. Snyder, *From Voting to Violence*.

66. Bensahel et al., *After Saddam*, 183.

67. Bensahel et al., *After Saddam*, 183.

68. "The Future of Iraq Project: Local Government Working Group," U.S. Department of State, June 22, 2005, https://nsarchive2.gwu.edu//NSAEBB/NSAEBB198/FOI%20Local%20Govt.pdf.

69. Hersh, "Chain of Command."

70. Hersh, "Torture at Abu Ghraib?"

71. Feldman, "Democratic Fatwa," 6. See also, Diamond, "What Went Wrong and Right in Iraq," 189–92.

72. Rahimi, *Ayatollah Sistani*, 1.

73. Rahimi, *Ayatollah Sistani*, 1. See also International Crisis Group, *Iraq's Constitutional Challenge*.

74. Bensahel et al., *After Saddam*, 181.

75. "Constitution of the Republic of Iraq," October 15, 2005, http://www .iraqinationality.gov.iq/attach/iraqi_constitution.pdf.

76. "Constitution of the Republic of Iraq."

77. Francis Gibb, "U.S. Sets Aside $75m for Putting Saddam on Trial," *London Times*, January 9, 2004, http://www.thetimes.co.uk/tto/news/world/middleeast /iraq/article1995164.ece.

78. Stephen Franklin, "Mass Graves 'Are Everywhere,'" *Chicago Tribune*, January 21, 2004, http://articles.chicagotribune.com/2004-01-21/news/0401210319 _1_mass-graves-iraqis-saddam-hussein.

79. For a summary of recommendations for Iraq's tribunal, see Miller, *Building the Iraqi Special Tribunal*.

80. Gerry G. Gillmore, "The Bulk of Iraq Reconstruction Monies 'Will Come from Iraqis,' Rumsfeld Says," American Forces Press Services, U.S. Department of Defense, October 2, 2003, http://www.defense.gov/news/newsarticle .aspx?id=28388.

81. "Oil Ministry an Untouched Building in Ravaged Baghdad," *AFP Report*, April 16, 2003, http://www.smh.com.au/articles/2003/04/16/1050172643895.html.

82. See, for example, Antonia Juhasz, "Why the War in Iraq Was Fought for Big Oil," *CNN*, April 15, 2013, http://www.cnn.com/2013/03/19/opinion/iraq -war-oil-juhasz/.

83. Johnson, "Iraq's Oil War."

84. Blanchard, "Iraq."

85. "Constitution of the Republic of Iraq."

86. Blanchard, "Iraq," 15.

87. Barlett and Steele, "Billions over Baghdad."

88. "Much of $60 B from U.S. to Rebuild Iraq Wasted, Special Auditor's Final Report to Congress Shows," *CBS News*, March 6, 2013, http://www.cbsnews .com/news/much-of-60b-from-us-to-rebuild-iraq-wasted-special-auditors-final -report-to-congress-shows/2/.

89. "Iraq: Agriculture," USAID, http://www.usaid.gov/iraq/agriculture.

90. Livingston and O'Hanlon, *Iraq Index: July 26, 2013*.

91. U.S. Department of Defense, *Measuring Stability and Security in Iraq*.

92. Livingston and O'Hanlon, *Iraq Index: November 2003*, 13.

93. "Declaration of the Shia in Iraq," Al-Bab.com, July 2002, http://www.al -bab.com/arab/docs/iraq/shia02a.htm.

94. "Declaration of the Shia in Iraq."

95. Diamond, "What Went Wrong in Iraq," 47.

6. Counterfactual State-, Nation-Building in Iraq

1. Livingston and O'Hanlon, *Iraq Index: October 1, 2007*, 51.

2. Livingston and O'Hanlon, *Iraq Index: October 1, 2007*, 55.

3. Livingston and O'Hanlon, *Iraq Index: November 19, 2003*, 13.

4. Kaldor, *Human Security*.

5. "7 Rules, 1 Oath," *Michael Yon Online Magazine*, July 19, 2007, https://www.michaelyon-online.com/7-rules-1-oath.htm.

6. "7 Rules, 1 Oath."

7. Bensahel et al., *After Saddam*, 183. See also William Booth, "U.S.-Run Local Election Touted as 'First Step' for Iraqis," *Washington Post*, May 25, 2003; Sabrina Tavernise, "Kurds Celebrate Elections of Mayor in Kirkuk," *New York Times*, May 29, 2003.

8. "Declaration of the Shia in Iraq," Al-Bab.com, July 2002, http://www.al-bab.com/arab/docs/iraq/shia02a.htm.

9. For more on bringing insurgents into the political process, see Gregg, "Setting a Place at the Table."

10. See, for example, Gregg, *Employment Handbook for Fighting Counterinsurgencies*.

11. See, for example, Schultheis, *Waging Peace*. See also Gavrilis, "Mayor of Ar Rutbah;" Stewart, *Prince of the Marshes*.

12. Meierhenrich, "Forming States after Failure," 156.

13. Verba, "Introduction to the Civic Culture Concept."

14. Diamond, "What Went Wrong in Iraq," 34–56.

15. For more on the NSP, see Ghani and Lockhart, *Fixing Failed States*, 206–11. See also Nagl, Exum, and Humayun, "*Pathway to Success in Afghanistan*.

16. Tom Hundley, "Surprising Iraq Thrills Its Fans," *Chicago Tribune*, August 16, 2004, http://articles.chicagotribune.com/2004-08-16/sports/0408160264_1_iraqi-team-uday-hussein-surprising-iraq.

17. James Klattel, "Iraqi Wins Arab 'Idol' Competition," CBS *News Online*, March 31, 2007, http://www.cbsnews.com/news/iraqi-wins-arab-idol-competition/.

18. Stewart, *Prince of the Marshes*, 86–100.

19. Erica Gies, "Restoring Iraq's Garden of Eden," *New York Times*, April 17, 2013.

20. "Iraq Aims to Unite with New Iraqi Flag, Anthem," *Daily Star: Lebanon*, September 24, 2004, http://www.dailystar.com.lb/News/Middle-East/2012/Sep-24/189006-iraq-aims-to-unite-with-new-national-anthem-flag.ashx. See also Nadir, "Iraqis Divided over New National Anthem."

7. State-Building in Afghanistan, 2001–2016

1. "Agreement on Provisional Arrangements in Afghanistan Pending the Re-Establishment of Permanent Government Institutions," United Nations, http://www.un.org/News/dh/latest/afghan/afghan-agree.htm. See also Howard French, "More Than $4.5 Billion Pledged Afghan Aid Effort," *New York Times*, January 22, 2002, http://www.nytimes.com/2002/01/22/international/asia/22AID.html.

2. Barfield, *Afghanistan*, 3–8.

3. For demographics, see "Country Profile: Afghanistan," *Library of Congress Country Studies on Afghanistan*, August 2008, http://web.archive.org/web/20140408085103/http://lcweb2.loc.gov/frd/cs/profiles/Afghanistan.pdf. For Sufis, see Dawood Azami, "Sufis Return to Afghanistan after Years of Repression," BBC *News*, February 23, 2011, http://www.bbc.com/news/world-south-asia-12539409.

4. Barfield, *Afghanistan*, 21, emphasis in original.

5. Barfield, *Afghanistan*, 21.

6. Barfield, *Afghanistan*, 8.

7. Barfield, *Afghanistan*, 99–105. See also Ewans, *Afghanistan*, 23–26.

8. For a detailed account of the First Anglo-Afghan War, see Norris, *First Afghan War*.

9. For a detailed account of the Second Anglo-Afghan War, see MacGregor, *War in Afghanistan 1879–80*.

10. Barfield, *Afghanistan*, 146–159, here 151.

11. Barfield, *Afghanistan*, 159.

12. Dupree, *Afghanistan*, 442–43.

13. Barfield, *Afghanistan*, 182–83.

14. Dupree, *Afghanistan*, 459.

15. Dupree, *Afghanistan*, 464.

16. Rubin, *Fragmentation of Afghanistan*, 62–66.

17. Dupree, *Afghanistan*, 579.

18. Dupree, *Afghanistan*, 565–87, here 565.

19. Ewans, *Afghanistan*, 131–32.

20. For a detailed account of the foreign backing of the mujahedeen, see Coll, *Ghost Wars*, 53–70.

21. Wright, *Looming Tower*.

22. "Afghanistan 10 Years After Soviet Pull Out," UNHCR, February 12, 1999, http://www.unhcr.org/cgi-bin/texis/vtx/search?page=search&docid=3ae6b81cf0&query=Return%20to%20afghanistan.

23. "Afghanistan," The Halo Trust, http://www.halotrust.org/where-we-work/afghanistan.

24. Rubin, *Fragmentation of Afghanistan*, 8.

25. Barfield, *Afghanistan*, 13.

26. Nojumi, *Rise of the Taliban*, 117–24.

27. Matinuddin, *Taliban Phenomenon*, 25–26.

28. For a detailed account of the first days of the war in Afghanistan, see Rothstein, *Afghanistan*.

29. "Agreement on Provisional Arrangements."

30. "Afghan Donors Pledge $4.5 Billion in Tokyo," Relief Web, http://reliefweb.int/report/afghanistan/afghanistan-donors-pledge-45-billion-tokyo.

31. Barfield, *Afghanistan*, 72.

32. Christia and Semple, "Flipping the Taliban."

33. "A Conversation with General William B. Caldwell, IV," Council on Foreign Relations, June 7, 2011, http://www.cfr.org/afghanistan/conversation-general-william-b-caldwell-iv/p25207.

34. Kelly, Bensahel, and Oliker, *Security Force Assistance in Afghanistan*, 21.

35. Kelly, Bensahel, and Oliker, *Security Force Assistance in Afghanistan*, 22. See also S. Jones, *Counterinsurgency in Afghanistan*, 67–78.

36. Kelly, Bensahel, and Oliker, *Security Force Assistance in Afghanistan*, xv–xvi.

37. Kelly, Bensahel, and Oliker, *Security Force Assistance in Afghanistan*, xiv.

38. Kelly, Bensahel, and Oliker, *Security Force Assistance in Afghanistan*, xvi.

39. Caldwell and Finney, "Security, Capacity and Literacy," 23–27.

40. Warren, *Afghanistan in 2014*, 31.

41. S. Jones, *Counterinsurgency in Afghanistan*, 73.

42. Roggio and Lundquist, "Green on Blue Attacks."

43. Kelly, Bensahel, and Oliker, *Security Force Assistance in Afghanistan*, 53–63.

44. Kelly, Bensahel, and Oliker, *Security Force Assistance in Afghanistan*, 54.

45. Eric Schmitt, "U.S. Envoy's Cables Show Worries over Afghan Plans," *New York Times*, January 26, 2010, http://www.nytimes.com/2010/01/26/world /asia/26strategy.html?pagewanted=all&r=0.

46. See, for example: Dressler, "*Haqqani Network*; Fair and Ganguly, "An Unworthy Ally."

47. Schmitt, "U.S. Envoy's Cables Show Worries."

48. Dressler, *Haqqani Network*.

49. Interview with a U.S. Special Forces officer on vso, July 17, 2012; interview with a U.S. Special Forces officer on Foreign Internal Defense and vso in Afghanistan, May 18, 2012; interview with a U.S. Special Forces officer on Foreign Internal Defense and vso in Afghanistan, July 17, 2012; interview with a U.S. Army Special Forces officer on vso at the company level across Nanghahar, Nuristan, Konar, and Laghman (n2kl) Provinces in Afghanistan, July 17, 2012; interview with a U.S. Army Special Forces nco on vso in Afghanistan, May 16, 2012.

50. Interview with a U.S. Special Forces officer on vso, July 17, 2012; interview with a U.S. Army Special Forces nco on vso in Afghanistan, May 16, 2012.

51. Jost, *Defend, Defect or Desert?*

52. Sopko, *Why ansf Numbers Matter*.

53. Barfield, *Afghanistan*, 283–92.

54. Torabi, *Growing Challenge of Corruption*.

55. Schmitt, "U.S. Envoy's Cables Show Worries."

56. Barfield, *Afghanistan*, 65–109.

57. Schmitt, "U.S. Envoy's Cables Show Worries."

58. "Afghanistan," cia *World Factbook*, https://www.cia.gov/library/publications /the-world-factbook/geos/af.html.

59. "A Survey of Public Perception on Elections and Civic Education: Afghanistan," usaid and Democracy International, April 2013, http://democracy international.com/sites/default/files/ECE%20Survey%20Report.pdf, 3.

60. Taylor, "Afghanistan: April 2014."

61. Peceny and Bosin, "Winning with Warlords in Afghanistan," 604.

62. Peceny and Bosin, "Winning with Warlords in Afghanistan."

63. Carlotta Gall, "In Pakistan Border Towns, Taliban Has a Resurgence," *New York Times*. May 6, 2003, http://www.nytimes.com/2003/05/06/international /asia/06STAN.html.

64. Guistozzi, Franco, and Baczko, *Shadow Justice*. See also Shawe, *Afghanistan in 2013*.

65. Alissa J. Rubin, "Assassination Deals Blow to Peace Process in Afghanistan," *New York Times*, September 20, 2011, http://www.nytimes.com/2011/09/21/world/asia/Burhanuddin-Rabbani-afghan-peace-council-leader-assassinated.html?r=1&hp.

66. For data on Afghanistan's elections, see "Afghanistan Election Data," http://afghanistanelectiondata.org/front.

67. National Democratic Institute for International Affairs, *"September 2005 Parliamentary and Provincial Elections.*

68. National Democratic Institute for International Affairs, *2010 Wolesi Jirga Elections in Afghanistan.*

69. "Provincial Reconstruction Teams," USAID, http://www.usaid.gov/provincial-reconstruction-teams. PRTS were also used in Iraq from 2008 on.

70. Abbaszadeh et al., "Provincial Reconstruction Teams."

71. McNearny, "Stabilization and Reconstruction in Afghanistan."

72. "Agreement on Provisional Arrangements."

73. "Agreement on Provisional Arrangements."

74. International Crisis Group, *Afghanistan's Flawed Constitutional Process*; Thier, *Making of a Constitution in Afghanistan.*

75. Benard and Hachigian, *Democracy and Islam*, 1.

76. International Crisis Group, *Afghanistan's Flawed Constitutional Process*, 6–10.

77. "Islamic Republic of Afghanistan: The Constitution of Afghanistan," January 26, 2004, http://www.afghanembassy.com.pl/afg/images/pliki/TheConstitution.pdf.

78. International Crisis Group, *Afghanistan's Flawed Constitutional Process*, i.

79. U.S. Department of Defense, *Report on Progress towards Security*, 32–37.

80. U.S. Department of Defense, *Report on Progress towards Security*, 33.

81. U.S. Department of Defense, *Report on Progress towards Security.*

82. Guistozzi, Franco, and Baczko, *Shadow Justice.*

83. Azam Ahmed, "Taliban Justice Gains Favor as Official Afghan Courts Fail," *New York Times*. January 31, 2015, http://www.nytimes.com/2015/02/01/world/asia/taliban-justice-gains-favor-as-official-afghan-courts-fail.html?r=0.

84. See, for example, Sachs, "Notes on a New Sociology"; and Collier, *Bottom Billion.*

85. "Afghanistan: Agriculture," USAID, http://www.usaid.gov/afghanistan/agriculture.

86. Charles Q. Choi, "$1 Trillion Trove of Rare Minerals Revealed under Afghanistan," Livescience, September 4, 2014, http://www.livescience.com/47682-rare-earth-minerals-found-under-afghanistan.html.

87. Ahmadzai, *Investment Opportunities.*

88. French, "More Than $4.5 Billion Pledged."

89. Dobbins et al., *America's Role in Nation-Building*, 156–58.

90. Poole, *Afghanistan.*

91. The Afghan Reconstruction Trust Fund, http://www.artf.af/who-we-are.

92. "Securing Afghanistan's Future: Accomplishments and the Strategic Path

Forward," Afghan Government and Interagency, March 17. 2004, http://www.cmi
.no/afghanistan/background/docs/SecuringAfghanistansFuture-18–03–04.pdf.

93. "Afghanistan National Development Strategy: A Strategy for Security, Governance, Economic Growth & Poverty Reduction, 2008–2013," Islamic Republic of Afghanistan, http://www.undp.org.af/publications/KeyDocuments/ANDS
_Full_Eng.pdf.

94. Poole, *Afghanistan*.

95. Ghani and Lockhart, *Fixing Failed States*, 98.

96. Ghani and Lockhart, *Fixing Failed States*, 100.

97. For the fraud conviction of the Louis Berger Group, see James Risen, "War Reconstruction Fraud Draws Big Fine," *New York Times*, November 5, 2010, http://www.nytimes.com/2010/11/06/world/asia/06contractor.html?r=0.

98. "Infrastructure Fact Sheet: Afghanistan," USAID: Afghanistan, August 2014, http://www.usaid.gov/sites/default/files/documents/1871/Infrastructure
%20sector%20fact%20sheet%20aug%202014.pdf.

99. Kevin Sieff, "After Billions in U.S. Investment, Afghan Roads Are Falling Apart," *Washington Post*, January 30, 2014, https://www.washingtonpost.com
/world/asia_pacific/after-billions-in-us-investment-afghan-roads-are-falling-apart
/2014/01/30/9bd07764-7986-11e3-b1c5-739e63e9c9a7_story.html.

100. Danielle Piskadlo and Jeffrey Riecke, "The Military as Providers of Micro Grants in Conflict Areas," Center for Financial Inclusion, April 14, 2014, http://cfi-blog.org/2014/04/04/the-military-as-a-provider-of-microgrants-in
-conflict-areas/.

101. Ghani and Lockhart, *Fixing Failed States*, 206–11; Nagl, Exum, and Humayun, *Pathway to Success in Afghanistan*.

102. Lynne O'Donnell, "Afghanistan's Plan to Jumpstart Economy with Chinese Mining Investment under Threat," *South China Morning Post*, September 20, 2013, http://www.scmp.com/news/asia/article/1313161/afghanistans-plan
-jumpstart-economy-chinese-mining-investment-under-threat.

103. Downs, "China Buys into Afghanistan," 65–84.

104. Lynne O'Donnell, "China's MCC Turns Back on US$3b Mes Aynak Afghanistan Mine Deal," *South China Morning Post*, March 20, 2014, http://
www.scmp.com/news/world/article/1453375/chinas-mcc-turns-back-us3b-mes
-aynak-afghanistan-mine-deal.

105. Louis Charbonneau, "Taliban Changing from Religious Group to Criminal Enterprise: UN," *Reuters*, June 13, 2014, http://www.reuters.com/article/2014
/06/14/us-afghanistan-taliban-un-idUSKBN0EP02920140614.

106. This plan was updated in 2006; see Islamic Republic of Afghanistan Ministry of Counternarcotics, *National Drug Control Strategy*, 17.

107. Rubin and Sherman, *Counter-Narcotics to Stabilize Afghanistan*, 6.

108. Felbab-Brown, *Shooting Up*, 138–54.

109. Rubin and Sherman, "*Counter-Narcotics to Stabilize Afghanistan*," 6.

110. "Poppy Cultivation in Afghanistan: After a Decade of Reconstruction and over $7 Billion in Counternarcotics Efforts, Poppy Cultivation Levels Are at

an All-Time High," Special Inspector General for Afghanistan Reconstruction, October 2014, http://www.sigar.mil/pdf/special%20projects/sigar-15-10-sp.pdf.

111. May Jeong, "Afghan Opium Crop Set for Record High," *Guardian*, November 12, 2014, http://www.theguardian.com/world/2014/nov/12/afghan-opium-crop-record-high-united-nations.

112. International Crisis Group, *Aid and Conflict in Afghanistan*.

113. United Nations Development Program and Islamic Republic of Afghanistan, *Security with a Human Face*, 17–18.

114. Accera et al., "Rebuilding the Health Care System," 78–79.

115. Livingston and O'Hanlon, *Afghanistan Index Report: August 26, 2005*, 25. See also Livingston and O'Hanlon, *Afghanistan Index Report: February, 10 2015*, 22.

116. Livingston and O'Hanlon, *Afghanistan Index: February 23, 2005*, 7. The next Afghanistan Index was not compiled until August 26, 2008.

117. "High Stakes: Girls' Education in Afghanistan," Care International, February 24, 2011, http://www.care-international.org/uploaddocument/news/publications/reports%20and%20issue%20briefs/english/afghanistan_joint%20report_girls%20education_240211.pdf.

118. Heather Barr, "In Afghanistan, Women Betrayed," Human Rights Watch, December 11, 2013, http://www.hrw.org/news/2013/12/11/afghanistan-women-betrayed.

119. "UN Reports 'Slow, Uneven' Use of Afghan Law to Protect Women," UN News Centre, December 8, 2013, http://www.un.org/apps/news/story.asp?NewsID=46685#.VSqYgl50zIU.

120. See, for example, Yunus, *Banker to the Poor*, 31–84; Sen, *Poverty and Famines*.

121. United Nations Development Program and Islamic Republic of Afghanistan, *Security with a Human Face*, 28. In 2015 the Afghan government conducted a follow-up survey and its HDI had improved only slightly.

122. United Nations Development Program and Islamic Republic of Afghanistan, *Security with a Human Face*, 31–34.

123. Livingston and O'Hanlon, *Afghanistan Index Report: February 10, 2015*, 22.

124. "Infrastructure Fact Sheet."

125. See "Audit Reports," Special Inspector General for Afghanistan Reconstruction," http://www.sigar.mil/audits/inspection-reports.html.

126. United Nations Development Program and Islamic Republic of Afghanistan, *Security with a Human Face*, 2–3.

127. United Nations Development Program and Islamic Republic of Afghanistan, *Security with a Human Face*, 2–3. See also "Afghanistan Human Development Report," UN Development Program 2013, http://hdr.undp.org/sites/default/files/Country-Profiles/AFG.pdf. The report notes that methods for measuring the index had changed between 2007 and 2013.

8. Counterfactual State-, Nation-Building, Afghanistan

1. Barfield, *Afghanistan*, 277–78.

2. Barfield, *Afghanistan*, 278.

3. Barfield, *Afghanistan*, 274.

4. Sopko, *Why ANSF Numbers Matter.*

5. Warren, *Afghanistan in 2014*, 32.

6. Shawe, *Afghanistan in 2013*, 6.

7. Akseer, Warren, and Rieger, *Afghanistan in 2017*, 42.

8. Warren, *Afghanistan in 2014*, 31.

9. Warren, *Afghanistan in 2014*, 31.

10. Shawe, *Afghanistan in 2013*, 29.

11. Akseer, Warren, and Rieger, "*Afghanistan in 2017*, 54.

12. Interview with a U.S. Army Special Forces officer on vso in Afghanistan, May 17, 2012.

13. Thruelson, *From Soldier to Civilian*, 7.

14. Afghanistan Justice Organization/Global Partner for the Prevention of Armed Conflict, *Transitional Justice in Afghanistan.*

15. Jon Boone, "Afghanistan Quietly Brings into Force Taliban Amnesty Law," *Guardian*, February 11, 2010, http://www.theguardian.com/world/2010/feb/11/taliban-amnesty-law-enacted.

16. Warren, *Afghanistan in 2014*, 31.

17. "UN Assistance Mandate in Afghanistan," UN Peacekeeping, http://www.betterworldcampaign.org/un-peacekeeping/missions/afghanistan.html.

18. "Islamic Republic of Afghanistan National Elections, April 5, 2014," *ElectionGuide: Democracy Assistance and Election News*, http://www.electionguide.org/elections/id/2316/.

19. I am indebted to an NPS student for pointing this out to me.

20. Although Barfield points out that using *jirgas* to elect a state leader is a relatively new use of this consensus-building process. Historically *jirgas* were used to ratify constitutions, laws, or other similar issues. See Barfield, *Afghanistan*, 294–300.

21. Lockhart, *Prepared Testimony.*

22. Lockhart, *Prepared Testimony*, 2.

23. Barfield, *Afghanistan*, 320–321. See also Biddle, Christia, and Thier, "Defining Success in Afghanistan." 48–60.

24. Barfield, *Afghanistan*, 303. Similar points are made by Biddle, Christia and Thier, "Defining Success in Afghanistan."

25. Peceny and Bosin, "Winning with Warlords in Afghanistan."

26. Biddle, Christia, and Thier, "Defining Success in Afghanistan," 2.

27. North, "Institutions."

28. Warren, *Afghanistan in 2014*, 8.

29. Warren, *Afghanistan in 2014*, 25.

30. Akseer, Warren, and Rieger, "*Afghanistan in 2017*, 14, 167–78.

31. U.S. Army Special Forces officer on vso in Afghanistan, May 17, 2012; interview with U.S. Army Special Forces officer on vso in Afghanistan, July 17, 2012.

32. Staff Sergeant Felix R. Fimbres, "Civil Affairs Team Gets Dirty to Learn New Ways to Help Afghans," *Army Times*, February 10, 2012, http://www.army.mil/article/73151/.

33. Ghani and Lockhart, *Fixing Failed States.*

34. See "Midwifery in Afghanistan," UNICEF, http://www.unicef.org/sowc09/docs/SOWC09-Panel-3.4-EN.pdf.

35. "How Has Rwanda Saved the Lives of 590,000 Africans?," *BBC News,* April 29, 2015, http://www.bbc.com/news/world-africa-32438104.

36. Chickering et al., *Strategic Foreign Assistance,* 45–70.

37. Ghani and Lockhart, *Fixing Failed States,* 142.

38. Ghani and Lockhart, *Fixing Failed States,* 142.

39. I am indebted to an NPS student for making this point to me.

40. Barfield, *Afghanistan,* 317.

41. Ben Farmer, "Afghanistan Launches First Professional Football League," *Telegraph,* September 28, 2012, http://www.telegraph.co.uk/news/worldnews/asia/afghanistan/9574387/Afghanistan-launches-first-professional-football-league.html.

42. In my U.S. primary school education, I learned songs from across the country, including "Oh Suzanna," "The Erie Canal," and "Oh Shenandoah," and learned folk tales about Paul Bunyan and Davey Crockett, despite growing up in a town of 3,500 in Northern California. The curriculum also required education about the U.S. Constitution and a test in the eighth grade to show proficient knowledge of the subject.

43. Afghanistan National Institute of Music, http://www.afghanistannationalinstituteofmusic.org/.

44. Turquois Mountain, http://turquoisemountain.org/.

45. Akseer, Warren, and Rieger, *Afghanistan in 2017,* 6, 10.

9. Program for Population-Centric State-, Nation-Building

1. Ruiz, "Report."

2. This approach mirrors, to a large extent, the National Solidarity Program initiated in Afghanistan. See Ghani and Lockhart, *Fixing Failed* States, 206–11; Nagl, Exum, and Humayun, *"Pathway to Success in Afghanistan."*

3. I am deeply indebted to Reverend Dr. Mitri Raheb of Dar al-Kalima School in Bethlehem, Palestine, for making these points clear to me.

4. Gregg, "Setting a Place at the Table."

5. Barfield, *Afghanistan,* 274.

6. Khilkhal, "Islamic State Conspiracy Theories Sway Iraqis."

7. I am indebted to several NPS students for their thoughtful points on this discussion.

8. For DOD budget, see U.S. Office of the Undersecretary of Defense, Chief Financial Officer, *Fiscal Year 2015 Budget Request.* For U.S. Department of State and USAID budget and overseas budget, see "Congressional Budget Justification: Department of State, Foreign Operations and Related Programs: Fiscal Year 2015," http://www.state.gov/documents/organization/222898.pdf.

9. Gentile, "War Is about Killing and Destruction"; Krahenbuhl, "Militarization of Aid and Its Perils."

BIBLIOGRAPHY

Interviews on culture and biometric data gathering in Iraq and Afghanistan, 2010

NPS IRB determination: NPS IRB# 2010.0075-IR-EP7-A

U.S. Marine Corps officer deployed to Iraq twice. Interview conducted at the Naval Postgraduate School, Monterey, California, on August 4, 2010.

U.S. Army Infantry officer deployed to Afghanistan. Interview conducted at the Naval Postgraduate School, Monterey, California, on August 5, 2010.

U.S. Marine Corps officer deployed to Iraq and Afghanistan. Interview conducted at the Naval Postgraduate School, Monterey, California, on August 6, 2010.

U.S. Marine Corps Combat Engineer officer deployed to Afghanistan. Interview conducted at the Naval Postgraduate School, Monterey, California, on August 9, 2010.

U.S. Army Infantry officer deployed to Iraq and Afghanistan. Interview conducted at the Naval Postgraduate School, Monterey, California, on August 11, 2010.

U.S. Army Special Forces officer deployed to Iraq three times. Interview conducted at the Naval Postgraduate School, Monterey, California, on August 11, 2010.

Interviews on gathering "atmospherics" from populations in Iraq and Afghanistan, 2011

NPS IRB determination: NPS IRB# NPS.2011.0035-IR-EP7-A

U.S. Army Special Forces officer deployed to Iraq twice. Interview conducted at the Naval Postgraduate School, Monterey, California, on February 1, 2011.

U.S. Army Special Forces officer deployed to Afghanistan. Interview conducted at the Naval Postgraduate School, Monterey, California, on February 3, 2011.

U.S. Army Special Forces officer deployed to Iraq twice. Interview conducted at the Naval Postgraduate School, Monterey, California, on February 3, 2011.

U.S. Army Field Artillery officer deployed to Iraq. Interview conducted at the Naval Postgraduate School, Monterey, California, on February 7, 2011.

U.S. Army Civil Affairs officer deployed to Iraq and Afghanistan. Interview conducted at the Naval Postgraduate School, Monterey, California, on February 8, 2011.

U.S. Army Civil Affairs officer deployed to Iraq. Interview conducted at the Naval Postgraduate School, Monterey, California, on February 9, 2011.

U.S. Army Civil Affairs officer deployed to Afghanistan twice. Interview conducted at the Naval Postgraduate School, Monterey, California, on February 10, 2011.

U.S. Army Civil Affairs officer deployed to Afghanistan three times. Interview conducted at the Naval Postgraduate School, Monterey, California, on February 10, 2011.

Interviews on vso and Cultural Support Teams in Afghanistan, 2012

IRB determination *not* human subject, no NPS determination number

U.S. Army Special Operations officer on Cultural Support Team training. Interview conducted at Fort Bragg, North Carolina, on May 9, 2012.

U.S Army Special Operations officer on Cultural Support Team Training. Interview conducted at Fort Bragg, North Carolina, on May 9, 2012.

U.S. Army Special Operations NCO on vso in Afghanistan. Interview conducted at Fort Bragg, North Carolina, on May 9, 2012.

U.S. Army Special Forces NCO on vso in Afghanistan. Interview conducted at Fort Bragg, North Carolina, on May 16, 2012.

U.S. Army Special Forces officer on vso in Afghanistan. Interview conducted at Fort Bragg, North Carolina, on May 17, 2012.

U.S. Army Special Forces officer on Foreign Internal Defense and vso in Afghanistan. Interview conducted at Fort Bragg, North Carolina, on May 18, 2012.

U.S. Army Special Forces officer on Foreign Internal Defense and vso in Afghanistan. Interview conducted at Fort Bragg, North Carolina, on July 17, 2012.

U.S. Army Special Forces officer on vso at the company level across Nanghahar, Nuristan, Konar, and Laghman (N2KL) provinces in Afghanistan. Interview conducted at Fort Bragg, North Carolina, on July 17, 2012.

U.S. Army Special Forces officer on vso in Afghanistan. Interview conducted at Fort Bragg, North Carolina, on July 17, 2012.

U.S. Army Special Forces officer on vso in Kandahar Province. Interview conducted at Fort Bragg, North Carolina, on July 18, 2012.

U.S. Army Special Forces officer on vso in Zabul Province. Interview conducted at Fort Bragg, North Carolina, on July 18, 2012.

Interviews on Cultural Support Teams and Female Engagement Teams in Iraq and Afghanistan, 2013

NPS IRB determination: NPS IRB NPS.2013.0025-IR-EP7-A

U.S. Army Ranger NCO on CST in Afghanistan. Telephone interview conducted on February 12, 2013.

U.S. Army officer CST program manager, USASOC. Interview conducted at Fort Bragg, North Carolina, on February 19, 2013.

U.S. Army Special Operations officer responsible for CST course development. Interview conducted at Fort Bragg, North Carolina, on February 20, 2014.

U.S. Army female officer who deployed as part of CST to Afghanistan. Interview conducted at Fort Bragg, North Carolina, on February 20, 2013.

U.S. Army Ranger officer, Ranger program manager, and two CST who deployed to Afghanistan in support of Rangers. Interview conducted at Fort Bragg, North Carolina, on February 20, 2013.

U.S. Army Special Forces NCO who was a CST course developer. Interview conducted at Fort Bragg, North Carolina, on February 20, 2013.

U.S. Army Civil Affairs officer CST course developer. Interview conducted at Fort Bragg, North Carolina, on February 20, 2013.

Published Sources

Aaron, Daniel, and Melissa Meyers. "Cost of Exile: The Role of Returning Exiles in Post-2003 Iraq." *Imes Capstone Paper Series: The George Washington University Elliott School of International Affairs* (May 2014): 29–33.

Abbaszadeh, Nima, Mark Crow, Marianne El-Khoury, Jonathan Gandomi, David Kuwayama, Christopher MacPherson, Meghan Nutting, Nealin Parker, and Taya Weiss. "Provincial Reconstruction Teams: Lessons and Recommendations." *Woodrow Wilson School of Public Policy.* January 2008, http://wws.princeton.edu/sites/default/files/content/docs/news/wws591b.pdf.

Accera, John R., Kara Iskyan, Zubair A. Qureshi, and Rahul K. Sharma. "Rebuilding the Health Care System in Afghanistan: An Overview of Primary Care and Emergency Services." *International Journal of Emergency Medicine* 2, no. 2 (June 2009): 77–82.

Afghanistan Justice Organization/Global Partner for the Prevention of Armed Conflict. *Transitional Justice in Afghanistan: "We Should Not Repeat Old Issues?"* October 2013. http://www.gppac.net/documents/130492842/0/GPPAC+AJO+Policy+Note+Transitional+Justice+in+Afghanistan+final.pdf/300e8c02-6e10-445a-9e19-8bfe91fbd7c5.

Ahmadzai, Mirwais. *Investment Opportunities in Textile & Clothing Industry of Afghanistan.* Afghanistan Investment Support Agency, 2013. http://www.aisa.org.af/study/Final%20Afghanistan%20Textile%20Industry%20Paper%20-%20MA.pdf.

Akseer, Tabasum, Zach Warren, and John Rieger, eds. *Afghanistan in 2017: A Survey of Afghan People.* Asia Foundation, 2017. https://asiafoundation.org/publication/afghanistan-2017-survey-afghan-people/.

Al-Rawi, Ahmed K. *Media Practice in Iraq.* London: Palgrave, 2012.

Anderson, Benedict. *Imagined Communities: Reflections on the Origins and Spread of Nationalism.* London: Verso, 1991.

Armstrong, John A. *Nations before Nationalism.* Chapel Hill: University of North Carolina Press, 1982.

Armstrong, Karen. *A Short History of Myth.* Edinburgh: Canongate, 2005.

Baram, Amatzia. "Neo-Tribalism in Iraq: Saddam Hussein's Tribal Policies 1991–1996." *International Journal of Middle East Studies* 29, no. 1 (February 1997): 1–31.

Barfield, Thomas. *Afghanistan: A Cultural and Political History*. Princeton NJ: Princeton University Press, 2010.

Barlett, Donald L., and James B. Steele. "Billions over Baghdad." *Vanity Fair*, October 2007. https://www.vanityfair.com/news/2007/10/iraq-billions200710.

Bayar, Murat. "Reconsidering Primordialism: An Alternative Approach to the Study of Ethnicity." *Ethnic and Racial Studies* 32, no. 9 (2009): 1639–57.

Beard, Charles A. "Written History as an Act of Faith," *American Historical Review* 39, no. 2 (January 1934): 219–31.

Benard, Cheryl, and Nina Hachigian, eds. *Democracy and Islam in the New Constitution of Afghanistan*. Conference Proceedings. Santa Monica CA: RAND, 2003.

Bensahel, Nora, Olga Oliker, Keith Crane, Richard R. Brennan Jr., Heather S. Gregg, Thomas Sullivan, and Andrew Rathmell. *After Saddam: Prewar Planning and the Occupation of Iraq*. Santa Monica: RAND, 2008.

Bereday, George Z. F. "An Introduction." In *The Making of Citizens*, edited by Charles E. Merriam, 1–26. New York: Columbia University Press, 1966.

Biddle, Steven, Fotini Christia, and J. Alexander Thier. "Defining Success in Afghanistan: What Can the United States Accept?" *Foreign Affairs* 89, no. 4 (July/August 2010): 48–60.

Blanchard, Christopher M. "Iraq: Oil and Gas Legislation, Revenue Sharing, and U.S. Policy," *Congressional Research Services*, November 3, 2009. https://fas .org/sgp/crs/mideast/RL34064.pdf.

Blanning, T. C. W. *The Culture of Power and the Power of Culture: Old Regime Europe, 1660–1789*. New York: Oxford University Press, 2003.

Bogdanos, Matthew. "The Casualties of War: The Truth about the Iraq Museum." *American Journal of Archaeology* 109, no. 3 (July 2005): 477–526.

———. "The Thieves of Baghdad: Combatting Global Traffic in Stolen Iraqi Antiquities." *Fordham International Law Journal* 31, no. 3 (2007): 725–40.

Boli, John, Francis O. Ramirez, and John W. Meyer. "Explaining the Origins and Expansion of Mass Education." *Comparative Education Review* 29, no. 2 (May 1985): 145–70.

Braun, Rudolph. "Taxation in Britain and Prussia." In *The Formation of National States in Western Europe*, edited by Charles Tilly, 243–327. Princeton NJ: Princeton University Press, 1975.

Breuilly, John. *Nationalism and the State*. Chicago: University of Chicago Press, 1982.

Brown, Michael E., ed. *Ethnic Conflict and International Security*. Princeton NJ: Princeton University Press, 1993.

———, ed. *Nationalism and Ethnic Conflict*. Cambridge MA: MIT Press, 2001.

Brubaker, Rogers. "In the Name of the Nation: On Nationalism and Patriotism." *Citizenship Studies* 8, no. 2 (June 2004): 115–27.

———. *Nationalism Reframed: Nationalism and the National Question in the New Europe*. Cambridge: Cambridge University Press, 1996.

Buzan, Barry. *People, States and Fear: An Agenda for International Security in the Post-Cold War Era*. 2nd ed. New York: Harvester Wheatsheaf, 1991.

Caldwell, Lieutenant General William B., and Captain Nathan K. Finney, U.S. Air Force. "Security, Capacity and Literacy." *Military Review* (January–February 2011): 23–27.

Campbell, Joseph. *The Power of Myth*. New York: Anchor Books, 1991.

Cannidine, David. "The Context, Performance, and Meaning of Ritual: The British Monarchy and the 'Invention of Tradition,' c. 1820–1977." In *The Invention of Tradition*, edited by Eric Hobsbawm and Terrence Ranger, 101–64. Cambridge: Cambridge University Press, 1983.

Cerulo, Karen A. "Symbols and the World System: National Anthems and Flags." *Sociological Forum* 8, no. 2 (1993): 243–71.

Chickering, A. Lawrence, Isobel Coleman, P. Edward Haley, and Emily Vargas-Baron, eds. *Strategic Foreign Assistance: Civil Society and International Security*. Palo Alto CA: Hoover Press, 2006.

Christia, Fotini, and Michael Semple. "Flipping the Taliban: How to Win in Afghanistan," *Foreign Affairs* 8, no. 44 (July–August 2009): 38–48.

Clawson, Patrick, ed. *How to Build a New Iraq after Saddam*. Washington DC: Washington Institute for Near East Policy, 2002.

Coll, Steve. *Ghost Wars: The Secret History of the CIA, Afghanistan, and Bin Laden, from the Soviet Invasion to September 10, 2001*. New York: Penguin, 2004.

Collier, Paul. *The Bottom Billion: Why the Poorest Countries Are Failing and What Can Be Done about It*. New York: Oxford University Press, 2008.

Connor, Walker. *Ethnonationalism: The Quest for Understanding*. Princeton NJ: Princeton University Press, 1994.

———. "Nation-Building or Nation-Destroying?" *World Politics* 24, no. 3 (April 1972): 319–55.

———. "The Timelessness of Nations." *Nations and Nationalism* 10, no. 1–2 (2004): 35–47.

Copeland, David A. *Colonial American Newspapers: Character and Content*. Wilmington: University of Delaware Press, 1996.

Deady, Colonel Timothy, U.S. Army Reserve (Ret.). "MiTT Advisor: A Year with the Best Division in the Iraqi Army." *Military Review* (November–December 2009): 43–56.

Deutsch, Karl. *Nationalism and Social Communication: An Inquiry into the Foundations of Nationality*. Cambridge MA: Harvard University Press, 1953.

Diamond, Larry. "What Went Wrong and Right in Iraq." In *Nation-Building: Beyond Afghanistan and Iraq*, edited by Francis Fukuyama, 173–95. Baltimore: Johns Hopkins University, 2006.

———. "What Went Wrong in Iraq." *Foreign Affairs* 83, no. 5 (September–October 2004): 34–56.

Dobbins, James, et al. *America's Role in Nation-Building: From Germany to Iraq*. Santa Monica CA: RAND, 2003.

———. *The Beginner's Guide to Nation-Building*. Santa Monica CA: RAND, 2007.

———. *Europe's Role in Nation-Building*. Santa Monica CA: RAND, 2008.

———. *Occupying Iraq: A History of the Coalition Provisional Authority*. Santa Monica CA: RAND, 2009.

———. *The UN's Role in Nation-Building: From the Congo to Iraq*. Santa Monica CA: RAND Corporation, 2005.

Dodge, Toby. *Inventing Iraq: The Failure of Nation-Building and a History Denied*. New York: Columbia University Press, 2003.

———. "Iraq: The Contradiction of Exogenous State-Building in Historical Perspective." In *From Nation-Building to State-Building*, edited by Mark T. Berger, 183–96. New York: Routledge, 2013.

Downs, Erica. "China Buys into Afghanistan." *SAIS Review* 32, no. 2 (Summer–Fall 2012): 65–84.

Dressler, Jeffry A. *The Haqqani Network: From Pakistan to Afghanistan*. Afghanistan Report no. 6. Washington DC: Institute for the Study of War, 2010.

Dupree, Louis. *Afghanistan*. Princeton NJ: Princeton University Press, 1978.

Eliade, Mircea. *Myth and Reality*. San Francisco: Harper & Row, 1963.

———. *The Myth of Eternal Return*. Princeton NJ: Princeton University Press, 1971.

Eller, Jack David. *From Culture to Ethnicity to Conflict: An Anthropological Perspective on International Ethnic Conflict*. Ann Arbor: University of Michigan Press, 1999.

Eller, Jack David, and Reed M Coughlan. "The Poverty of Primordialism: The Demystification of Ethnic Attachments." *Ethnic and Racial Studies* 16, no. 2 (1993): 183–202

Epstein, S. R. "The Rise and Fall of Italian City States." London School of Economics Working Paper 51, no. 99, July 1999.

Etzioni, Amitai. "A Self-Restrained Approach to Nation-Building by Foreign Powers." *International Affairs* 80, no. 1 (2004): 1–17.

Ewans, Martin. *Afghanistan: A Short History of Its People and Politics*. New York: HarperCollins, 2002.

Fair, C. Christine, and Sumit Ganguly. "An Unworthy Ally: Time for Washington to Cut Pakistan Loose." *Foreign Affairs* 94, no. 5 (September/October 2015): 160–70.

Felbab-Brown, Vanda. *Shooting Up: Counterinsurgency and the War on Drugs*. Washington DC: Brookings Institution Press, 2010.

Feldman, Noah. "The Democratic Fatwa: Islam and Democracy in the Realm of Constitutional Politics." *Oklahoma Law Review* 58, no. 1 (Spring 2005): 1–9.

Finer, Samuel E. "State- and Nation-Building in Europe: The Role of the Military." In *The Formation of National States in Western Europe*, edited by Charles Tilly, 84–163. Princeton NJ: Princeton University Press, 1975.

Fox, Stephen. *John Muir and His Legacy: The American Conservation Movement*. Madison: University of Wisconsin Press, 1986.

Fukuyama, Francis. *The Great Disruption: Human Nature and the Reconstruction of Social Order*. New York: Touchstone, 1999.

———, ed. *Nation-Building: Beyond Afghanistan and Iraq*. Baltimore: Johns Hopkins University, 2006.

———. "Social Capital." In *Culture Matters: How Values Shape Human Progress*, edited by Lawrence Harrison and Samuel Huntington, 98–111. New York: Basic Books, 2000.

———. *State-Building: Governance and World Order in the 21st Century*. Ithaca NY: Cornell University Press, 2004.

Gellner, Ernest. "Nationalism." *Theory and Society* 10, no. 6 (November 1981): 753–76.

———. *Nations and Nationalism*. Oxford: Oxford University Press, 1983.

Gavrilis, James A. "The Mayor of Ar Rutbah." *Foreign Policy*, October 20, 2009, http://foreignpolicy.com/2009/10/20/the-mayor-of-ar-rutbah/.

Gentile, Gian P. "War Is about Killing and Destruction, It Is Not Armed Social Science: A Short Response to Andrew Mackay and Steve Tatham." *Small Wars Journal*, 2009. file:///C:/Users/Laptop/Downloads/334-gentile.pdf, accessed June 7, 2015.

Ghani, Ashraf, and Clare Lockhart. *Fixing Failed States: A Framework for Rebuilding a Fractured World*. New York: Oxford University Press, 2008.

Ghani, Ashraf, Clare Lockhart, and Michael Carnahan. "Closing the Sovereignty Gap: An Approach to State-Building." Overseas Development Institute Working Paper 253, London, September 2005. http://www.odi.org/sites/odi.org .uk/files/odi-assets/publications-opinion-files/2482.pdf.

Greenfeld, Liah. *Nationalism: Five Roads to Modernity*. Cambridge MA: Harvard University Press, 1992.

Gregg, Heather S. *Employment Handbook for Fighting Counterinsurgencies: A Toolkit for How to Build Rapport, Create Jobs and Work towards a Viable State*. Naval Postgraduate School Technical Report NPS-DA-09–001 (November 2009).

———. *The Path to Salvation: Religious Violence from the Crusades to Jihad*. Washington DC: Potomac Press, 2014.

———. "Setting a Place at the Table: Ending Insurgencies through the Political Process," *Small Wars and Insurgencies* 22, no. 4 (2011): 644–68.

Guistozzi, Antonio, Claudio Franco, and Adam Baczko. *Shadow Justice: How the Taliban Run Their Judiciary?* Kabul: Integrity Watch Afghanistan, 2012. http://www.iwaweb.org/_docs/reports/research/shadow_justice-how_the _taliban_run_their_judiciary.pdf.

Habermas, Jürgen. *The Structural Transformation of the Public Sphere: An Inquiry into a Category of Bourgeois Society*. Translated by Thomas Burger. Cambridge MA: MIT Press, 1989.

Habermas, Jürgen, Sara Lennox, and Frank Lennox. "The Public Sphere: An Encyclopedia Article." *New German Critique* 3 (Autumn 1974): 49–55.

Hersh, Seymour. "Chain of Command: How the Department of Defense Mishandled the Disaster at Abu Ghraib." *New Yorker*, May 17, 2004. https:// www.newyorker.com/magazine/2004/05/17/chain-of-command-2.

———. "Torture at Abu Ghraib: How Far Up Does the Responsibility Go?" *New Yorker*, May 10, 2004. https://www.newyorker.com/magazine/2004/05/10 /torture-at-abu-ghraib.

Hobbes, Thomas. *The Elements of Law*. 2nd ed. Edited by F. Tönnies. London: Frank Cass, 1979.

———. *Leviathan*. Edited by Richard Tuck. London: Cambridge University Press, 1992.

Hobsbawm, Eric J. "Introduction: Inventing Traditions." In Hobsbawm and Ranger, *Invention of Tradition*, 1–14.

———. *Nations and Nationalism since 1780*. 2nd ed. Cambridge: Cambridge University Press, 1992.

Hobsbawm, Eric, and Terrence Ranger, eds. *The Invention of Tradition*. Cambridge: Cambridge University Press, 1983.

Horowitz, Donald. *Ethnic Groups in Conflict*. Berkeley: University of California Press, 1985.

Hutchinson, John, and Anthony Smith, eds. *Nationalism*. New York: Oxford University Press, 1994.

International Crisis Group. *Afghanistan's Flawed Constitutional Process*. ICG Asia Report no. 56, June 12, 2003. http://www.crisisgroup.org/en/regions/asia /south-asia/afghanistan/056-afghanistans-flawed-constitutional-process.aspx.

———. *Aid and Conflict in Afghanistan*. ICG Asia Report no. 210, August 4, 2011. http://www.crisisgroup.org/~/media/Files/asia/south-asia/afghanistan/210 -%20Aid%20and%20conflict%20in%20Afghanistan.

———. *Iraq: Building a New Security Structure*. ICG Middle East Report no. 20, December 23, 2003. https://d2071andvip0wj.cloudfront.net/20-iraq-building -a-new-security-structure.pdf.

———. *Iraq's Constitutional Challenge*. ICG Middle East Report no. 19, November 13, 2003. https://www.crisisgroup.org/middle-east-north-africa/gulf -and-arabian-peninsula/iraq/iraqs-constitutional-challenge.

———. *Shiite Politics in Iraq: The Role of the Supreme Council*. ICG Middle East Report no. 70, November 15, 2007. https://www.crisisgroup.org/middle -east-north-africa/gulf-and-arabian-peninsula/iraq/shiite-politics-iraq-role -supreme-council.

Islamic Republic of Afghanistan Ministry of Counternarcotics. *National Drug Control Strategy*. Kabul, 2006. htps://www.gov.uk/government/uploads/system /uploads/attachment_data/file/36443/fco_nationaldrugcontrolstrategy.pdf.

Johnson, Keith. "Iraq's Oil War." *Foreign Policy*, January 17, 2014. http:// foreignpolicy.com/2014/01/17/iraqs-oil-war/.

Jones, Philip. *The Italian City-State: From Commune to Signoria*. New York: Oxford University Press, 1997.

Jones, Seth. *Counterinsurgency in Afghanistan*. Santa Monica CA: RAND, 2008.

Jost, Tyler. *Defend, Defect or Desert? The Future of the Afghan Security Forces*. Center for New American Security policy brief. Washington DC: Center for a New American Security, 2015. http://www.cnas.org/sites/default/files /publications-pdf/CNAS_Afghan_ANF_policybrief_Jost.pdf.

Juergensmeyer, Mark. *The New Cold War? Religious Nationalism Confronts the Secular State*. Berkeley: University of California Press, 1992.

————. *Terror in the Mind of God*. Berkeley: University of California Press, 2000.

Kaldor, Mary. *Human Security*. Cambridge: Polity Press, 2007.

Karadaghi, Kamran. "Managing Ethnic Tensions." In *How to Build a New Iraq after Saddam*, edited by Patrick Clawson, 31–43. Washington DC: Washington Institute for Near East Policy, 2002.

Kaufmann, Chaim. "Possible and Impossible Solutions to Ethnic Civil Wars." *International Security* 20, no. 4 (1996): 136–75.

Kelly, Terrence K., Nora Bensahel, and Olga Oliker. *Security Force Assistance in Afghanistan: Identifying Lessons for Future Efforts*. Santa Monica CA: RAND, 2011.

Khilkhal, Shukur. "Islamic State Conspiracy Theories Sway Iraqis." *Al-Monitor*. February 27, 2015. http://www.al-monitor.com/pulse/originals/2015/02/iraq -doubts-us-eliminate-islamic-state.html#, accessed June 4, 2015.

Kilcullen, David. *The Accidental Guerilla: Fighting Small Wars in the Midst of a Big One*. New York: Oxford University Press, 2009.

Kiser, Edward, and April Linton. "Determinants of the Growth of the State: War and Taxation in Early Modern France and England." *Social Forces* 80, no. 2 (2001): 411–48.

Krahenbuhl, Pierre. "The Militarization of Aid and its Perils." *ICRC Resource Center*. February 22, 2011. https://www.icrc.org/eng/resources/documents /article/editorial/humanitarians-danger-article-2011-02-01.htm.

Kyridis, Argyris, Anna Mavrikou, Christos Zagkos, Paraskevi Golia, Ifigenia Vamvakidou, and Nikos Fotopoulous. "Nationalism through State Constructed Symbols: The Case of National Anthems." *International Journal of Interdisciplinary Sciences* 4 (2009): 1–22.

Lemay-Hébert, Nicolas. "Statebuilding without Nation-Building? Legitimacy, State Failure and the Limits of the Institutional Approach." *Journal of Intervention and Statebuilding* 3, no. 1 (March 2009): 21–45.

Levi-Strauss, Claude. *Myth and Meaning: Cracking the Code of Culture*. Toronto: University of Toronto Press, 1978.

Lipset, Seymour Martin. *Political Man*. New York: Doubleday, 1960.

Livingston, Ian S., and Michael O'Hanlon. *Afghanistan Index Report*. Brookings Institution, 2005–17. http://www.brookings.edu/about/centers/middle -east-policy/afghanistan-index.

————. *Iraq Index: Tracking Variables of Reconstruction & Security in Iraq*. Brookings Institution, 2003–13. http://www.brookings.edu/about/centers/middle -east-policy/iraq-index.

Locke, John. *An Essay concerning Human Understanding*. Pennsylvania State University Electronic Classic Series, 1999. http://www2.hn.psu.edu/faculty /jmanis/locke/humanund.pdf.

————. *Political Writings*. Edited by David Wootton. New York: Penguin Books, 1993.

————. *Second Treatise of Government*. Edited by Jonathan Bennett. http://www .earlymoderntexts.com/pdfs/locke1689a.pdf.

Lockhart, Clare. *Prepared Testimony for the Senate Committee on Foreign Affairs.* Institute for State Effectiveness, September 17, 2009, http://www.foreign .senate.gov/imo/media/doc/LockhartTestimony090917a1.pdf.

Loewen, James W. *Lies My Teacher Told Me: Everything Your American History Textbook Got Wrong.* New York: Touchstone Books, 2007.

Lubragge, Michael T. "Manifest Destiny: The Philosophy That Created a Nation." *American History: From Revolution to Reconstruction and Beyond.* http://www .let.rug.nl/usa/essays/1801-1900/manifest-destiny, accessed July 8, 2014.

Lytle, Scott. "Robespierre, Dalton and Levee en Masse." *Journal of Modern History* 30, no. 4 (December 1958): 325–37.

MacGregor, Charles Metcalfe. *War in Afghanistan 1879–80: The Personal Diary of Major General Sir Charles Metcalfe MacGregor.* Edited by William Trousdale. Detroit: Wayne State University, 1985.

Machiavelli, Niccolò. *Discourses on Livy.* Translated by Harvey M. Mansfield and Nathan Tarcov. Chicago: University of Chicago Press, 1996.

Madden, David. "Flags." *Callaloo* 24, no. 1 (2001): 123–25.

Mann, Fritz. "The Sociology of Taxation." *Review of Politics* 5 (1943): 225–35.

Mansfield, Edward D., and Jack Snyder. "Democratization and War." *Foreign Affairs* 74, no. 3 (1995): 79–97.

Marr, Phebe. *The Modern History of Iraq.* 2nd ed. Boulder CO: Westview Press, 2004.

Matinuddin, Kamal. *The Taliban Phenomenon, Afghanistan 1994–1997.* New York: Oxford University Press, 1999.

McNearny, Michael J. "Stabilization and Reconstruction in Afghanistan: Are PRTS a Model or a Muddle?" *Parameters* 35, no. 4 (Winter 2005–6): 32–46.

Meierhenrich, Jens. "Forming States after Failure." In *When States Fail: Causes and Consequences,* edited by Robert I. Rotberg, 155–69. Princeton NJ: Princeton University Press, 2004.

Meringolo, Denise D. *Museums, Monuments, and National Parks: Towards a New Genealogy of Public History.* Amherst: University of Massachusetts Press, 2012.

Merriam, Charles E. *The Making of Citizens.* New York: Columbia University Press, 1966.

Mill, John Stuart. *Considerations on Representative Government.* An Electronic Classic Series Publication. Pennsylvania State University, 2004. http://www2.hn .psu.edu/faculty/jmanis/jsmill/considerations.

Miller, Laurel. *Building the Iraqi Special Tribunal: Lessons from Experiences in International Criminal Justice.* United States Institute of Peace Special Report no. 122, June 13, 2004. http://www.usip.org/publications/building-the-iraqi -special-tribunal-lessons-experiences-in-international-criminal.

Montesquieu, Charles de Secondant. *The Spirit of Laws.* Translated by Thomas Nugent. 1748. http://socserv2.socsci.mcmaster.ca/econ/ugcm/3ll3 /montesquieu/spiritoflaws.pdf.

Nadir, Rabih. "Iraqis Divided Over New National Anthem." *Al Monitor.* January 29, 2014. http://www.al-monitor.com/pulse/originals/2014/01/iraq-political -dispute-new-national-anthem.html#, accessed February 9, 2015.

Nagl, John A., Andrew M. Exum, and Ahmed A. Humayun. *A Pathway to Success in Afghanistan: The National Solidarity Program*. Center for New American Security, March 2009. http://www.cnas.org/files/documents/publications/CNAS%20Policy%20Brief%20-%20Supporting%20Afghanistans%20NSP%20March%202009.pdf.

National Democratic Institute for International Affairs. *The 2010 Wolesi Jirga Elections in Afghanistan*. 2011. https://www.ndi.org/files/Afghanistan-2010-election-observers-final-report.pdf.

———. *The September 2005 Parliamentary and Provincial Elections in Afghanistan*. 2006. https://www.ndi.org/files/2004_af_report_041006.pdf.

Nojumi, Neamatollah. *The Rise of the Taliban in Afghanistan: Mass Mobilization, Civil War and the Future of the Region*. New York: Palgrave, 2002.

Norris, James Alfred. *The First Afghan War, 1838–1842*. New York: Cambridge University Press, 1967.

North, Douglas C. "Institutions." *Journal of Economic Perspectives* 5, no. 1 (Winter 1991): 97–112.

Oliver, Bette W. *From Royal to National: The Louvre Museum and the Bibliotheque Nationale*. Lanham MD: Lexington Books, 2006.

Parker, Geoffrey. *The Thirty Years' War*. London: Routledge, 1984.

Peceny, Mark, and Yury Bosin. "Winning with Warlords in Afghanistan." *Small Wars and Insurgencies* 22, no. 4 (2011): 603–18.

Perito, Robert. M., ed. *Guide for Participants in Peace, Stability, and Relief Operations*. Washington DC: US Institute of Peace, 2007.

Pohlsander, Hans. *National Monuments and Nationalism in 19th Century Germany*. Bern: Peter Lang, 2008.

Poole, Lydia. *Afghanistan: Tracking Major Resource Pools, 2002–2010*. Global Humanitarian Assistance, January 2011. http://www.globalhumanitarianassistance.org/wp-content/uploads/2011/02/gha-Afghanistan-2011-major-resource-flows.pdf.

Porter, Gareth. "Iraqi Prime Minister Al-Maliki Draws U.S. Troops into Crackdown on Sunnis." *Washington Report on Middle East Affairs* 28, no. 4 (May/June 2009): 24–25.

Posner, Daniel N. "Civil Society and the Reconstruction of Failed States." In *When States Fail: Causes and Consequences*, edited by Robert I. Rotberg, 237–55. Princeton NJ: Princeton University Press, 2004.

Putnam, Robert D., et al. *Making Democracy Work: Civic Traditions in Modern Italy*. Princeton NJ: Princeton University Press, 1993.

Rahimi, Babak. *Ayatollah Sistani and the Democratization of Post-Ba'athist Iraq*. U.S. Institute of Peace Special Report no. 187, June 2007.

Ramet, Sabrina. *Balkan Babble: The Disintegration of Yugoslavia from the Death of Tito to the Fall of Milosevic*. Boulder CO: Westview Press, 2002.

Rashid, Ahmed. *Taliban: Militant Islam, Oil and Fundamentalism in Central Asia*. London: I. B. Tauris 2010.

Renan, Ernst. "What Is a Nation?" 1882. Translated by Ethan Rundell. http://ucparis.fr/files/9313/6549/9943/What_is_a_Nation.pdf.

Ricks, Thomas E. *Fiasco: The American Military Adventure in Iraq*. New York: Penguin Press, 2006.

Robinson, Glenn. "Notes on Iraqi Identity." In *The Three Circles of War: Understanding the Dynamics of Conflict in Iraq*, edited by Heather S. Gregg, Hy Rothstein, and John Arquilla, 11–24. Washington DC: Potomac, 2010.

Roggio, Bill, and Lisa Lundquist. "Green on Blue Attacks in Afghanistan: The Data." *Long War Journal*, June 17, 2017. http://www.longwarjournal.org/archives /2012/08/green-on-blue_attack.php.

Rose, David. "Heads in the Sand." *Vanity Fair*, May 2009. http://www.vanityfair .com/news/2009/05/iraqi-insurgents200905.

Rotberg, Robert I. "The Failure and Collapse of Nation-States: Breakdown, Prevention and Repair." In *When States Fail: Causes and Consequences*, edited by Robert I. Rotberg, 1–50. Princeton NJ: Princeton University Press, 2004.

Rothstein, Hy S. *Afghanistan and the Troubled Future of Unconventional Warfare*. Annapolis MD: U.S. Naval Institute Press, 2006.

————. "Lessons from Reconstructing Security Forces in Iraq." In *The Three Circles of War: Understanding the Dynamics of Conflict in Iraq*, edited by Heather S. Gregg, Hy S. Rothstein, and John Arquilla, 45–58. Washington DC: Potomac Press, 2010.

Rousseau, Jean-Jacques. *The Social Contract*. New York: Carlton House, 1968.

Rubin, Barnett R. *The Fragmentation of Afghanistan*. New Haven CT: Yale University Press, 2002.

Rubin, Barnett R., and Jake Sherman. *Counter-Narcotics to Stabilize Afghanistan: The False Promise of Crop Eradication*. Center on International Cooperation, February 2008. http://cic.es.its.nyu.edu/sites/default/files/counternarcoticsfinal.pdf.

Ruiz, Rebecca. "Report: A Million Veterans Injured in Iraq, Afghanistan." *Forbes*, November 4, 2013. http://www.forbes.com/sites/rebeccaruiz/2013/11/04/report -a-million-veterans-injured-in-iraq-afghanistan-wars/.

Saalman, Howard. *Haussmann: Paris Transformed*. New York: George Braziller, 1971.

Sachs, Jeffrey. "Notes on a New Sociology of Economic Development." In *Culture Matters: How Values Shape Human Progress*, edited by Lawrence E. Harrison and Samuel P. Huntington, 29–43. New York: Basic Books, 2000.

Schultheis, Rob. *Waging Peace: A Special Operations Team's Battle to Rebuild Iraq*. New York: Gotham Books, 2005.

Segal, Robert A. *Myth: A Very Short Introduction*. London: Oxford University Press, 2004.

Sen, Amartya. *Poverty and Famines: An Essay on Entitlement and Deprivation*. New York: Oxford University Press, 1981.

Shawe, Keith, ed. *Afghanistan in 2013: A Survey of the Afghan People*. Asia Foundation, 2013. http://asiafoundation.org/country/afghanistan/2013-poll.php.

Smith, Anthony. "Dating the Nation." In *Ethnonationalism and the Contemporary World: Walker Connor and the Study of Nationalism*, edited by Daniele Conversi, 53–71. London: Routledge, 2002.

————. "The Ethnic Sources of Nationalism." In *Ethnic Conflict and Interna-*

tional Security, edited by Michael Brown, 27–42. Princeton NJ: Princeton University Press, 1993.

———. *National Identity*. Reno: University of Nevada Press, 1991.

Smith, Whitney, ed. *Flags throughout the Ages and across the World*. New York: McGraw Hill, 1975.

Snyder, Jack. *From Voting to Violence: Democratization and National Conflict*. New York: Columbia University Press, 2000.

Sopko, John F. *Why ANSF Numbers Matter: Inaccurate and Unreliable Data and Limited Oversight of On-Budget Assistance Put Millions of U.S. Tax Payer Dollars at Risk*. Testimony before the Subcommittee on National Security, Committee on Oversight and Government Reform, U.S. House of Representatives, April 29, 2015. http://oversight.house.gov/wp-content/uploads/2015/04/SIGAR-15-56-TY-ANSF-Data-Statement11.pdf.

Stark, Rodney. *The Victory of Reason*. New York: Random House, 2005.

Strayer, Joseph. *The Medieval Origins of the Modern State*. Princeton NJ: Princeton University Press, 1970.

Stewart, Rory. *The Prince of the Marshes: And Other Occupational Hazards of a Year in Iraq*. Orlando FL: Harcourt Press, 2006.

Taylor, Alan. "Afghanistan: April 2014." *Atlantic Photo*, April 30, 2014. http://www.theatlantic.com/photo/2014/04/afghanistan-april-2014/100725/.

Thier, J. Alexander. *The Making of a Constitution in Afghanistan*. London School of Economics and Politics Occasional Paper, June 1, 2003. http://eprints.lse.ac.uk/28380/1/Thier_LSERO_version.pdf.

Thomas, Evan, and John Barry. "A New Way of War: How Do You Stop Foes Who Kill with Devices Built for the Price of a Pizza? Maybe the Question Is, Can You Stop Them?" *Newsweek*, August 20–27, 2007. http://www.newsweek.com/id/32259.

Thruelson, Peter Dahl. *From Soldier to Civilian: Disarmament, Demobilization and Reintegration in Afghanistan*. Danish Institute for International Studies Report no. 2006:7. http://www.diis.dk/files/media/documents/publications/rp2006-7web.pdf.

Tilly, Charles, ed. *The Formation of National States in Western Europe*. Princeton NJ: Princeton University Press, 1975.

———. "Reflections on the History of European State Making." In Tilly, *Formation of National States*, 3–83.

———. "War Making and State Making as Organized Crime." In *Bringing the State Back In*, edited by Peter Evans, Dietrich Rueschemeyer, and Theda Skocpol, 169–87. New York: Cambridge University Press, 1985.

Tocqueville, Alexander de. *Democracy in America*. Vol. 1. New York: Alfred A. Knopf Vintage Books, 1990.

Torabi, Yama. *The Growing Challenge of Corruption in Afghanistan: Reflections on a Survey of Afghan People, Part 3 of 4*. Asia Foundation Occasional Paper no. 15, July 2012. https://asiafoundation.org/resources/pdfs/FNLcorruptionchapterOccasionalPaperJuly30.pdf.

Trachtenberg, Marvin. *The Statue of Liberty*. New York: Viking Press, 1976.

Tripp, Charles. *A History of Iraq*. New York: Cambridge University Press, 2007.

United Nations Development Program and Islamic Republic of Afghanistan. *Security with a Human Face: Challenges and Responsibilities*. Afghanistan: National Human Development Report, 2004. http://hdr.undp.org/sites /default/files/afghanistan_2004_en.pdf.

U.S. Department of the Army. "FM 3-07: Stability Operations." 2008. https:// usacac.army.mil/cac2/repository/FM307/FM3-07.pdf.

———. "FM 3-07: Stability Operations." 2014. https://www.globalsecurity.org /military/library/policy/army/fm/3-07/fm3-07_2014.pdf.

U.S. Department of Defense. *Measuring Stability and Security in Iraq*. Report to Congress, November 2006. http://www.defense.gov/pubs/pdfs/9010quarterly -Report-20061216.pdf.

———. *Report on Progress towards Security and Stability in Afghanistan*. Report to Congress in Accord with the 2008 National Defense Authorization Act (Section 1230, Public Law 110–181), June 2008. http://www.defense.gov /pubs/Report_on_Progress_toward_Security_and_Stability_in_Afghanistan _1230.pdf.

U.S. Institute of Peace and U.S. Army Peacekeeping and Stability Operations Institute. *Guiding Principles for Stabilization and Reconstruction*. 2009. https:// www.usip.org/sites/default/files/guiding_principles_full.pdf.

U.S. Office of the Undersecretary of Defense, Chief Financial Officer. *United States Department of Defense Fiscal Year 2015 Budget Request*. March 2014. http://comptroller.defense.gov/Portals/45/Documents/defbudget/fy2015 /fy2015_Budget_Request_Overview_Book.pdf.

Vagts, Alfred. *A History of Militarism*. New York: Meridian Books, 1959.

Van Evera, Stephen. "Hypotheses on Nationalism and War." *International Security* 18, no. 4 (1994): 5–39.

Van Geldern, Martin, and Quentin Skinner, eds. *Republicanism*. Vol. 2, *The Values of Republicanism in Early Modern Europe: A Shared European Heritage*. London: Cambridge University Press, 2002.

Van Zanden, Jan Luiten, and Maarten Prak. "Towards an Economic Interpretation of Citizenship: The Dutch Republic between Medieval Communes and Modern Nation-States." *European Review of Economic History* 10, no. 2 (2006): 111–45.

Verba, Sidney. "Introduction to the Civic Culture Concept." In *The Civic Culture Revisited*, edited by Gabriel A. Almond and Sidney Verba, 1–36. Newbury Park CA: Sage, 1989.

Warren, Zach, ed. *Afghanistan in 2014: A Survey of Afghan People*. Asia Foundation, 2014. http://asiafoundation.org/publications/pdf/1425, accessed March 15, 2015.

Weber, Max. *Economy and Society*. Translated and edited by G. Roth and C. Wittich. Los Angeles: University of California Press, 1968.

———. "Politics as Vocation." 1919. http://www.sscnet.ucla.edu/polisci/ethos /Weber-vocation.pdf, accessed July 6, 2015.

———. *The Theory of Social and Economic Organization*. Translated by A.M. Henderson and Talcott Parsons. New York: Free Press, 2009.

Widner, Jennifer A. "Building Effective Trust in the Aftermath of Severe Conflict." In *When States Fail: Causes and Consequences*, edited by Robert I. Rotberg, 222–36. Princeton NJ: Princeton University Press, 2004.

Wilbanks, Mark, and Efraim Karsh. "How the 'Sons of Iraq' Stabilized Iraq." *Middle East Quarterly* 17, no. 4 (Fall 2010): 57–70.

Wright, Lawrence. *The Looming Tower: Al-Qaeda and the Road to 9/11*. New York: Alfred A. Knopf, 2006.

Yunus, Muhammad. *Banker to the Poor: Micro-Lending and the Battle against World Poverty*. New York: Public Affairs, 2003.

Zakaria, Fareed. *The Future of Freedom: Liberal and Illiberal Democracy at Home and Abroad*. New York: Norton, 2003.

INDEX

"Declaration of Shia in Iraq," 103, 122–23, 135, 136

democracy: in Afghanistan's state-building, 151, 160, 166–68, 189, 190, 196–97; and civic nationalism, 31–32, 37; coalition actions in state-building, 124; and governance, 81–83; in Iraq's state-building, 2, 91, 99, 109–14, 122–23; theories on, 18, 27, 66, 109; U.S. foundation in, 61. See also civic nationalism; governance in state- and nation-building

Democracy in America (Tocqueville), 51

Development Fund for Iraq, 119

Diamond, Larry, 123

Discourses on Livy (Machiavelli), 43

Dodge, Toby, 72, 93–94

Dost Mohammed, 154

Dupree, Louis, 156

Durand, Mortimer, 155

Durand Line, 155

Durrani Dynasty, 154, 167

Dutch Republic, 43

economic development in state- and nation-building: in Afghanistan, 177–84, 187, 202–6, 215; in Iraq, 117–20, 124, 137–39, 149; pillars in, 84–86, 89

Economy and Society (Weber), 22

education: in Afghanistan, 201, 212–13; for girls and women, 161, 185, 209; nationalism in U.S. curriculum, 60–61, 83–84, 258n42; programs of mass, 50–52, 62; service development of, 64–65, 144–45, 185. See also government services and programs; language for national unity

Eikenberry, Karl, 164, 167–68, 169

Eliade, Mircea, 25–26

Eller, Jack David, 14, 16, 34

England, 46, 56. See also Great Britain

Enlightenment, 45–46

Epstein, S. R., 42

ethnic groups, 14

ethnic nationalism, 14, 24–28

Etzioni, Amitai, 71–72

Europe: nation-building in, 49–58; social contract in state-building in, 45–46, 49, 62; state creation in, 41–47

failing or failed states, identification of, 81

Faisal, King of Iraq, 94

Faulkner, William, 59

The Federalist Papers, 48–49

Felbab-Brown, Vanda, 183

Fiasco (Ricks), 98–99

Finer, Samuel, 52

fire departments, 133, 144, 239

First Anglo-Afghan War (1838–42), 154

Fixing Failed States (Ghani and Lockhart), 84, 179

flags. See national flags

FM 3–07, "Stability Operations" (U.S. Army), 67

football, 143–44, 209–10

forests. See national forests

France: French Revolution, 46; Napoleon's use of levee en masse, 52–53; national literature, 59; national symbols of, 60

Fukuyama, Francis, 7, 68–69, 73–74, 79, 86

The Future of Iraq (U.S. Department of State), 101–2, 105, 110, 113

Garner, Jay, 102

gay rights in U.S., 141

Gellner, Ernest, 23–24, 52, 55

Gemeinschaft, 79

genocide, 96

George III, 57

George IV, 57–58

German nationalism, 59, 60, 156

Ghani, Ashraf, 16, 70, 83, 171, 205, 208

GI Bill (1944, United States), 83

girls' education, 161, 185, 209

Global Humanitarian Assistance, 179

"good enough" governance, 197

governance in state- and nation-building: in Afghanistan, 166–73, 187, 195–200, 215; community-based, 228–30; "good enough" governance type, 198; in Iraq, 2, 109–14, 124, 134–36, 149; pillars in, 81–84, 89. See also democracy

government services and programs, 50–54, 64–65. See also education; health care, service department of

Great Britain: flags of, 56; independence of, 236; military and political efforts in Afghanistan, 154–55; military and political efforts in Iraq, 93–94, 97, 138

Islamic and National Revolution Movement of Afghanistan, 157
Islamic Republic of Iran. *See* Iran
Islamic State in Iraq and the Levant (ISIL): 2014 Iraq takeover by, 1–2, 90, 92, 125, 223; conditions for success of, 3, 4, 7, 11, 126, 132, 139; current state of power of, 218; misconceptions about U.S. connection to, 231
Islamic Union for the Liberation of Afghanistan, 157
Islamic Unity of Afghanistan Mujahedeen, 157
Islamism, as term, 29. *See also* religious nationalism
Israel, 30

Jamiat-e-Islami, 157
Jay, John, 48
Jewish populations, 30
jirgas, 166–67, 185, 197, 215, 257n20. *See also* Loya Jirga; Meshrano Jirga; Wolesi Jirga
Joint Task Force Phoenix, 162
Juergensmeyer, Mark, 28–29

Kandahar, Afghanistan, 159
Karzai, Hamid, 167–68, 171, 173
Kaufmann, Chaim, 35
Kenya, 159
Keyes, Francis Scott, 56
Khalis group, 157
Kho'ei, Sayyed Abdul Majid al-, 110
Kilcullen, David, 71, 77
Kirkuk, Iraq, 113, 118, 131, 135, 223
Kuchi, 185
Kurdistan Regional Government (KRG), 118
Kurds in Iraq: coalition support for, 135; Peshmerga military, 92, 97; political parties of, 97; under Saddam's rule, 96–97; takeover attempt of Kirkuk by, 113, 118, 131, 223; transitional leadership by, 102–3
Kuwait, 96
Kyridis, Argyris, 55

language for national unity, 8, 50, 55, 62
law. *See* rule of law in state- and nation-building
Law on Elimination of Violence against Women (EVAW), 185

Lazarus, Emma, 57
leadership sources, 82–84
Lemay-Hébert, Nicolas, 73, 76
levee en masse, 52–53, 219
Levi-Strauss, Claude, 26
literacy programs, 163, 210–11
literature. *See* national literature
Locke, John, 46
Lockhart, Clare, 16, 70, 83, 197, 205, 208
Loewen, James, 61
London Times, 116
Louis Berger Group, 180
Louvre, 58
Loya Jirga: about, 160–61, 235; Bonn Agreement on, 173, 196, 197; "Peace," 199; ratifications by, 156, 157, 167, 171, 187, 197, 200
Lubragge, Michael T., 33
Luiten van Zanden, Jan, 43
Luther, Martin, 43–44

Machiavelli, Niccolò, 43
Madden, David, 56
Madison, James, 48
Magna Carta, 42–43
The Making of Citizens (Merriam), 74
Maktab al-Khidamat, 157–58. *See also* Al-Qaeda
Mamluks, 93
Manifest Destiny, 33
Mansfield, Edward D., 82
Massachusetts Spy, 51
Massoud, Ahmad Shah, 157
mature democracies. *See* democracy
media for national-unity building, 62
Meierhenrich, Jens, 69–70, 219
Merriam, Charles E., 74
Meshrano Jirga, 171
Midhat Pasha, 95
military, mass-based, 52–53, 62. *See also* rule of law in state- and nation-building
military forces, formal: Afghan National Army, 162–64; of Great Britain, 93–94, 97, 138, 154–55; Iraqi Army, 94, 101, 105–7; ISIL, 1–2, 90, 92; of Soviet Union, 154, 156, 157, 158; of U.S., 67, 105–6, 162, 237–39. *See also* police forces
Military Review, 107
Military Transition Teams (MITTS), 107–8

Samara, Iraq, 1, 113, 122
Saudi Arabia, 157
Schmalkaldic League of Lutherans, 44
SCIRI (Supreme Council for the Islamic
  Revolution in Iraq), 96, 110
Scotland, 56
Second Anglo-Afghan War (1878–80), 154
Second Treatise on Government (Locke), 46
Security Force Assistance (SFA), 162–63
security in state- and nation-building: in
  Afghanistan, 161–66, *187*, 191–95, *215*;
  in Iraq, 104–9, *124*, 129–34, *149*; pillars
  in, 77–79, *89*
Segal, Robert A., 26
Semple, Michael, 162
September 11, 2001 attacks, 159
sharia law, 1, 140–41, 156, 175. *See also*
  rule of law in state- and nation-building
Shia Islam, 30
Shia population in Afghanistan, 153
Shia population in Iran, 30
Shia population in Iraq: cultural and polit-
  ical history of, 93–98; "Declaration of
  Shia in Iraq," 103, 122–23, 135, 136; ISIL
  violence against, 1; role in transitional
  governance, 110–11, 114; Sunni violence,
  121–22; transitional leadership by, 102–3
Shinseki, Eric, 100
Shinwari Pashtuns, 156
shura councils, 166–67, 170
Sikh nationalism, 30
Sistani, Ayatollah Ali, 115
slavery, 81, 141, 237
Smith, Anthony, 19, 24–25
Smithson, James, 58
Smithsonian Institution, 58
Snyder, Jack, 35, 82
soccer, 143–44, 209–10
social contract: in Afghanistan, 154, 188,
  203, 204, 206; creation of, 54, 219, 222,
  231; in Europe and U.S., 45–46, 49,
  62; in Iraq, 128, 129; needed in state-
  building, *62*, 71, 84, 85, *89*
social well-being in state- and nation-
  building: in Afghanistan, 184–86, *187*,
  206–10, *216*; in Iraq, 120–23, *124*, 142–
  45, *149*; pillars of, 86–87, *89*. *See also*
  health care, service development of

Sons of Iraq (SOI) group, 108–9, 132
sovereignty: in Afghanistan, 168, 196–97;
  criteria for measuring, 70–71; de facto
  sovereignty, 16; de jure sovereignty,
  16; and ethnic nationalism, 25, 41; history of concept, 4–5, 12, 15, 19, 42, 219;
  locally led governance, 81, 134
Soviet-Afghan War (1979–89), 157, 158, 167
Soviet Union involvement in Afghanistan, 154, 156, 157, 158
Spain, 236
sports: in Afghanistan, 209, 210, 213, *216*;
  in Iraq, 143–44, 146, *149*; for nation-
  building, 32, 87, 227. *See also* football
Sri Lanka, 30
"Stability Operations" (FM 3–07, U.S.
  Army), 67
stabilization, post-conflict. *See* nation-
  building; state-building
state: as concept, 15–18; as term, 9, 14
state-building: economic pillars in, 84–
  86, *89*; in Europe, 41–47; Fukuyama
  on, 69; governance and democracy
  pillars in, 81–84, *89*; in Iraq, 91–93,
  103–24; Meierhenrich on, 69–70;
  national unity pillars in, 4–8, 74–76,
  87–88, *90*; ongoing work on, 236–
  37; in post-9/11 security environment,
  65–69; rule of law pillars in, 79–81,
  89; security in, 77–79, *89*, 104–9, *124*;
  social well-being in, 86–87, *89*; as
  term, 64
state bureaucracies, 54
state services. *See* government services
  and programs
Stewart, Rory, 144–45
Sufis, 1, 153
Sunni population in Afghanistan, 153, 157
Sunni population in Iran, 30
Sunni population in Iraq: Daughters of
  Iraq group, 109; effects of U.S. policies on, 5, 108, 222; history of, 93–94;
  ISIL's reception by, 1–2, 92; Mamluks,
  93; role in transitional governance,
  108–12, 135; and Saddam Hussein's
  rule, 96; Shia violence, 121–22; Sons
  of Iraq (SOI) group, 108–9, 132. *See
  also* Iraq